Lecture Notes in Computer Scie

Commenced Publication in 1973
Founding and Former Series Editors:
Gerhard Goos, Juris Hartmanis, and Jan van Leeuwen

John Domingue   Dieter Fensel
Paolo Traverso (Eds.)

Future Internet – FIS 2008

First Future Internet Symposium, FIS 2008
Vienna, Austria, September 29-30, 2008
Revised Selected Papers

 Springer

Volume Editors

John Domingue
The Open University
Knowledge Media Institute
Walton Hall, Milton Keynes MK6 7AA, UK
E-mail: j.b.domingue@open.ac.uk
and
STI International
Amerlingstraße 19/35, 1060 Vienna, Austria
E-mail: john.domingue@sti2.org
www.sti2.org

Dieter Fensel
University of Innsbruck
Semantic Technology Institute (STI) Innsbruck
Technikerstraße 21a, 6020 Innsbruck, Austria
E-mail: dieter.fensel@sti2.at

Paolo Traverso
FBK Center for Information Technology IRST
Via Sommarive 18, Povo 38100, Trento, Italy
E-mail: traverso@fbk.eu

Library of Congress Control Number: Applied for

CR Subject Classification (1998): C.2, D.4.4, D.2, H.3.5, H.4, K.6.5

LNCS Sublibrary: SL 5 – Computer Communication Networks
and Telecommunications

ISSN   0302-9743
ISBN-10   3-642-00984-0 Springer Berlin Heidelberg New York
ISBN-13   978-3-642-00984-6 Springer Berlin Heidelberg New York

springer.com

© Springer-Verlag Berlin Heidelberg 2009
Printed in Germany

Typesetting: Camera-ready by author, data conversion by Scientific Publishing Services, Chennai, India
Printed on acid-free paper   SPIN: 12648719   06/3180   5 4 3 2 1 0

Preface

The First Future Internet Symposium was held during September 28–30, 2008 in Vienna, Austria. FIS 2008 provided a forum for leading researchers and practitioners to meet and discuss the wide-ranging scientific and technical issues related to the design of a new Internet. The sentiment shared in Vienna was that we are at the beginning of something very exciting and challenging and that FIS 2008 has played a role in forming a community to address this.

With over a billion users, today's Internet is arguably the most successful human artifact ever created. The Internet's physical infrastructure, software, and content now play an integral part in the lives of everyone on the planet, whether they interact with it directly or not. Now nearing its fifth decade, the Internet has shown remarkable resilience and flexibility in the face of ever-increasing numbers of users, data volume, and changing usage patterns, but faces growing challenges in meetings the needs of our knowledge society. Globally, many major initiatives are underway to address the need for more scientific research, physical infrastructure investment, better education, and better utilization of the Internet. Japan, the USA and Europe are investing heavily in this area. The EU is shaping around the idea of the Future Internet its research programmes for the Seventh Framework. EU commissioners, national government ministers, industry leaders and researchers met in Bled, Slovenia during March 31–April 2, 2008, to begin developing a vision of a future Internet that will meet Europe's needs a decade from now, and beyond.

A broad programme of scientific research is essential to supporting the aims of the Future Internet initiative. To complement the agenda-setting activity emerging from the Bled conference, the Future Internet Symposium (FIS 2008) is a new open international event designed to bring together leading researchers to collaborate and contribute to the science behind the vision. FIS 2008 has dealt with the main requirements our Future Internet must satisfy: an "Internet of Things," where every electronic device will be an active participant in the network; an "Internet of Services," where applications live in the network, and data become an active entity; an "Internet of Content and Media," where most of the contents are generated by end-users; an "Internet of Publicity, Privacy and Anonymity," where people and software must understand how much trust to extend to others; an "Internet of Mobility and Ubiquity," where connectivity everywhere is expected, and depended upon. All these nascent Internets, and the others that we have yet to imagine, require further research activity, especially at the interdisciplinary boundaries where opportunities lie and problems lurk.

Ten technical papers were accepted for presentation at FIS 2008. Authors presented works proposing novel ideas and results related to the future Internet infrastructure, user-generated content, content visualization, usability, trust and security, collaborative workflows, the Internet of services and service science.

Beyond the papers submitted and accepted for publication, four papers were invited and presented at FIS 2008: "The Nature of Our Digital Universe" by Michael L. Brodie, "The Internet of Things in an Enterprise Context" by Stephan Haller et al., "Security-By-Contract for the Future Internet" by Fabio Massacci et al., and "eServices in a Networked World: From Semantics to Pragmatics" by Jaap Gordijn et al. FIS 2008 had two keynote speakers: one keynote was by Joao da Silva, Director of the Network and Communication in Directorate of DG-INFSO. He presented a survey of all the R&D work relating to mobile communications, broadband networks including satellite communications, audio-visual and home networks; trust and security, software engineering and ICT for business applications. The other keynote was by Alexander Hauptmann, Senior Systems Scientist in Computer Science at Carnegie Mellon University, and a faculty member in the Language Technologies Institute at CMU. His talk was on multi-media analysis and retrieval.

February 2009

John Domingue
Dieter Fensel
Paolo Traverso

Organization

Chair

John Domingue   The Open University, UK

Programme Chairs

Dieter Fensel   STI International, Austria
Paolo Traverso   FBK IRST, Italy

Local Organization

Eva Zelechowski   STI International, Austria

Programme Committee

Alessandro Armando
Luciano Baresi
Paolo Bouquet
Keke Chen
Luca Compagna
John Davies
Hervé Debar
Elisabetta Di Nitto
Zeta Dooly
Marcello Federico
Andreas Friesen
Alex Galis
Sergio Gusmeroli
Christopher Kruegel
Domenico Laforenza
Tiziana Margaria
Fabio Massacci
Corrado Moiso

Barry Norton
Massimo Paoluccci
Carlos Pedrinaci
Charles Petrie
Radoslaw Piesiewicz
Marco Pistore
Lakshmish Ramaswamy
Elena Simperl
Rudi Studer
Rahim Tafazolli
Wolfgang Theilmann
Dirk Trossen
Luca Viganò
Matthias Wagner
Nick Wainwright
Hannes Werthner
Michal Zaremba
Frank van Harmelen

External Reviewers

Marco Bakera	Daniel Oberle
Sven Buschbeck	Alessandro Petri
Laura Ferrari	Serena Ponta
Christoph Grün	Tirdad Rahmani
Steffen Lamparter	Marc Richardson
Jens Lemcke	Alessandro Sorniotti
Thomas Motal	Christian Wagner

Table of Contents

The Nature of Our Digital Universe

Michael L. Brodie

Verizon Communications
117 West Street, Waltham, MA, USA 02140
Michael.Brodie@Verizon.com

Abstract. A compelling question for the 21st Century is "What is the nature of our digital universe?" In designing the Future Internet, we have a remarkable opportunity and need for a deeper understanding of this question. Based on the profound importance of our Future Digital World and on the role of the Future Internet in shaping it, this paper suggests holistic objectives for the design process and some thoughts on challenges and opportunities that the design process may face.

Keywords: Future Internet, digital worlds, grand challenges.

1 Introduction

Shortly after World War II physicists captivated the world's imagination with a simple but profound question "What is the nature of our physical universe?" The compelling question for the 21st Century is "What is the nature of our digital universe?" - a question that has immediate and long-term relevance for our planet in both challenges and opportunities.

20th Century physicists convinced the world that understanding our physical universe required Big Science characterized by instruments, laboratories, staff, and budgets on a scale far beyond that of previous scientific endeavors. The most recent example of Big Science is the Large Hadron Collider (LHC) that went into operation at European Organization for Nuclear Research (CERN) in 2008 at a cost of approximately €5 billion.

The Big Science pursuit of the grand challenges of our physical universe was motivated by practical and theoretical relevance. A better understanding of the structure of matter has had practical relevance with urgent applications such as better harnessing energy to diminish global warming. For fifty years, these efforts have contributed to improved theoretical models of matter and of the forces that govern our physical universe. An intended theoretical objective of the LHC is to prove the existence of the elusive Higgs boson and thus make a "significant step in the search for a Grand Unified Theory, which seeks to unify three of the four known fundamental forces: electromagnetism, the strong nuclear force, and the weak nuclear force, leaving out only gravity."[1] The underlying premise is that a better understanding of the physical universe provides a basis for problem solving involving matter and energy plus insight into the nature of our physical universe.

J. Domingue, D. Fensel, and P. Traverso (Eds.): FIS 2008, LNCS 5468, pp. 1–13, 2009.

A compelling and profound question for the 21st Century is "What is the nature of our digital universe?" *Our real world is increasingly digital and our digital world is increasingly real.* As we enter the 21st Century the Future Internet initiatives provide an opportunity to redefine our digital world and thus shape the real world. But how can we redefine what we do not understand? We are far from understanding our digital world - how we shape it and how it shapes us.

The Future Internet is 21st Century Big Science. The scale of the Future Internet surpasses the scale of 20th Century Big Science in terms of instruments, laboratories, staff, and budgets. The Internet is the largest human artifact ever created and continues to grow at unbelievable rates. The technologies and tools must address web-scale challenges. The Future Internet will be distributed globally with, collectively, web-scale instruments, laboratories, staff, and budgets. The European Future Internet [2] includes a worldwide experimental facility – a web-scale experimental environment – that, like the Internet, is a network of experimental facilities around the world. Hence, the Future Internet should be pursued as a global activity, as a network of Future Internet activities.

21st Century Big Science should be pursued holistically. The current focus of the Future Internet is on the digital infrastructure – the technical solutions - and on policies that will govern it. The dramatic and significant positive and negative impacts of our current digital world on local and global society, business, and the economy demonstrate that we cannot pursue the infrastructure of our Future Digital World without understanding the human endeavors or domains that it will serve and the relationship between the two. An improved infrastructure may address known challenges and limitations of our current digital world, but will it help us envisage its needs and opportunities? To define and create a better world we must understand the nature of our digital universe. This requires a deep understanding of the requirements of our digital infrastructure, as proposed in [2], and of our Future Digital Worlds (domains), and of the relationships between the two. We must extend the scope of the Future Internet initiatives to include Future Digital Worlds – the requirements of the domains that the infrastructure will serve - and the relationship between the digital world and the human endeavors that it will realize, as proposed for Web Science [3].

Based on the importance of the current and the Future Internet and the opportunities it offers to define our Future Digital World, this paper expands on the cross-disciplinary objective of the Future Internet Manifesto [4] to suggest taking a more holistic approach. The paper proposes objectives for a design process for the Future Internet that includes the communities that will be served by the Future Internet. The paper offers thoughts on the extensive and profound challenges and opportunities that the process must as address such as how to envisage the future, the innovation and competition that might result from eliminating traditional technical and industrial boundaries, and the creation of a more realistic digital world.

2   The Future Internet Will Shape Our World

The Internet, 40 years ago, and the World Wide Web, 15 years ago, marked some of the most significant events in the history of computing and communications that led to substantial innovation not only in the underlying technologies but also in the local and global communities, businesses, and economies that they enabled. Innovative products, services, processes, and behaviours significantly impact our personal and professional lives. The things, actions, and processes that make up our real world are increasingly rendered, manipulated, analyzed, and communicated in digital form. *Our real world is increasingly digital and our digital world is increasingly real.*

The scope and scale of our digital world never ceases to amaze us [8]. Our digital world impacts every human endeavor – entertainment, retail, health care, manufacturing, communications, agriculture, science, the arts – by improving existing products, services, and processes, or by replacing them with fundamentally new innovations. Entire industries such as recorded entertainment and communications are becoming predominantly digital. Our digital world directly impacts most people with almost 75% of the developed world online today and with 25% of the world online by 2011. The developing world is catching up to the developed world at unbelievable rates since it skips errors and evolutionary stages and jumps right into 21st Century digital technologies.

The Internet is the largest human artifact ever created and continues to grow at astounding rates. Cisco, a leading authority on Internet size and traffic, increased its 2008 five year projections by a factor of two over its 2007 projections. Internet traffic will increase by a factor of six between 2007 and 2012 at which time the Internet will be 75 times larger than it was in 2002 [9], each year growing by more information than was created in the preceding 5,000 years. The growth and adoption rates and the trends continue to amaze the most ardent proponents and exceed projections [8] and overwhelm the current Internet and its supporting technologies.

The Future Internet initiatives around the world are bold and to be praised for their vision. The Future Internet initiatives are responding to the need to address known technical and policy limitations and challenges. Technologists are pursuing problems and limitations such as capacity, traffic, security, trust, quality of service, stability, robustness, and reliability; and to enhance the Internet to accommodate opportunities such as mobility and ubiquity. The European initiative [2] is considering the Future Internet in terms of six technology domains: networks; services; content; security, trust, and privacy; and experimental facilities. Governments and economic policy makers are addressing issues such as universal access, barriers to entry, enabling and empowering users, the support of government services and education, and the Internet as a public good. The OECD wants to "Ensure an Internet Economy that will improve the quality of life by developing opportunities for employment, productivity, education, health and public services, enterprises and communities, civic engagement, safety, and create a global information society."[5][6][7] The Bled Future Internet Manifesto [4] calls us to: "Coordinate our efforts to foster cross-disciplinary innovation and creativity." These initiatives propose additional, noble objectives.

Based on the premise that the Future Internet will shape our future world in ways that we cannot anticipate, this paper proposes to build on already noble and challenging objectives for the Future Internet with the objective of being holistic in an attempt to anticipate aspects of the future worlds that the Future Internet will serve.

Just as the current World Wide Web came about in response to the needs of physicists 15 years ago, the Future Internet should serve the needs of physicists over the next 25 years. What will be the requirements of the digital models of physics that the Future Internet should meet? The Future Internet should serve the future needs of all other human endeavors, just as it should serve physicists. Given the impact of Internet on our current economy, it is likely that the Future Internet will shape our future economy. Alternatively, the requirements of future digital economic models could be defined as requirements for the Future Internet so that the Future Internet is shaped by future requirements rather than *vice versa*. Innovation and trends in Internet search suggest that a substantial portion of human knowledge and information will be digitally accessible to every person on the planet. What are the evolving visions for web-scale knowledge representation, search, and presentation and how will Future Internet accommodated them? These positively posed challenges have negative counterparts. Just as the Internet enables efficient, worldwide business endeavors, it also enables worldwide crime and terrorism, and provides means that can threaten privacy and civil rights [17]. How will visions of security, trust, privacy, safety, and democracy in our Future Digital World lead to requirements that the Future Internet will serve? While establishing policies and guidelines [5][6][7] for these domains is a start, we need visions – models of how they might operate – and their requirements for the Future Internet.

Consider for a moment the view that the vision for the Future Internet should be a vision of our Future Digital World and that its enabling technologies are mere implementation details. The term *mere* is used to emphasize the importance of human endeavors that it will serve such as the economy, social interactions, health care, science, and education, over technology. *Mere* also reminds us that technology serves the needs of society and not *vice versa*. The Future Internet and future information and communications technologies can no longer be seen as support technologies but as the means by which we shape and create our world.

In the 21st Century we can, more than ever, redefine our world with the aid of technology. What an Amazing opportunity! The Future Internet will be a worldwide technology platform – the computing/communications infrastructure - for our Future Digital Worlds. This leaves the Future Internet initiatives with the challenge of formulating visions for the Future Internet and the Future Digital Worlds that it will serve. We lack both. Happily in our already digital world, each domain of human endeavor has been formulating digital models for years. Unhappily, we all lack a vision for the current Internet let alone the Future Internet. Year after year for over 30 years, we have been astounded by the growth of the Internet and the related innovations. This suggests that we do not yet have an appropriate mental model of the Internet, how it operates, and how it interacts with the real world[1]. How can we envisage a Future Internet if we do not understand the current Internet? We should not initiate the design of the Future Internet without a reasonable vision or model of the Internet and of the digital worlds that it will serve. So how should we design the Future Internet?

3   Designing The Future Internet

Let's consider how a design process for the Future Internet by analogy with a design process for a family home.

---

[1] Suggested by Dr. Gérard Berry - a French computer scientist, member of French Academy of Sciences (Académie des sciences), French Academy of Technologies (Académie des technologies), and Academia Europaea.

Dick and Jane, newly married and newly graduated are embarking on new careers and need a home. How should they design their first home with a very limited vision of how they want to live? Pragmatics led them to acquire an existing house that they extended over time to meet anticipated and unanticipated needs. Ultimately they found the house to be too limited for their maturing needs. Let's call this initial phase a practice phase with a practice house.

As Dick and Jane matured as people, a couple, and as professionals, their requirements grew and matured relative to the limitations and problems of the practice house and initial life style, and to a vision of their future life – how they want the house to serve them. How should Dick and Jane design their future home? Should they select, based on the limitations of the practice house, the very best location, plumbing, wiring, foundations, and building materials? That bottom-up approach might address known problems of the practice phase that are unlikely to be as critical as the values and needs of their future life together. While a top-down vision of their future may be impossible to define clearly, they both have a substantial base of concrete and anecdotal evidence of what they like and don't like and possibly more mature visions of the life they want to live – recreation, rest, entertain, work, health, family, etc. There are also many expert resources to draw on to assist in planning these aspects of their future life and in designing their new home. The top-down and bottom-up approaches are both valuable and can inform and inspire each other in a virtuous cycle. The homeowners pose to the builder visions for the home including functions or requirements that the builder may not have imagined. The builder discusses with the homeowners the feasibility of the vision and poses alternatives including capabilities that the homeowners may not have considered. Mutually they evolve a home design. Since no one can predict the future, they attempt to include flexibility to facilitate modifications for inevitable unanticipated needs and opportunities.

Now that we have had our practice Internet and Web and have a detailed list of technical problems and limitations, but no clear model of the Internet how should we design the Future Internet? The Future Internet initiatives have identified technologists, policy makers, and economists with the intent of addressing bottom-up issues - known technical limitations and problems – and top-down issues – guided by policies intended to support innovation, creativity and economic growth. In comparison with the home design analogy, the house is being designed by builders and those responsible for building codes. The prospective homeowners are not involved. E-Government and Healthcare [2] are mentioned as policy domains but not as user communities with digital models of e-Government or healthcare. The current design process for the Future Internet includes the technologists who will build it and the policy makers who will govern it, but not the user communities that it will serve.

The design process for the Future Internet should include, in addition to the problem solvers - technologists, policy makers, and economists - the problem owners - the user communities who will create and operate their Future Digital Worlds on the Future Internet. The user communities are the well established and emerging industries, sectors, disciplines, and domains, and their ultimate end-user communities consisting of individuals, consumers, customers, patients, employees, and students – the ultimate beneficiaries of the Future Digital world. The citizens or inhabitants of our Future Digital World must have a voice. The process must also accommodate those that the Future Internet will impact but who do not have the means or resources to participate, such as those outside our current digital world. Since some communities are more advanced than others, some requirements will be better formulated for consideration for inclusion while others must be considered premature for inclusion. The competition for inclusion should spur learning and innovation.

As with the home design analogy, the design process should be collaborative with problems owners providing problem solvers with visions and requirements and problem solvers providing problem owners with models to evaluate, feasibility analysis, and possibly alternatives that the problem owners had not considered. Ideally the collaborative interaction between problem owners and problem solvers should operate in a virtuous cycle [8] that inspires problem solvers to innovate enabling technologies and solutions that in turn inspire problem owners to envisage more ambitious models and challenges for better and better digital worlds.

Due to the rapid pace of innovation and evolution in user communities and in Future Internet technologies and policies, and due to the enormous number of communities that should be included, the design process must be evolutionary. It must solicit, motivate, educate, review, evaluate, and compare design requirements iteratively. The scale of the endeavor, beyond that for any engineering artifact ever designed, will require new methods of continuous collaboration, modeling, evaluation, and evolution. A fundamental requirement is that the Future Internet and its design process be evolutionary – designed to evolve constantly and robustly.

Who will decide what requirements to include in the design of the Future Internet? The design process must accommodate and govern the full scope and scale of the objective – the Future Digital World – and that is as global as any human endeavor could be. It encompasses technologists, policy makers, and economists, and every human endeavor that could be impacted in our Future Digital World. It must encompass every nation. The Future Internet should be governed by a global body that can balance competing interests. As with the current Internet, the power and richness of the Future Internet may be based on a diversity of Future Internets each supporting a diversity of digital worlds in a competition that leads to innovation and Darwinian evolution.

Using the above principles, a health care system, for example, should be designed involving all stakeholders, including the patients or beneficiaries, the doctors, the administrators, the relevant policy makers, and the builders. The design process should start with a vision of how the digitally enabled process would operate which evolves iteratively and collaboratively amongst the stakeholders who decide on the solution before it is released. This ideal is seldom achieved as was the case in which the British Medical Association and most (55%) British doctors rejected the £12.4 billion Choose and Book system built by the British National Health Service as part of its "Connecting for Health - the worlds largest non-military computerization programme" designed to allow patients, advised by their doctors, to choose the treatments and to book appointment [13].

The above ideal can be achieved, as was the case for the Traditional Chinese Medicine (TCM) system developed in China [14]. It addressed deep issues such as the digital rendering of the relevant artifacts and processes, including 3,000 years of canonized case histories and the actual TCM processes of practitioners, including rural treatment and collaborative problem solving. The system was developed holistically and iteratively, following TCM practices, in a virtuous cycle involving patients, doctors, practitioners, administrators, drug companies, and the government (i.e., the insurer). The relevant digital worlds of the stakeholder were simple augmentations of the corresponding, age-old, non-digital worlds. Consequently the system was deployed almost transparently in 200 hospitals and via handheld devices to 1,000s of rural practitioners.

The challenges of designing a Future Internet based on the Future Digital Worlds that it will serve under the constraints above seem overwhelming, especially if the design process is seen as separate from the real world. As with the TCM example above, the design process should be an integral part of each component of the digital world, as is the case in most domains. Designing, creating, and evolving the Future Digital World of any one component should be considered a normal step in solving problem in that component.

4 Lesser Grand Challenges

The paper concludes with a few thoughts on the profound opportunities and challenges offered by the design of our Future Digital World.

4.1 Envisaging the Future

An obvious grand challenge for the design of our Future Digital Worlds is "How do we envisage the future?" Happily the answer has a simple starting point based on the observation:

> "The future is here. It's just not evenly distributed yet." -- William Gibson

A half-century history of creating digital worlds – in applying information and communications technologies – has produced digital models in almost every human endeavor. Indeed the challenge is not a lack but a plethora of future digital visions – typically incomplete and rapidly evolving. Each domain of human endeavor is replete with concepts for Future Digital Worlds - unified communications, ubiquitous computing, high performance workplace, cloud computing, social networking, and digital ecosystems. This is wonderful. The competition amongst these alternatives is the soul of innovation. To contribute requirements for its Future Digital Worlds to the design of the Future Internet, each domain will have to cooperate and develop its own selection and definition process or choose not to contribute.

A significant challenge in every domain is overcoming the legacy. Replacing the legacy – analog or previous digital models – with new digital models is costly and challenging. These challenges should be overcome based on improvements in quality and reduction in total cost of deploying the improved products, services, and processes. For example, e-business and e-retail while significant components in our economy account for less than 15% of business and retail transactions. Legacy, pre-Internet technologies, such as Electronic Data Interchange (EDI), still dominate business and retail transactions. EDI supports over 90% of all e-business transactions. Future Digital Worlds should be used to modernize domains by replacing less efficient, legacy technologies with the most efficient technologies and methods. New digital models and technologies should be selected based on the their value that should be enough to justify, over a reasonable period of time, migration from the legacy.

Web-scale information, processing, and communications will change our world. To direct that change for the better we must understand Future Digital Worlds and their potential for good and ill. Look at the impact of the Internet and the Web on our world today. The continued ascendance of the digital world can be seen in the adoption rates of digital rendering and traffic [9]. But adoption rates do not even hint at the fundamental changes that the digital world enables. The most obvious changes are new technologies that replace the legacy. Greater impacts are seen in fundamental changes in the business models that underlie a domain, such as automating end-to-end supply chains across all stakeholders and selling and distributing books and music over the Internet. Deeper still are the changes that alter the fundamentals principles of the domain, as illustrated in examples in the next two paragraphs. The design of the Future Internet should include these future digital visions to support advancement in all human endeavors.

Almost every domain of human endeavor has or is about to change qualitatively due to digitization. Wired magazine [10] describes such fundamental changes in medicine, law, air travel, disease control, surveillance, astronomy, news, counterterrorism, and proclaims *The End of Science* [11]. Science has been based on creating and verifying hypotheses. Scientists create hypotheses about the part of the world that they are investigating – from astrophysics to nanophysics – make models based on the hypothesis, and run experiments on the model to prove or disprove the hypothesis. I recall to this day the thrill of understanding the 1887, Nobel Prize winning Michelson-Morley experiment that itself marked a qualitative change in science, called the Second Scientific Revolution [12]. But models sometimes elude experimentation, as has the Higgs boson. In the Petabyte Age, objects of study from DNA to the cosmos, can be rendered in digital form and analyzed to find correlations and patterns that lead to an understanding of the phenomenon without using man-made, thus limited models, as Craig Venter did for DNA sequencing.

Telescopes have been the primary instrument for astrophysicists for 100s of years before Galileo's 17th Century version. Today individual astrophysicists schedule observation time in Arizona on the $120 million Large Binocular Telescope. In the Petabyte Age, any astrophysicists anywhere can search a digital image of sky scanned by the Sloan Digital Sky Survey or the ten times more powerful Large Synoptic Survey Telescope. Indeed software can be used to find things in the digital image that the human eye could never see. If you wonder if true scientific discoveries can be made by database search consider these two recent examples. In August 2008, Dr Andrew Becker of the University of Washington, using the Sloan Digital Sky Survey discovered almost 50 new asteroid-sized bodies in the outer regions of our Solar System. Based in results obtained from the Sloane Survey and the Two Degree Field Galaxy Redshift Survey, Prof Carlos Frenk, of the University of Durham, UK said, "It's an amazing new insight into how the Universe works." The results "essentially explains why we are here - why matter created in the Big Bang came together to create everything we see around us" [15].

The Next Generation of Technology, shaped by the Future Internet, may qualitatively change the nature of science. The challenges of empirically identifying the

Higgs boson may signal the limits of the LHC, of Big Science, and of the scientific method itself, as suggested in *The End of Science* [11] and call for new scientific methods enabled by massive data and digital methods [10]. The information from the LHC introduces the possibility that science becomes a search for understanding the world in terms of correlations found via analysis of massive digital representations (datasets) without predetermined models (theories).

4.2 A Digital Industrial Revolution

The Internet is famous for eliminating physical boundaries such as location and geography thus providing global access and eliminating distance as a cost metric in communications and access but has confounded legal, regulatory, and other boundaries that define our non-digital world. The Future Internet is about to eliminate technical and industrial boundaries with equally significant opportunities and threats.

The Future Internet is intended to integrate existing, disjoint communications and computing networks and technologies to achieve a single, pervasive, and trustworthy network and services infrastructure that will resolve the known problems and limitations of the existing networks. The impact of this convergence will be far beyond technology. The Future Internet will provide a basis for the convergence and redefinition of the industries whose products and services are digital in some aspect of their lifecycle. This will lead to massive innovation and competition.

Entire industries (e.g., communications, computing, entertainment) and within them sub-industries (e.g., fixed, wireless, and cable in communications; TV, radio, film, and video in entertainment) live on technology islands based on their own core technology (broadcast technology, physical and digital film, wireline and wireless technologies, cable technologies, Internet Protocol). Historically, the complexity, cost, and legacy aspects of these islands limited innovation within an industry and protected the industry incumbents from external competition. Moving from the legacy networks to the Future Internet will enable each industry to re-envisage itself not only to improve the quality and reduce the cost of existing products and services, but also to reinvent its products and services. This alone should lead to massive innovation and improvements. But the threats and opportunities are far greater. The previous technology-based boundaries will disappear together with the protections that they offered. The power of our digital world will permit entire industries to re-invent themselves – their products, their services, and their operations – innovating with any product or service that could be rendered digitally and drawing on products and services from every industry that lived on the previous networks and technologies. This head-to-head competition across industries with products and services that could be rendered and delivered digitally may initially be limited only by regulation and policy but those restrictions are being rethought [5][6][7]. Managed well, the design and development of our Future Digital World on the Future Internet could result in one of the most innovative periods since the Industrial Revolution, one of the most productive periods in history with correspondingly large economic growth – a Digital Industrial Revolution.

4.3 Technology Should Disappear

One of the greatest challenges of modern computing and communications is complexity. How do you select it? How do you configure it to work, let alone meet your personal needs – as the vendor promised? When it breaks, how do you fix it? While these technology challenges are stunningly evident to consumers of digital products, it is even more obvious and critical in more sophisticated technologies. Database management systems (DBMSs) is a bedrock technology for modern business. DBMSs may be the most successful ($15 billion annual sales) and sophisticated infrastructure technology. The sophistication of DBMSs permits them to meet the need of a vast array of data management applications. It also impedes the efficient and effective use that powerful technology. The efficient use of a DBMS for a modestly sophisticated application is beyond the capability of most database administrators and engineers, not only due to the range of choices but also to the 200 or more new choices introduced each year. The DBMS community has a long way to go to achieve the 20-year goal of self-management. A similar story applies to most of the 30 major infrastructure software categories. The recent achievements of the Service Oriented Architecture (SOA) community indicate the wrong way to go. SOA has become one of the most complex forms of middleware in history and may require more expertise and knowledge than DBMSs. The requirement that technology disappear and manage itself is not simply a desire for reduced complexity and increased productivity through higher levels of automation and self-management. The scope and scale of databases already exceeds the human resource cost barrier to keep databases cost efficient. The scope and scale of our Future Digital World will do the same for all technology.

A major requirement for our Future Digital Worlds and specifically for the Future Internet is that technology should disappear and manage itself or be managed transparently by experts. It should transparently offer its capabilities when needed in a form that suits your requirements and preferences. A model to aspire to might be more mature technologies such as electricity, car engines, refrigerators, and washing machines.

4.4 Our Digital World Should Be Realistic

As our real world becomes more digital, our digital worlds should become more real. My current digital worlds – my calendar, my contacts, my health care records - are crisp, delineated, deterministic, and compartmentalized unlike my real world that can at times be vague, approximate, ambiguous, changing, and deeply connected to the real worlds of others. My real world is holistic; my digital worlds are not.

Bringing reality to our digital worlds involves at least three challenges - achieving greater realism in rendering, manipulating, and analyzing our digital worlds; sharing digital things, actions, and processes across digital worlds to achieve more holistic, connected worlds, and finally aligning our real and digital worlds. Achieving more realistic renderings, manipulations, and analysis requires extending currently discrete means to accommodate non-deterministic, ambiguous, and approximate aspects of our reality. These capabilities must be supported by the most basic representation technologies such as databases to store and manage the data representations and technologies with which to query, modify, and manipulate them. Achieving more holistic digital worlds, e.g., healthcare, family relationships, entertainment, or retail, requires that those worlds be able to share different digital representations while maintaining the veracity of each world. Finally, our real and digital worlds will shape each other and should be adjusted according to needs and realities. Being immersed in a highly digital world will impact our notions of privacy, trust, and security and lead to a deeper understanding of the concepts and their feasibility, e.g., "security is an illusion and only neurotics think they can use technology to control the real world."[16] Finally, law and regulations are often defined in terms of the technologies just prior to enactment. As with other human endeavors it may be possible to develop digital legal and regulatory models that could be used to define the Future Internet and our digital worlds rather than *vice versa* [17].

4.5   Integrity in the Digital World Requires Collaboration

Our real world is holistic and deeply connected, no matter how we look at it. Our digital world must also be holistic and deeply connected. How do we design, develop, and evolve digital worlds so that they retain the connectedness of the real world? The philosophical and scientific premise that the world can be decomposed into separate and disjoint realms or disciplines may have run its course since the premise does not tell us how to reconnect the realms to regain an integral world.

Consider the challenge facing the design of the Future Internet. The requirements for the Future Internet should reflect the requirements of each digital world – each human endeavor – that it will support. The number is clearly enormous. The requirements for each digital world should be combined so that each thing, action, and process that exists in two or more digital worlds can be seen as one, in each digital world while retaining its integrity in each digital world in which it takes part. How do you combine the representations or design them to achieve integrity? The design must be collaborative across all participating digital worlds.

The Traditional Chinese Medicine application [14] is an excellent example of a collaborative process across nine realms – those of the patient, the rural practitioner, the hospital practitioner, the hospital, the drug company, the regulator, the insurer, the computing solution, and the communications solution. The trick was that the design and development team were experts in most realms. Team members were active TCM practitioners as well as computing and communications technologists. Due to the role of government in healthcare and to the 3,000 year TCM tradition, there was an intimate relationship between the hospital, the government, and practitioners, and the drug company. For example, the 3,000 year TCM cannon often leads to a specific pathology that typically leads to a small set of prescriptions each of which is approved by the government that is also the insurer, and provided by the drug company. The team, as TCM practitioners, sees 100's of patients per week. While this level of collaboration and strong holistic requirements is rare, it provides a model to emulate.

For decades, the requirement for collaborative, interdisciplinary work has been acknowledged and promoted to achieve holistic, end-to-end solutions, with little perceptible impact. There are walls not only between domains, but also within domains. As our real worlds become increasingly digital they must become more real, hence holistic versus separate and disjoint. This will require collaboration across the relevant digital worlds and disciplines. The process to design the Future Internet faces the interdisciplinary challenge more than previous computing and communications initiatives. Future Internet initiatives should take a bold step and break down walls and require collaborative steps towards realistic and holistic digital worlds.

5 Can We Free Our Minds?

Each realm of human endeavor continues to create Future Digital Worlds in which to represent its things, actions, and processes. These digital worlds will be built on the Next Generation computing and communications platform, the Future Internet. Collectively these digital worlds will shape our future digital universe that will increasingly shape our lives. The requirements for these digital worlds should drive the design of the Future Internet rather than *vice versa*. The amazing opportunity to re-think and redesign our world requires us to envisage a better future, eliminate artificial boundaries, eliminate the drudgery of technology, and strive for realism through collaboration towards holistic digital worlds.

Perhaps the greatest challenge in envisaging our Future Digital World is to free our minds and overcome our intellectual, technical, and social history to create new visions of the future and to work holistically across currently disjoint domains.

These grand challenges are steps towards answering the compelling question for the 21st Century "What is the nature of our digital universe?"

References

1. Large Hadron Collider, Wikipedia
2. The Future Internet, European Commission: Information and Communications Technologies Programme, http://www.future-intenet.eu
3. Web Science, http://webscience.org/
4. Bled Future Internet Manifesto. The Future of the Internet: Perspectives emerging from R&D in Europe, Bled, Slovenia (March 31, 2008)
5. Shaping Policies for the Future of the Internet Economy. OECD Ministerial Meeting on the Future of the Internet Economy, Seoul, Korea (June 17-18, 2008)
6. Declaration on the Future of the Internet Economy. OECD Ministerial Meeting on the Future of the Internet Economy, Seoul, Korea (June 17-18, 2008)
7. Social and Economic Factors Shaping the Future of the Internet. In: NSF/OECD Workshop proceedings (January 31, 2007)
8. Brodie, M.L.: The End of the Computing Era: Hephaestus meets The Olympians. In: IEEE/IES Digital Ecosystem and Business Intelligence Conference, Phitsanulok, Thailand (February 26-29, 2008)
9. Approaching the Zetabyte Era, White Paper, Cisco Systems (July 18, 2008)
10. The Petabyte Age: Because More Isn't Just More - More Is Different, Wired Magazine, issue 16.07, 06.23.08
11. The End of Theory: The Data Deluge Makes the Scientific Method Obsolete, Wired Magazine, issue 16.07, 06.23.08
12. Michelson-Morley experiment, Wikipedia
13. The electronic bureaucrat: A special report on technology and government. The Economist (February 16, 2008)

14. Wong, A.K.Y., Lin, W.W.K., Wong, J.H.K.: Telemedicine: Application to Traditional Chinese Medicine. In: IEEE/IES Digital Ecosystem and Business Intelligence Conference, Phitsanulok, Thailand, Hong Kong Polytechnic University and PuraPharm International (H.K.) Ltd. of the Hong Kong SAR (February 26-29, 2008)
15. Sky surveys reveal cosmic ripples, BBC News (January 12, 2005),
    http://news.bbc.co.uk/2/hi/science/nature/4161323.stm
16. Claburn, T.: Black Hat: Security Offers Illusion Of Control. InformationWeek (August 6, 2008)
17. Protecting Individual Privacy in the Struggle Against Terrorism: A Framework for Program Assessment, Committee on Technical and Privacy Dimensions of Information for Terrorism Prevention and Other National Goals, National Research Council, Washington, D.C (2008) ISBN-10: 0-309-12488-3 ISBN-13: 978-0-309-12488-1

The Internet of Things in an Enterprise Context

Stephan Haller[1], Stamatis Karnouskos[2], and Christoph Schroth[3]

[1] SAP (Schweiz) AG, SAP Research CEC Zürich,
Kreuzplatz 20, CH-8008 Zürich, Switzerland
[2] SAP AG, SAP Research CEC Karlsruhe,
Vincent-Priessnitz-Strasse 1, D-76131Karlsruhe, Germany
[3] SAP (Schweiz) AG, SAP Research CEC St.Gallen,
Blumenbergplatz 9, CH-9000 St.Gallen, Switzerland
{stephan.haller,stamatis.karnouskos,christoph.schroth}@sap.com

Abstract. This paper puts the Internet of Things in a wider context: How it relates to the Future Internet overall, and where the business value lies so that it will become interesting for enterprises to invest in it. Real-World Awareness and Business Process Decomposition are the two major paradigms regarding future business value. The major application domains where the Internet of Things will play an important role and where there are concrete business opportunities are highlighted. But there are also many technical challenges that need to be addressed. These are listed and it is shown how they are tackled by existing research projects with industrial participation.

Keywords: Internet of Things, Future Internet, Real-World Visibility, Business Process Decomposition, Business Value, SOA, Enterprise Services.

1 Introduction

The Internet of Things is a term that has been around for several years. It was first introduced by the MIT Auto-ID Center, the precursor to the current EPCglobal organisation, and at that time stood for the vision of a world where all physical objects are tagged with an RFID transponder with a globally unique ID – the EPC or electronic product code. RFID easily allows tracking the objects, and the EPC serves as a link to data which can be queried over the Internet about each individual object. Since then, the meaning of the Internet of Things has expanded. Using sensors or sensor networks, additional information about the objects or the environment that they are in can be recorded as well. Software embedded in the objects enables data processing directly on the item, and in combination with actuators, local control loops can be implemented.

The Internet of Things is a key part of the Future Internet. Many new opportunities can be foreseen for citizens as well as for businesses and other organisations, but also for the society as a whole.

2 The Internet of Things and the Future Internet

There are currently many terms flying around when trying to characterise the future development of the Internet: In addition to the Internet of Things, there is the Internet

J. Domingue, D. Fensel, and P. Traverso (Eds.): FIS 2008, LNCS 5468, pp. 14–28, 2009.

of Services, 3D Internet, Internet of Content, and Next-Generation Networks, just to name a few. It is important to note that these terms should not be regarded as different "Internets" that will exist in parallel, but rather as different aspects of a common Future Internet. The European Commission has understood this and is therefore taking concerted action and clustering the research projects it is funding in the 7th Framework Programme into what it calls the *Future Internet Assembly*. Furthermore, collaborations are on-going and likely will be intensified with similar efforts in the USA and Japan.

From an enterprise and economic perspective, the Future Internet is the basis for a *web-based service economy* [1]. There will be service platforms and a multitude of services available over the Internet, hence the term Internet of Services. The granularity of these services will be very different, ranging from high-level business services to low-level sensor services provided by the Internet of Things. The role of the Internet of Things is to bridge the gap between the physical world and its representation in information systems. This leads us to our definition of the Internet of Things:

> *"A world where physical objects are seamlessly integrated into the information network, and where the physical objects can become active participants in business processes. Services are available to interact with these 'smart objects' over the Internet, query their state and any information associated with them, taking into account security and privacy issues."*

It is noteworthy that in this definition, we don't talk about technologies. RFID, sensor networks, embedded systems etc. are just enabling technologies, and we will see the technologies change over the years, but the main concept behind the Internet of Things will remain. Furthermore, the objects can be passive, as is the case with RFID-tagged objects, or active as in the case of machines with embedded process logic. Key is though the seamless integration into the business processes.

3   The Business Value of the Internet of Things

For the Internet of Things to become reality and not just stay at the buzz-word and concept level, investments will be needed: to solve current research challenges, to develop the necessary hard- and software, and to deploy the infrastructure required. This will only happen if there is a clear economic benefit. We see two major paradigms from which business value can be derived, which we term *real-world visibility* and *business process decomposition*. In the following, we define and explain both these terms before looking at some of the application areas that stand to profit most from the possibilities in the Internet of Things.

3.1   Real-World Visibility

The term real-world visibility denotes the fact that through the use of automated identification and data collection technologies like RFID and sensors it will be possible for a company to better know what actually is happening in the real world, i.e., how its operations are performing and what the status and whereabouts of its assets and products in the supply chain are. This enables what Fleisch et al. call *high-resolution management* [2]. The increased accuracy and timeliness of information about the business processes provides competitive advantages in terms of process optimisation [3]. The deeper insights gained into the processes allows a better understanding of them at the operational level and leads to their optimisation. Low data entry costs offset the considerable investment currently required, enabling organizations to benefit from automated entry and, largely, from continuous, near real-time measurement. Optimized shelf replenishments serve here as a well-known example where 'out-of-shelf' situations are avoided, thereby providing optimal product availability for the customer. Shop floor control can similarly be optimized with lot and equipment tracking functionalities that provide MES and ERP systems with more accurate information about the physical state and conditions of manufacturing inventories, thereby potentially increasing the efficiency and availability of production plants [4].

These example applications make use of the monitoring of the real world and the derived data in order to better control and manage business processes that deal with products and assets, the environment or persons. Sensory information increases the accuracy of real world checks and thus is the foundation of event-driven management. Automated sensing enables a new and much finer granularity of management, since it helps to control what was before uncontrollable. With a network architecture that supports the easy discovery, communication, and usage of events across the enterprise, events enriched with contextual business information will improve business data quality on all levels.

Additionally, (near) real-time analytics combines the usage of enterprise data with incoming sensory information to discover patterns and derive more timely and accurate business insight. New strategies and predictions can be generated based on certain pre-configured criteria.

3.2 Business Process Decomposition

Real-world visibility as described above is what basically is done today with RFID and sensing. Data is collected and sent to a central application, where it is processed and decisions about actions are taken. Business process decomposition takes this a step further, as shown in Fig. 1: A business process is decomposed into process steps, some of which are executed in a distributed manner, even at the edges of the network and on physical items themselves. Hence sometimes the term edge processing is used, and the physical items that can process some business logic are called *smart items*.

Current enterprise strategies already acknowledge a few interfaces to smart items, but with increased computational and communication capabilities of these items, the power shifts towards the edges of the network. Intelligent mechanisms for data aggregation, filtering, fusion and conversion can be deployed to and executed at the network edge, or within the network, as appropriate. The decomposition and decentralization of existing business processes increases scalability and performance, allows better decision making and could even lead to new revenue streams through entitlement management of software products deployed on smart items. Software is already the key innovation driver in many industries and many new business models of the future will heavily rely on the use of such items [5].

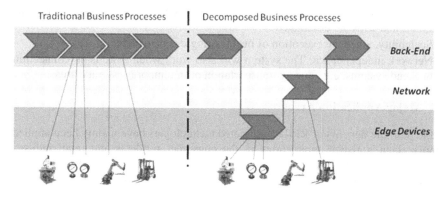

Fig. 1. Traditional vs. decomposed and distributed business processes

Edge processing and business process decomposition allows applications to make (part of their) decisions locally in a decentralized manner and act accordingly. It thereby extends the real world visibility concept with real world interaction.

In addition to a (central) business application, data is processed locally in a distributed fashion. Actuators, which directly influence the real world, can be integrated as well. Smart items become thereby active participants in the overall business process.

Utilizing the computing power and intelligence on smart items or other edge devices allow enterprise systems to propagate data and services to these new, potentially underutilised, run time environments. It allows local decision-making and early aggregation and filtering of raw sensor data. However, it also requires innovation in distributed computing and network utilization.

Based on this paradigm shift, a new need arises for design time environments that allow modelling of business applications through a decentralized optimization strategy, taking into account all business objects, business processes, services, as well as processing, sensing and communication capabilities of smart items. New and optimized business processes can be modelled as collections of these 'artefacts' based on specific policies. Self-organisation in this context describes the adaptability of the model during deployment. Changes in the environment (e.g. location change, connectivity outage, reconfiguration of business processes etc.) require reorganization of the deployed components during run time to meet given Quality of Service (QoS) constraints.

In summary, edge processing can bring significant benefits, but this comes at a cost of increased management complexity. The decomposition of business processes can be seen as an evolutionary continuation of *enterprise service-oriented architectures* (E-SOA). E-SOA enables the efficient decomposition of large segments of functionality into largely decoupled components. In essence, E-SOA is a set of architectural components for building autonomous yet interoperable composites. The convergence of computing and networking technologies and the trends to increased intelligence of smart items opens the opportunity of applying these concepts to the real world. Because of the increased management complexity however, it has to be determined for each application on a case-by-case basis if distributed business logic is appropriate. The following are criteria that indicate an advantage for a decentralized approach:

- Responsiveness of the overall system, since unnecessary 'expensive' communication round-trips are eliminated
- Scalability, since the execution of business logic is distributed
- Network independence: The system will also work when there is no connection to backend systems, e.g., during transportation or in temporary storage areas.

3.3 Major Application Areas

In the past, the benefits of RFID and related technologies have mainly been applied to supply chain logistics applications in the consumer products and retail industries. While these will remain an important cornerstone also in the future, we see with the expanded definition of the Internet of Things many other interesting application domains. Some of the most promising ones are discussed below.

Manufacturing. Due to the rapid advances in the embedded systems domain, the manufacturing domain is undergoing significant changes as ubiquitous computing is applied to the shop floor. An entirely new dynamic network of cooperating devices can be created which effectively shows that the Internet of Things can reshape the manufacturing domain. Currently, shop floor intelligent systems based on distributed embedded devices concentrate the programming of the behaviour and intelligence on a handful of large monolithic computing resources accompanied by large numbers of "dumb" devices. The intelligence and behaviour are tailored and individually programmed for each application.

As SOA concepts are becoming the de-facto standard to connect to enterprise applications, there has been a move also in the automation domain towards putting web services on the devices themselves and giving them the capability of providing their functionality as a service. This will create eventually cross-layer web service mash-ups, with services hosted at the enterprise, middleware and device level [6].

The key idea is to provide the same interoperability and ease of integration of devices as is the case with service mash-ups. All the devices would offer their functionality as a web service. Device integration thus means service integration, focusing on the functionality a device offers and not on the particular device technology. This not only creates a new paradigm on the shop floor, but it also would encourage the development of new devices in the automation industry that offer embedded web services. Furthermore, it would kick-start collaboration at the lowest level, i.e., among the devices themselves, as well as offer new opportunities by effectively connecting the vendor-locked isolated islands of today.

Supply Chain Integrity. Internet of Things technologies allow the tracking of the location and the state of an object throughout the full product life-cycle and throughout the supply chain. Nowadays this is already used to detect diversions into illicit or grey markets as well as the introduction of counterfeit products [7]. But this is just one part of ensuring complete integrity of the supply chain. Complete integrity though includes many other aspects. First of all, there is the physical integrity of the product itself. Sensors can be used to ensure that the product was never exposed to potentially damaging environmental conditions, e.g., that safe temperature or shock levels never were exceeded. Secondly, there is the integrity of the transportation routes, i.e. that the product never was in an area where it was not allowed to be. For example, hazardous goods may not be transported through heavily populated or environmentally sensitive areas because of the severe effects of an accident. For the same reason, some means of transportation may be forbidden, and other areas might be off-limits due to fears of unauthorized access to a product. And thirdly, there is the integrity of a product and all its subcomponents regarding the means of production. Here in particular environmental compliance is important. It must be ensured that the final product doesn't exceed certain levels regarding emissions and carbon footprint. With the problem of global warming, we believe that especially this last point will be a driving factor for research and development. Internet of Things technologies will enable the recording of all the emissions that were generated in the production and transportation of every subcomponent across multiple levels of a complex supply chain. In general, the new technologies will be used to ensure full *compliance* of all participants of the supply chain to a set of agreed-upon rules: legal regulations, internal policies and service-level agreements. Time is important in most cases: The violation of certain temporal boundaries would mean a possible breach of integrity.

Energy. In the quest for providing abundant clean, secure and affordable energy, Europe and the rest of the world are investing heavily in ICT in the energy domain. The usage of modern technologies, coupled with concepts coming from the Internet of Things and the Internet of Services will lead to a paradigm change. Innovative new technologies and concepts will emerge as we move towards a more dynamic, service-based, market-driven infrastructure, where energy efficiency and savings can be better addressed though interactive distribution networks. One example from the energy area that shows the importance of the Internet of Things is the creation of an advanced metering infrastructure (AMI).

AMI refers to systems that measure, collect, and analyze energy usage from advanced devices such as electricity, gas, and water meters. Communication can either be on request or on a pre-defined schedule. These devices are usually referred to as *smart meters*. Smart meters can be either considered as sensors with wireless capabilities themselves, or they are expected to cooperate with (wireless) sensor networks at home in order to deliver their data. Driven by new regulation and the global energy crisis, in the United States advanced metering with embedded wireless sensor networks has grown from a few thousand units in 2004 to 1.5 million smart meters this year, according to a survey by ON World. ON World projects that the global wireless sensor networking smart meter and demand response market will be worth $1.6 billion in 2011.

Smart meters empower an advanced metering infrastructure which is able to react almost in real time, provide fine-grained energy production or consumption info and adapt its behaviour proactively. These smart meters will be multi-utility ones, managing not only electricity but also gas and heat, and they will depend on multiple (wireless) sensors. New information-dependent intelligent energy management systems will be needed for an infrastructure capable of supporting the deregulated energy market. Smart meters will have to be installed for millions of households and companies and get connected to transaction platforms.

Smart meters provide new opportunities and challenges in networked embedded system design and electronics integration. They will be able not only to provide (near) real-time data, but also process them and take decisions based on their capabilities and collaboration with external services. That in turn will have a significant impact on existing and future energy management models. Decision and policy makers will be able to base their actions on real-world, real-time data and not just on simple predictions. Households and companies will be able to react to market fluctuations by increasing or decreasing consumption or production, thus directly contributing to increased energy efficiency.

Health. In the health sector, RFID is now being used by some hospitals like the Jena University hospital in Germany [8] to optimise both the logistics processes as well as to provide better care, to track equipment, patients – in particular, new-born babies – and medications. This benefits both the health care providers in the form of cost savings as well as the patients, since false treatments can be avoided. The expected usage of wireless sensors as well as the emerging interconnection of all devices in the hospitals will increasingly change the landscape. Even bigger potential comes though with the expected ageing of society with the associated rise of health care costs: The Internet of Things will be essential in realising the vision of ambient assisted living.

Automotive. In the automotive industry, sensors and embedded systems already play a large role. These will become even more important when these are integrated into a future "Internet of Vehicles": *Car-to-X Communication*, as it is more commonly known, denotes communication between vehicles as well as between vehicles and certain road-side infrastructure. This has turned into a very important research area over the last few years: Several different use-cases have been proposed and analyzed which range from safety-related warning systems over information and entertainment applications to Car-to-Business scenarios. In case the vehicles are wireless enabled (car manufacturers are currently investing into the definition of a common standard), feature a communication module and sensors for detecting road conditions and local dangers, they may autonomously connect to each other and exchange information (we refer to these temporary and autonomously organized connections as Vehicular Ad hoc Networks). When detecting hazards or blockings on the road as visualized, these vehicles can generate appropriate messages containing a description, their geographical position and many more application-dependent pieces of information. Messages may be immediately broadcasted to all other cars within communication range, which in turn can store, evaluate and forward them.

Besides such applications with a safety improvement focus, other scenarios encompass the communication of vehicles with backend business services. Based on car-to-infrastructure communication technologies, cars may consume services such as remote diagnosis in case of break-downs, software version management, and other applications in the field of *Vehicle Relationship Management*. These exemplary scenarios show that vehicles are about to become smart items interacting over partly decentralized (ad-hoc) networks and partly over stable infrastructure-based Internet connections. The shift away from "mute and autistic" cars towards intelligent and proactive sensor nodes allows for both the above-mentioned real-world visibility and for business process decomposition: Firstly, cars are enabled to gather fine-granular information about their environments and their own status in order to facilitate better services (e.g., for central traffic management, anti-theft-, or smart insurance pricing applications). Secondly, vehicles become truly autonomous, intelligent items which are capable of performing event-based business logic in a decentralized fashion. Safety-related applications rely on cars being able to independently sense road conditions, create proper warning messages, disseminate them appropriately in temporary, ever-changing ad hoc networks and continuously evaluate them for their current relevance. Significant intelligence is thus allocated to the edges of vehicular networks, following the vision of an Internet of Vehicles.

Insurance. Insurance companies are assessing the consequences and potential benefits of new technologies and their applications. The considered technology trends lead potentially to a "high-resolution world", which will allow insurance companies to better estimate and manage risks, enabling the setting of individual insurance rates as well as better decisions what to underwrite. It will also allow them to minimise losses by preventing accidents and damage events or at least reducing their severity thanks to early detection and intervention, and by helping to locate missing persons, animals or things. Furthermore, costs can be reduced by automating the claims management processes. Besides direct benefits (e.g., less costs due to less damage events), the main opportunity for insurance companies is to use the technologies to differentiate their offering from the competition – innovative offerings – and to increase the number of contacts with their customers. While in the past insurance companies only dealt with customers when signing a policy and when settling a claim, now they can leverage technology to frequently discuss how individual risks could be measured or reduced and how this could influence existing contracts or initiate new ones. In the case of loss, the technology also enables the insurance company to provide immediate and better assistance to their customers.

4 Major Technical Issues

The Internet of Things promises many opportunities and socio-economic benefits. However, there still are a number of technical as well as governance issues that need to be solved in order to realize the vision. In the following, we highlight some of what we believe to be major issues in the years ahead.

4.1 Internet Scalability

The Internet currently consists of more than 540 million hosts [9] and 1.4 billion users [10]. The Internet of Things will possibly have trillions of things connected. As an example of scale, let's assume that each thing will have its own IP address. IPv6 could accommodate 2^{128} (about 3.4×10^{38}) things, which raises the number of possible participants in the Future Internet by several orders of magnitude. As a result of connectivity, the data volumes will significantly increase; and in addition to discrete data we will see more and more streaming data, e.g., from sensors and cameras being transmitted over the Internet. Traditional client-server paradigms and methods of data processing where all data is collected and processed in a central instance will not suffice. A paradigm change needs to be undertaken. Considering the advances in the computing capabilities that are now available within the network as well as on its edges, new models and algorithms will need to be developed that can depend on "in-network" and "on-edge" processing with the help of information fetched from enterprise systems.

Scalability has been recognized as an important topic since the days the term "Internet of Things" was first used. Several methods exist and will have to be used in combination to achieve the desired scalability: filtering of irrelevant data, aggregating data to a higher semantic level, event-driven architectures and complex event processing, as well as the execution of business logic at the edges and on physical items themselves. The key is to reduce the number of messages and the amount of data transmitted throughout all the layers of the system; to that end data should be evaluated locally and where it makes sense, while propagation should be done only if a network-wide usage is expected or where there are clear application requirements for doing so.

Regarding the management of networks and devices, the focus currently is on the self-* research that includes self-configuration (automatic configuration of components), self-healing (automatic discovery and correction of faults), self-optimization (automatic monitoring and control of resources to ensure the optimal functioning with respect to the defined requirements) and self-protection (proactive identification and protection from arbitrary attacks).

As an example of testing scalability issues, within the IST FP6 SOCRADES [11] project we have embedded web services on a variety of devices. These devices provide their functionality as a service to which other entities can subscribe and get the status of the device and/or its sensor results. In our preliminary research we have successfully managed to simulate approx. 25'000 such web-service enabled devices, generated and hosted within a single Java virtual machine. As expected however, the overhead on the communication channel increased tremendously (as every second each one of these devices would both try to propagate its values to the subscribers, as well as to answer new discovery requests). In the Future Internet such operations will be much more common, requiring the right architectural decisions to be made. Event-Driven Architectures and Complex Event Processing (CEP) will gain significance, as this will be one major tool to manage complex data evaluations and extract meaningful and business relevant correlations.

Continued development and testing for scalability is needed. The IST FP7 project SENSEI [12] is addressing this by setting up a large-scale distributed Pan-European test bed for sensor and actuator based ambient intelligence.

4.2 Identification and Addressing

In order to be able to address the billions of entities in the Internet of Things, we first need to be able to identify them with a unique ID. That ID can also be used to find other information about the entity of interest. The EPC Network [13] as proposed by EP-Cglobal is one possible implementation of such a scheme. The EPC is used as a unique ID, and via the ONS the EPCIS server of the manufacturer of the product can be found where further information on the product can be looked up. However, for the unique identification of objects other approaches exist: In Japan, the ucode [14] is gaining popularity, and other groups – especially when we are talking about smart items – propose to use IPv6 addresses for this purpose. Furthermore, there are many well-established industry-specific IDs that at least so far have not been mapped to EPCs.

Also the ONS has not gained the popularity yet that was originally envisioned. The reason is that there are concerns regarding security and privacy [15] as well as reliability, since currently a single company, VeriSign, is in charge of operating the ONS root server. To achieve the necessary level of confidence globally, a more distributed model is required with a set of geographically distributed, but synchronized root servers, as is the case with DNS today. A first step has been taken in that direction with the awarding of a contract to Orange to operate a (still regional) ONS server by GS1 France [16].

Tracking and tracing objects as they are moving along the supply chain is one of the most important basic functions of the Internet of Things. It provides the foundation for product authentication, anti-counterfeiting and other supply chain integrity applications. To implement this functionality, discovery services are required that allow dynamically finding all information about a specific object. In an EPC context, this means a service that can find all EPCIS instances that contain some information about a certain object. One of the key difficulties here is to be able to find all relevant information in a world with multi-level adaptive supply chains where business relationships change quickly, and to still keep the necessary confidentiality. Such discovery services are currently being developed in the BRIDGE project; and a joint requirements group has also started to work on this within EPCglobal. Like with ONS, discussions centre here around the issue of centralisation vs. decentralisation. A centralised discovery service is certainly easier to implement and manage, but it raises concerns regarding confidentiality as well as availability. A decentralised or even peer-to-peer model therefore seems more acceptable in industry.

The ID used to uniquely identify an object can also be used when we want to communicate with the object. In the case of IPv6 addresses, the ID and the technical address are the same. In the case of EPCs, some mapping is required. Implementing such a mapping is trivial though, since the EPC can be used to look up the physical address; the technical address is simply another property of the object.

In contrast to this technical, direct addressing, from a business application perspective another method of addressing that we call *logical addressing* is needed as well. This denotes a method to address a group of objects or any random object within that group based on certain properties. For example, all drums in storage area A that contain isopropyl alcohol. Or, an arbitrary temperature sensor in meeting room B. This issue has been recognized in the research community. For example, in the IST FP6 CoBIs project [17], a reliable multicast dissemination protocol was developed and used to transmit business rule updates to a group of sensor nodes [18]. The SENSEI project is currently developing a service framework to interact with wireless sensor & actuator networks and semantically annotated service interfaces as well as context and actuation models, where this issue will also need to be addressed. However, a lot of work still needs to be done to develop both appropriate methods as well as globally accepted standards for logical addressing.

4.3 Heterogeneity

For connecting and integrating all the objects into the Internet of Things, there are and will be many different technologies. RFID is one of the most prominent ones, but sensors, wireless sensor & actuator networks and embedded systems will also play an important role.

In all these areas standards are in place or standardisation efforts are underway. For example, EPCglobal as well as ISO offer a family of standards for RFID, ZigBee [19] and 6LoWPAN [20] are gaining popularity in the wireless sensor networking area, and OPC [21] is well accepted in factory automation. But the technologies are too different to expect any standard to be able to cover them all. Furthermore, as shown in the section above regarding unique identification, there are also competing standards in the same field.

For all these reasons, it is clear that we will have to deal with heterogeneity when building the software infrastructures for the Internet of Things. Standards are helpful, but they alone cannot be the solution. Rather asked for here is *interoperability*. The key is to separate the functionality from its technical implementation. Service-oriented architectures are ideally suited for this, since they encapsulate functionality in services with a common interface, abstracting from the underlying hardware and protocols. This has already been understood in several domains, e.g., in the home automation with the usage of DPWS or in factory automation with the usage of OPC-UA.

Having infrastructures that allow connecting and integrating a diverse set of technologies is in our opinion not just a "necessary evil", but rather a strength, since it offers two key benefits. Firstly, it allows applying different solutions to different applications. Depending on the application requirements, the best-fitting technology can be used. For example, in the CoBIs project three different sensor network platforms – Particles, µNodes and Sindrion, all exhibiting different properties [22] – were used. µNodes are best suited regarding energy efficiency, Particles offer more flexible and powerful programming capabilities and Sindrion is superior regarding standards support and commercialisation. All these platforms were integrated into the same CoBIs framework using a service-oriented concept based on UPnP [23] on the lower levels and web services towards the applications.

Secondly, an infrastructure where diverse technologies can easily be integrated into will be future-proof. Especially in the area of wireless sensor networks, the technical developments are not complete and we can expect that new technologies, protocols and standards will arise. These will have to be interoperable with existing and already deployed devices and networks. An infrastructure built with heterogeneity in mind will easily allow this. The framework under development in the SENSEI project is a good example of such a system: It not only defines a plug & play service interface to connect heterogeneous wireless sensor & actuator network islands to the system, but also offers a framework to orchestrate different services provided by the islands into higher-level context and actuation services.

4.4 Service Paradigms

Service-Oriented Architecture (SOA) has been recognized as *adequate architectural style for the organization of large-scale and distributed business logic* since a number of years. Many definitions of SOA have already been published [24]. The normative OASIS Reference Model for SOA [25] defines SOA as "...a paradigm for organizing and utilizing distributed capabilities that may be under the control of different ownership domains.

It provides a uniform means to offer, discover, interact with and use capabilities to produce desired effects consistent with measurable preconditions and expectations". According to this model, the major components of a basic SOA and their possible interactions are: a service provider publishes his service interface via a service registry where a service requester/consumer can find it and subsequently may bind to the service provider. The central concept of the SOA reference model is the existence of services which provide access to capabilities by well-defined interfaces to be exercised following a service contract with constraints and policies. This enables a loose coupling of services (thereby minimizing mutual dependencies) and complies with some of the probably most-known principles in software-engineering, information-hiding and modularisation [26]. Services are provided by entities, the service provider, and are to be used by others, the service consumers. Services may be composed on the basis of other, existing services, thereby adhering to the principle of reuse. They are autonomous in the sense that they solely control the logic they encapsulate, uniformly described and publicly retrievable via certain discovery mechanisms. The concept of supporting loosely coupled, business-aligned and networked services as introduced above can be realized with the help of numerous different technologies such as the Web Services stack. This stack comprises WSDL as a uniform format for service interfaces, UDDI as standard for specifying publicly available service registries, SOAP as data exchange protocol and BPEL as language for orchestrating services according to specific business logic.

However, to enable the seamless and agile interoperation of smart items in the Internet of Things, a number of challenges still exist with respect to the organization and implementation of services.

First of all, the lack of comprehensive, trustworthy and widely accepted *service intermediaries* in the Internet of today still prevents the establishment of a Future Internet as described above. The few globally available UDDI-based registries are mostly only usable for technical experts, do not offer any additional functionality such as service performance monitoring and only feature a small number of references to different web services. As a part of the so called Web 2.0 movement, novel and richer kinds of intermediaries have already been established [27]. These allow for improved navigation by facilitating the efficient retrieval of services which match a given user need, service performance transparency through permanent monitoring of service quality and availability, and governance, i.e., controlling and enforcing the delivery of service levels as defined in Service-Level Agreements (SLA). Although promising, these intermediaries are still at an early stage of maturity and also rarely reach into the world of physical items; mostly they focus on simple information services.

Secondly, the *lack of means for composing diverse services* towards higher-order services meeting actual user demands imposes additional challenges to the emergence of the Future Internet. A phenomenon sometimes referred to as "corporate household" problem today prevents web services-based SOAs from being set up quickly and easily. Companies and their respective systems are subject to rigid governance mechanisms and adhere to different conventions with respect to business documents and also internal business processes. For this reason, the information objects which need to be exchanged between services are virtually guaranteed to have inconsistency in both syntax and semantics. Novel technologies will be required to annotate the business meaning of services and their input as well as output objects in a comprehensible way. Semantically organized services are believed to improve retrievability and seamless composability significantly. The EU-funded project FAST [28] deals with these challenges as it aims to develop a method as well as a tool enabling human users to quickly find electronic resources in the Web, and compose them with other resources in order to model a service-based scenario.

Thirdly, services in the Internet of today can be considered as *mute and autistic*. In the Future Internet, services are expected to become more open and reactive to their respective environments particularly in two respects: First, existing service interfaces (e.g., WSDL-based) are not designed to be interpreted and used by humans but rather by machines. This frequently prevents the long tail of Internet users from easily discovering and interacting with them. In the course of the above mentioned FAST project, novel methods are currently being developed which allow designers to "put a face" on services and to thus improve user-service interaction. Second, today's Internet-based services are rarely context-sensitive. However, in order to realize the business process decomposition which has been discussed as a fundamental advantage of the Future Internet, services need to be aware of different aspects of the environment they are acting in [29]. Context services can provide such information to the application services that implement local control loops and that trigger specific actions. Such context services will be composed of several lower-level services which deliver individual sensor readings. However, this is not enough. For the application services to base their decisions on context data, some notion of *Quality of Information* is needed. Quality of Information provides meta information to what degree the information that a service provides is accurate – i.e., how well the measured value reflects the true value in the real world –, as well as timely, reliable and trustworthy. The EU-funded project SENSEI has taken on this challenge and will provide novel means for modelling, quantifying, representing and processing of Quality of Information of individual sensor services as well as the aggregated context information itself.

5 Outlook

While we believe that there are many business opportunities ahead, industry is still reluctant to widely adopt the new technologies that will lead to the realisation of the vision set by the Internet of Things. The reason behind this is many-fold: As outlined above, many technical challenges still need to be resolved. But more importantly, often the real business cases are not clear yet. While many papers on this exist, the business cases have not been proven yet in the real world on a large-scale basis. Trust in the technology – and thereby also wider adoption – will only come with real-world deployments that operate reliably and productively and have a real impact on a company's financial bottom line. Furthermore, there is a need for open global standards, in particular on the topics of unique identification and object addressing, service interfaces, decentralised object discovery services and service infrastructures.

A combined – and focused on real-world needs – effort of industry and academia is needed to overcome the challenges. The technical challenges need to be addressed, and the solutions have to be tested and proven in real settings. In addition, new business models and quantifiable business cases need to be developed. The 7th Research Framework Programme of the European Union provides the means to fund such collaborative efforts; however, open collaboration with initiatives in other regions of the world – in particular Asia and the Americas – will be essential.

Acknowledgments. This paper describes work undertaken in the context of the SENSEI project, 'Integrating the Physical with the Digital World of the Network of the Future' (www.sensei-project.eu). SENSEI is a Large Scale Collaborative Project supported by the European 7th Framework Programme, contract number: 215923. The authors would also like to thank the other colleagues working on Internet of Things topics at SAP Research.

References

1. ISTAG Working Group Report on Web-based Service Industry (February 2008), `ftp://ftp.cordis.europa.eu/pub/ist/docs/web-based-service-industry-istag_en.pdf`
2. Fleisch, E., Sarma, S., Subirana, B.: High-Resolution Management. IESE Alumni Magazine, 8–13 (July/September 2006)
3. Spiess, P., Karnouskos, S.: Maximizing the Business Value of Networked Embedded Systems through Process-Level Integration into Enterprise Software. In: Second International Conference on Pervasive Computing and Applications, pp. 536–541 (2007)
4. Karnouskos, S., Baecker, O., Moreira Sa de Souza, L., Spiess, P.: Integration of SOA-ready Networked Embedded Devices in Enterprise Systems via a Cross-Layered Web Service Infrastructure. In: 12th IEEE Conference on Emerging Technologies and Factory Automation, pp. 293–300 (2007)
5. Odenwald, T.: Putting M2M into Business Context. M2M Pioneer Magazine 5(2) (March/April 2007)
6. Moreira Sa de Souza, L., Spiess, P., Koehler, M., Guinard, D., Karnouskos, S., Savio, D.: SOCRADES: A Web Service based Shop Floor Integration Infrastructure. In: Floerkemeier, C., Langheinrich, M., Fleisch, E., Mattern, F., Sarma, S.E. (eds.) IOT 2008. LNCS, vol. 4952, pp. 50–67. Springer, Heidelberg (2008)
7. Lehtonen, M., Oertel, N., Vogt, H.: Features, Identity, Tracing, and Cryptography in Product Authentication. In: 13th International Conference on Concurrent Enterprising (2007)
8. SAP Press Release: Jena University Hospital Leads Healthcare Innovation with RFID Solution from SAP (May 2006), `http://www.sap.com/industries/healthcare/newsevents/Press.epx?PressID=6329`
9. ISC Domain Survey: Number of Internet Hosts, `http://www.isc.org/ds/host-count-history.html`
10. World Internet Users (March 2008), `http://www.internetworldstats.com/stats.htm`
11. IST FP6 Project SOCRADES, `http://www.socrades.eu/`
12. IST FP7 Project SENSEI, `http://www.sensei-project.eu/`
13. EPCglobal Architectural Framework, http://www.epcglobalinc.org/standards/architecture/
14. Sakamura, K.: Ubiquitous ID Technologies 2008, uID Center booklet (2008), `http://www.uidcenter.org/pdf/UID910-W001-080226_en.pdf`
15. Fabian, B., Günther, O., Spiekermann, S.: Security Analysis of the Object Name Service. In: First International Workshop on Security, Privacy and Trust in Pervasive and Ubiquitous Computing, pp. 71–76 (2005)

16. GS1 France Press Release: GS1 lance le premier service de l'Internet des Objets en Europe (May 2008),
    http://www.gs1.fr/gs1_fr/actualites__1/informations__1/commu
    niques_de_presse/communiques_de_presse_2008/gs1_lance_le_pre
    mier_service_de_l_internet_des_objets_en_europe
17. IST FP6 Project CoBIs, http://www.cobis-online.de/
18. Marin-Perianu, M., Havinga, P.: RMD: Reliable Multicast Data Dissemination within Groups of Collaborating Objects. In: 31st IEEE Conference on Local Computer Networks, pp. 656–663 (2006)
19. ZigBee Alliance, http://www.zigbee.org/
20. Kushalnagar, N., Montenegro, G., Schumacher, C.: IPv6 over Low-Power Wireless Personal Area Networks (6LoWPANs): Overview, Assumptions, Problem Statement, and Goals. RFC 4919, IETF (August 2007),
    http://www.ietf.org/rfc/rfc4919.txt
21. OPC Foundation, http://www.opcfoundation.org/
22. CoBIs Project Final Report,
    http://www.cobis-online.de/files/Deliverable_D104V2.pdf
23. UPnP Forum, http://www.upnp.org/
24. Alonso, G., Casati, F., Kuno, H., Machiraju, V.: Web Services Concepts, Architectures and Applications. Springer, Berlin (2004)
25. MacKenzie, M., Laskey, K., McCabe, F., Brown, P.F., Metz, R.: OASIS - Reference Model for Service Oriented Architecture 1.0 (2006),
    http://www.oasisopen.org/committees/tc_home.php?wg_abbrev=so
    a-rm
26. Parnas, D.L.: On the criteria to be used in decomposing systems into modules. Communications of the ACM 15(2) (1972)
27. Hierro, J.J., Janner, T., Lizcano, D., Reyes, M., Schroth, C., Soriano, J.: Enhancing User-Service Interaction Through a Global User-Centric Approach to SOA. In: Fourth International Conference on Networking and Services, pp. 194–203 (2008)
28. IST FP7 Project FAST, http://fast.morfeo-project.eu/
29. Schroth, C., Christ, O.: Brave New Web: Emerging Design Principles and Technologies as Enablers of a Global SOA. In: The 2007 IEEE International Conference on Services Computing, pp. 597–604 (2007)

Security-By-Contract for the Future Internet[*]

Fabio Massacci[1], Frank Piessens[2], and Ida Siahaan[1]

[1] Università di Trento, Italy
name.surname@disi.unitn.it
[2] Katholieke Universiteit Leuven, Belgium
name.surname@cs.kuleuven.be

Abstract. With the advent of the next generation java servlet on the smartcard, the Future Internet will be composed by web servers and clients silently yet busily running on high end smart cards in our phones and our wallets. In this brave new world we can no longer accept the current security model where programs can be downloaded on our machines just because they are vaguely "trusted". We want to know what they do in more precise details.

We claim that the Future Internet needs the notion of *security-by-contract*: In a nutshell, a contract describes the security relevant interactions that the smart internet application could have with the smart devices hosting them. Compliance with contracts should verified at development time, checked at depolyment time and contracts should be accepted by the platform before deployment and possibly their enforcement guaranteed, for instance by in-line monitoring.

In this paper we describe the challenges that must be met in order to develop a security-by-contract framework for the Future Internet and how security research can be changed by it.

1   The End of Trust in the Web

The World Wide Web evolved rapidly in 90's with a highlight in 1995 when the Java Applet enabled secure mobile code for the Web. In this millennium the notion of the Web has changed: rather than a network, the Web has become a platform where people migrate desktop applications. We have richer applications such as WebMail, Social Web sites, Mashups, Web 2.0 applications, etc. this is further supported by technologies such as Asynchronous JavaScript and XML (AJAX), .NET, XML, SOAP (Web Services).

Fact of Life 1. *The security model of the current version of the web is based on a simple assumption: the good guys develop their .NET or Java application, expose it on the web, and then spend the rest of their life letting other good guys using it while stopping bad guys from misusing it.*

The business trend of outsourcing processes [16] or the construction of virtual organizations [18] have slightly complicated this initially simple picture. Now running a

---

[*] Research partly supported by the Projects EU-FP6-IST-STREP-S3MS, EU-FP6-IP-SENSORIA, and EU-FP7-IP-MASTER. We would like to thank Eric Vetillard for pointing to us the domain of Next Generation Java Card as the Challenge for the Future Internet.

J. Domingue, D. Fensel, and P. Traverso (Eds.): FIS 2008, LNCS 5468, pp. 29–43, 2009.
© Springer-Verlag Berlin Heidelberg 2009

"service" means that different service (sub)components can be dynamically chosen and different partners are chosen to offer those (sub)services.

Hence we need different trust establishment mechanisms (see e.g. [23,22]). A large part of the WS security standards are geared to solve some of these problems: WS-Federation defines the mechanisms for federating trust; WS-Trust enables security token interoperability; WS-Security [3] covers the low level details such as message content integrity and confidentiality; WS-Security Policy [9] details lower level security policies .

Still, the assumption is the same: *the application developer and the platform owner are on the same side*. Traditional books on secure coding [20] or the .NET security handbook [24] are pervaded by this assumption.

Unfortunately, this assumption is no longer true for the brave new world of Web 2.0 and the Future Internet. Already now a user downloads a multitude of communicating applications ranging from P2P clients to desktop search engines, each of them ploughing through the user's platform, and springing back with services from and to the rest of the world. Most of these applications will be developed by people and companies that a lay user had never known they existed (at least before downloading the application).

It looks like we are simply back to the good old security model of Java applets [15] and good confinement would do the job. Nothing could be more wrong: applets are light pieces of code that would not need access to our platform. Indeed, to deal with the untrusted code either .NET [24] or Java [15] can exploit the mechanism of permissions. Permissions are assigned to enable execution of potentially dangerous or costly functionality, such as starting various types of connections. The drawback of permissions is that after assigning a permission the user has very limited control over how the permission is used. Conditional permissions that allow and forbid use of the functionality depending on such factors as bandwidth or the previous actions of the application itself (e.g. access to sensitive files) are also out of reach. Once again the consequence is that either applications are sandboxed (and thus can do almost nothing), or the user decided that they are trusted and then they can do almost everything.

The mechanism of signed assemblies from trusted third parties does not solve the problem either.

Fact of Life 2. *Currently a signature on a piece of code only means that the application comes from the software factory of the signatory, but there is no clear definition of what guarantees it offers. It essentially binds the software with nothing.*

Loosely speaking, the mobile software deployment process is identical to the hiring process of the aristocratic armies. In order to hire an officer you don't ask for his CV, you don't stipulate a contract with him and set targets. You just ask for his father's name and depending on that name you make him lieutenant, major or general. You grant him the privileges of the rank and trust that he'll not betray the name of the family.

The (once) enthusiast installers of UK Channel 4 on demand services 4oD [1] might tell a different story [29]. What is best than download a client that allows you to see almost free movies from your favorite TV channel? After all you are downloading from a reputable and trusted broadcaster. It is not shady software from a hacker web site. Only in the fine print of the legal terms of use (nowhere in the FAQs and only visible after a long scrolling down of legalese) you find something you most likely would like to know beforehand (extracted from the web site on 31st of July 2008):

> If you download Content to your computer, during the License Period, we may upload this from your computer (using part of your upstream bandwidth) for the purpose of transferring Content to other users of the Service. Please contact your Internet Service Provider ("ISP") if you have any queries on this.

As one of the many unfortunate users of the system noticed [29], there is no need of contacting your ISP. They will contact you pretty soon and will not be pleasant...

Fact of Life 3. *We end up in a stale-mate. We built our security models on the assumption that we could trust the vendors (or at least some of them). The examples from reputable companies such as Channel 4 (or BBC, Sky TV etc.) show that this is no longer possible. Still we really really want to download a lot of software.*

2   The Smart(Card) Future of the Web

The model that we have described above is essentially the web of the personal computers. We, as world-wide consumer[1], accept the idea that PC applications fails, that PC are ridden with viruses, spyware and so on. So we do not consider this a major threat.

Fact of Life 4. *None of the users complaining about 4oD [29] have considered their PC or their Web platform "broken" because it allowed other people to make use of it. They did not consider returning their PC for repair. They considered themselves being gullible users ripped off by an untrusted vendor.*

There is another domain at the opposite side of the psychological spectrum: smartcard technology. This technology enjoyed worldwide deployment in 90's with Java Card Applets and their strict security confinement. At the beginning of the millennium, many applications such as large SIM cards, emerging security and identity management businesses are implemented on smart-cards to address mobile devices security challenges [19]. Still, smart-cards have essentially led a sheltered life from the Web problems we have described. When used in mobile phones they just acted as authenticator and withdrawn from the picture immediately.

(Un)fortunately, the smartcard technology evolved with larger memories, USB and TCP/IP support and the development of the Next-Generation Java Card platform with Servlet engine. This latter technology is a full fledged Java platform for embedded Web applications and opens new Web 2.0 opportunities such as NG Java Card Web 2.0 Applications. It can also serve as alternative to personalized applications on remote servers so that personal data no longer needs to transmitted to remote third-parties.

Prediction 1. *The Future Internet will be composed by those embedded Java Card Platforms running on high end smart cards in our phones and our wallets, each of them connecting to the internet and performing secure transactions with distributed servers and desktop browsers without complicated middleware or special purpose readers.*

---

[1] We should distinguish between the computer scientist or security expert and the computer, even if savvy, user.

We still want to download a huge amount of software on our phones but there is a huge psychological difference from a consumer perspective.

Fact of Life 5. *If our PC is sluggish in responding,* we *did something wrong or down-loaded the wrong software, if our phone is sluggish,* it *is broken.*

Idea 1. *In the realm of next generation Java card platforms we cannot just download a software without knowing what it does. The smart card web platform must have a way to check what is downloading.*

3   Security by Contract for the Smart Future Internet

In the past millennium Sekar et al. [32] have proposed the notion of Model Carrying Code (MCC) as the seminal work on which our research agenda for the Smart Future Internet is based. MCC requires the code producer to establish a model regarding the safety of mobile code which captures the *security-relevant behavior* of the code. The code consumers checks their policies against the model associated with untrusted code to determine if this code will violate their policy.

The major limitation was that MCC had not fully developed the whole lifecycle and had limited itself to finite state automata which are too simple to describe realistic policies. Even a simple, basic policy such as "Only access url starting with http" could not be addressed. The *Security-by-Contract (S×C)* framework that we have developed for mobile code [11,10] builds upon the MCC seminal idea to address the *trust relationship* problem of the current security models in which a digital signature binds a contract with nothing.

Idea 2. *In S×C we augment mobile code with a claim on its security behavior (an* application's contract*) that could be matched against a mobile* platform's policy *before downloading the code. A digital signature does not just certify the origin of the code but also bind together the code with a contract with the main goal to provide a semantics for digital signatures on mobile code.*

This framework is a step in the transition from trusted code to trustworthy code.

This idea is nice but we must develop it fully in order to really make a significant advance over the initial intuition from model carrying code. So we should consider the full lifecycle. A contract should be negotiated and enforced during development, at time of delivery and loading, and during execution of the application by the mobile platform. Figure 1 summarizes the phases of the application/service life-cycle in which the contract-based security paradigm should be present.

At *development time* the mobile code developers are responsible for providing a description of the security behavior that their code finally provides. Such a code might also undergo a formal certification process by the developer's own company, the smart card provider, a mobile phone operator, or any other third party for which the application has been developed. By using suitable techniques such as static analysis, monitor in-lining, or general theorem proving, the code is certified to comply with the developer's contract. Subsequently, the code and the security claims are sealed together

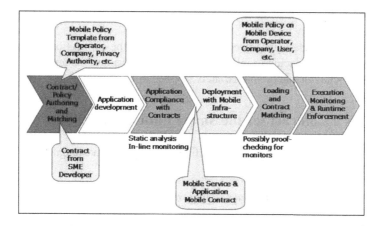

Fig. 1. Application/Service Life-Cycle

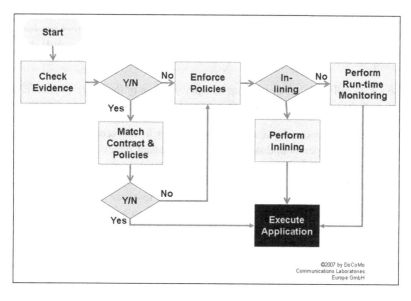

Fig. 2. SxCWorkflow

with the evidence for compliance (either a digital signature or a proof) and shipped for deployment.

At *deployment time*, the target platform follows a workflow similar to the one depicted in Fig.2 (see also [35]). First, it checks that the evidence is correct. Such evidence can be a trusted signature as in standard mobile applications [40]. An alternative evidence can be a proof that the code satisfies the contract (and then one can use PCC techniques to check it [28]).

Once we have evidence that the contract is trustworthy, the platform checks, that the claimed policy is compliant with the policy that our platform wants to enforce. If it is, then the application can be run without further ado. This may be a significant saving from in-lining a security monitor.

At *run-time* we might want to decide to still monitor the application. Then, as with vaccination, we might decide to inline a number of checks into the application so that any undesired behavior can be immediately stopped or corrected.

4   What Is a Contract for the Smart Future Internet?

The first challenge that we must address is finding an appropriate language for defining contracts and policies.

Definition 1. *A* contract *is a formal complete and correct specification of the behavior of an application for what concerns relevant security actions (Virtual Machine API Calls, Web Messages etc).*

By signing the code the developer certifies that the code complies with the stated claims on its security-relevant behavior.

On the other side we can see that users and mobile phone operators are interested that all codes that are deployed on their platform are secure. In other words they must declare their security policy:

Definition 2. *A* policy *is a formal complete specification of the acceptable behavior of applications to be executed on the platform for what concerns relevant security actions.*

Technically, a contract can be a security automaton in the sense of Schneider [17], and it specifies an upper bound on the security-relevant behavior of the application: the sequences of security-relevant events that an application can generate are all in the language accepted by the security automaton. We can have a slightly more sophisticated approach using Büchi automata [34] if we also want to cover liveness properties that can be enforced by Edit automata [4]. This definition can be sufficient for theoretical purposes but it is hardly acceptable for any practical use.

State-of-the-Art 1. *All theoretical papers [17,4,34] define the security behavior as a set of "actions" as ground terms but real programs are not made by "actions", they have API calls, OS calls, and those calls have a number of parameters. Even the most basic security policy if we simply instantiate the API parameters into ground actions will lead to automata with infinitely many transitions that we cannot even write down.*

Example 1. The policy of smart card provider may require that "After PIM (the Personal Identification Module) APIs were accessed only secure connections can be opened". This policy permits executing the Java `Connector.open(string url)` method only if the started connection is a secure one i.e. `url` starts with "https://".

Fig.3a represents an automaton for Ex. 1. Starting from state p_0, we stay in this state while PIM is not accessed (jop). As PIM is accessed we move to state p_1 and we stay in state p_1 only if the started connection Connector.open(string url) method is a secure one i.e. url starts with "https://" or we keep accessing PIM (jop). We enter state e_p if we

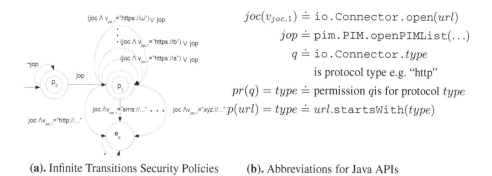

(a). Infinite Transitions Security Policies   **(b).** Abbreviations for Java APIs

Fig. 3. Infinite Transitions Security Policies

start an unsecure connection Connector.open(string url) e.g. url starts with "http://"
or "sms://" etc. These examples are from a Java VM. Since we do not consider useful to
invent our own names for API calls we use the javax.microedition APIs (though
a bit verbose) for the notation that is shown in Fig.3b.

Idea 3. *For SxCfor mobile code (.NET and Java) a variant of the PSLANG language
[2] has been proposed whose formal counterpart is the notion of automata modulo
theory [25] where atomic actions are replaced by expressions that can finitely capture
infinite values of API parameters.*

Challenge 1. *Identify a suitable language for the specification of contracts and policies
at a level of abstraction that is suitable for the smart future internet that can be used
for all phases of the life-cycle (Fig.1) both at development and deployment time (Fig.2)*

It is indeed important that the language is able to be used in all steps. A language
perfect for matching that cannot be enforced at run-time or that can only be verified
with a costly interactive theorem prover is not going to be very effective.

5   Application-Contract Compliance

So far we have only defined a language for describing the behavior of smart-card web
applications. There is no a-priori guarantee that this statement is correct.

Idea 4. *Static analysis can be used at development time to increase confidence in the
contract. With static analysis, program analysis and verification algorithms are used in
an attempt to prove that the application satisfies its contract.*

The major advantages of static analysis are that it does not impose any runtime
overhead, and that it shows that all possible executions of a program comply with the
contract. The major disadvantage is that the problem of checking application-contract
compliance is in general undecidable, and so automatic static analysis tools will typically only support restricted forms of contracts, or restricted forms of applications, or

the tool will be *conservative* in the sense that it will reject applications that are actually compliant, but the tool fails to find a proof for this.

The S3MS project for mobile code has shown that static analysis is feasible for limited forms of contracts (e.g. for contracts that are stateless), or in combination with runtime verification [37].

The programs and services running on the embedded servlet will be significantly more complex and have actions at different level of abstractions whose full security implications can be understood by considering all abstraction levels at once. The challenges for static analysis are many: with expressive notions of security contracts, verifying application-contract compliance is actually as hard as verifying compliance with an arbitrary specification [31].

Prediction 2. *Contracts for applications in the Smart Future Internet will have a complexity that that is comparable to the level of abstractions of current concurrent models that are used for model checking hardware and software systems (in 10^{10} states or transitions and beyond).*

A standard approach to make program verification and analysis algorithms scale to large programs is to make them *modular*: make sure that the algorithm can check parts (classes / methods / ...) of the program independently. This is particularly hard for application-contract compliance checking, because the security state of the contract is typically a global state, and the structure of the contract and its security state might not align with the structure of the application.

State-of-the-Art 2. *For modular verification algorithms, annotations are required on all methods to specify how they interact with the security state, and not only on methods that are relevant for the contract at hand.*

Clearly, this annotation overhead is prohibitive, so a key challenge is to look for ways to reduce the annotation burden.

Idea 5. *An interesting research question is whether a program transformation (similar to the security-passing style transformation used for reasoning about programs sandboxed by stack inspection [39,33]) can improve this situation.*

Idea 6. *A second approach to address scalability is to give up soundness of the analysis, and to use the contract as a model of the application in order to generate security tests by applying techniques from Model Based Testing [38].*

Losing soundness is a major disadvantage: an application may pass all the generated tests and still turn out to violate the contract once fielded. However, the advantages are also important: no annotations on the application source code are needed, and the tests generated from the contract can be easily injected in the standard platform testing phase, thus making this approach very practical.

Challenge 2. *One particularly interesting research challenge to be addressed here is how to measure the coverage of such security tests. When are there enough tests to give a reasonable assurance about security?*

It is easy to automatically generate a huge amount of tests from the contract. Hence it is important to know how many tests are sufficient, and whether a newly generated test increases the coverage of the testing suite.

6   Matching Contract and Policy on the Smart Future Internet

Suppose our language constructs allowed the developer to provide a verified contract. Now we are at the time of deployment and, as users, we would like precisely to check whether our intriguing application will not use our upward bandwidth as the 4oD unfortunate users. We must therefore identify the next key component of the SxC paradigm, namely *contract-policy matching*.

The operation of matching the application's claim with the platform policy requires that the contract is trustworthy, i.e. the application and the contract are sealed together with a digital signature when shipped for deployment or by shipping a proof that can checked automatically. We will return on this issue in a later section but for the moment let's take it for granted.

Idea 7. *We must show that the behavior described by the contract is acceptable according to our platform policy.*

A simple solution is to build upon automata theory, interpret contract and policy as automata and use language inclusion [6]. Given two such automata Aut^C (representing the contract) and Aut^P (representing the policy), we have a match when the language accepted by Aut^C is a subset of the language accepted by Aut^P.

As we have already shown in Figure3a this cannot be done just be instantiating the variables of API calls in order to obtain the usual set of ground actions. A solution that we have used in the S3MS project has been to introduce the notion of *automata modulo theory* in which actions labelling the transactions of the finite state automata are instead expressions constraining the value of the arguments of an API call [25]. In Figure4 we show the automaton modulo theory corresponding to the infinite automaton in Figure3a.

Once the policy and the contract are represented as automata then one can either use language inclusions [25] or simulation [26] to check whether the contract is acceptable according our platform policy.

Such solution is only partial because the automata that we have envisaged do not store the values of the arguments of allowed/disallowed APIs. As a result the policy below cannot be yet matched.

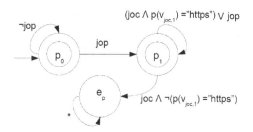

Fig. 4. Example of Automata Modulo Theory for the policy from Ex. 1

Example 2. After connecting to a URL X then the application is only allowed to connect to the same URL X".

Such policy would allow us to solve the 4oD problem: once the site connect to Channel4 web site it can only connect to this site again. So no bandwidth can be used while acting as a P2P servent.

In order to do this a potentially promising research could be to build a version of automata modulo theory that is able to exploit the usage of action arguments that is typical of process algebra approaches. For instance, one could exploit the works on history-dependent automata (HD-automata) [27,14] which extended automata by local names on states and labels.

Challenge 3. *Contracts and policies for the future internet must be history-dependent: the arguments of past allowed actions (API calls, WS invocations, SOAP messages) may influence the evolution of future access control decision in a policy.*

Further, in our current implementation of the matcher that runs on a mobile phone, security states of the automata are represented by variables over finite domains e.g. smsMessagesSent ranges between 0 to 5. [2,5]. A possible solution could be to extend the work on finite-memory automata [21] by Kaminski and Francez or other works [30] that studied automata and logics on strings over infinite alphabets through register and pebble automata.

Challenge 4. *Define matching for contracts and policies that allows to compactly represent states with potentially infinite state spaces without giving up effective matching.*

The last clause of the challenge ("without giving up effective matching") is essential. Remember that our model of the Future Internet is built up by powerful smartcards running their own web servers and clients and sitting on our mobile phones, devices and cars. We cannot wait for two hours of BBD construction using current model checking technologies before deciding that an interesting travel program discovered at our arriving airport is not good for our phone.

Hence we arrive here in the same corner that we ended up during the discussion on static analysis.

Idea 8. *Another approach to address scalability is to give up soundness of the matching and use algorithms for simulation and testing.*

Also in this case losing soundness is a major disadvantage: a contract may pass the matching and still turn out to violate the policy once fielded. However, the advantages are also important. A quick decision with high probability of correctness is significantly better than no decision due to memory consumption: if users get tired of waiting or the device has not enough battery to run a full test, users might decide to run the program anyhow and we would end up in a bad situation.

Challenge 5. *One particularly interesting research challenge to be addressed here is how to measure the coverage of approximate matching. Which value should give a reasonable assurance about security? Should it be an absolute value? Should it be in proportion of the number of possible executions? In proportion to the likely executions?*

An interesting approach could be to recall to life a neglected section of the classical paper on model checking by Courcoubetis et al [7] in which they traded off a better performance of the algorithm in change for the possibility of erring with a small probability.

7 Inlining a Monitor on Future Internet Applications

What happens if matching fails? or what happens if we do not trust the evidence that the code satisfies the contract? If we look back at Fig.2 monitor inlining of the *contract* can provide strong assurance of compliance. Here, we highlighting the research challenges that still remain.

With *monitor inlining* [13], code rewriting is used to push contract checking functionality into the program itself. The intention is that the inserted code enforces compliance with the contract, and otherwise interferes with the execution of the target program as little as possible. Monitor inlining is a well-established and efficient approach [12], and the S3MS project has shown that inlining can be used today as a contract compliance technique [36].

However a major open question is how to deal with concurrency efficiently.

Prediction 3. *Servents in the Smart Future Internet will need to monitor the concurrent interactions of tens of untrusted multithreaded programs.*

An inliner needs to protect the inlined security state against race conditions. So all accesses to the security state will happen under a lock. A key design choice for an inlining algorithm is whether to lock across security relevant API calls, or to release the lock before doing the API call, and reacquiring it when the API call returns.

The first choice (locking across calls) is easier to get secure, as there is a strong guarantee that the updates to the security state happen in the correct order. This is much trickier for an inliner that releases the lock during API calls. However, an inliner that locks across calls can introduce deadlocks in the inlined program, because some of the security relevant API calls will themselves block. And even if it does not lead to deadlock, acquiring a lock across a potentially blocking method call can cause serious performance penalties.

The S3MS project has provided a partial solution by partitioning the security state into disjoint parts, and replacing the global lock, by per-part locks. This improves efficiency, but depending on application and policy, it can still introduce deadlocks.

Challenge 6. *How to inline a monitor into a concurrent program so that it cannot create a deadlock in future interactions with other unknown programs yet to be downloaded.*

The ability to resist to changes in context (i.e. new concurrent programs downloaded after the inlined program) is essential for usability. The inlined version of 4oD should not get in the way if later on I want to download a (inlined) role-playing game. Of course it is possible that two malicious software downloaded at different instants might try to cooperate in order to steal some data. The security monitor should be able to spot them but not be deadlocked by them.

If inlining is performed by the code producer, or by a third party, the code consumer (the client that actually runs the application) needs to be convinced that inlining has been performed correctly. Without a secure transfer of the guarantees of application-contract compliance to the client, it would be easy for an attacker to modify either the application or the contract, or it would be possible for an application developer to lie about the contract.

Cryptographic signatures by a trusted (third) party is a first solution even if it transfer the risk from the technical to the legal domain. The trusted party vouches for application-contract compliance. Note the difference with the use of signatures in the traditional mobile device security model. In the security-by-contract approach, a signature has a clear semantics [11]: the third party claims that the application respects the supplied contract. Moreover, what is important is the fact that the decision whether the contract is acceptable or not remains with the end user. If an application claims that it will not connect to the internet and instead it does, at least you can bring the signatory to the court for fraudulent commercial claims.

An alternative solution is whether we can use the techniques of Proof-Carrying-Code (PCC) [28] for this. In PCC, the code producer produces a proof that the code has certain properties, and ships this proof together with the code to the client. By verifying the proof, the client can be sure that the code indeed has the properties that it claims to have.

State-of-the-Art 3. *Proof verification is a relatively simple process, so the key issue in PCC systems is how to generate the proofs (and how to keep them compact). Currently proof generation requires essentially PhD students working on an interactive theorem prover for hours or months using complicated logics and type systems. In other words, it is unfeasible.*

The difficulty of the endeavour is that the code has not been produced to be verified compliant against a security property but usually to actually do some business. In other words, the code producer is not aware of the property and the property producer is not aware of the code. In this scenario verification is clearly an uphill path.

Idea 9. *When we inline a contract we know precisely what code we are inlining and also what property the inlined code should satisfy. So, instead of asking a PhD student to annotate the code, we can ask the inliner to do this automatically for us. Indeed we could ask the inliner to generate the proof directly.*

This should make it relatively easy to check that code complies with the contract: the generation of a proof should be easier, and the size of the proof would also be acceptable for inlined programs. Preliminary results from the S3MS project for PCC for inlined sequential Java [8] show that this is indeed the case.

Challenge 7. *Identify automatic inlining mechanisms that inline a monitor for a security contract and generate an easily checkable proof for industrial applications in the Smart Future Internet.*

8 Beyond Micro-security for the Future Internet

In the discipline of economics there is a traditional distinction between micro-economics and macro-economics. According the Wordnet dictionary at Princeton University, the former is "the branch of economics that studies the economy of consumers or households or individual firms" while the latter is "the branch of economics that studies the overall working of a national economy".

Idea 10. *We can now draw a parallel of the notion of micro- and macro- research into the realm of security research.*

microsecurity *is the branch of IT security research that studies the security of individual digital services, components, or organizations*
macrosecurity *is the branch of IT security research that studies the overall security behavior of a large population of digital entities.*

State-of-the-Art 4. *All our ideas and challenges and the 99.9% of all security research in the world has been in the field of microsecurity. We have been fixing, breaking and proving correct an individual service or protocol or the interaction between N entities discussing the individual interactions between them.*

The picture is slowly changing as epidemiological studies on viruses appeared and research targeting population is starting. For example, researchers at NEC Japan are considering solutions to the problem of SPAM mails that do not focus on better filtering algorithms on the client (i.e. a micro-security solutions) and works if a "population" of servers as a whole adopts the much simpler measures of throttling email invoices to the average rate.

Challenge 8. *In the Future Internet few millions of smart servents will adopt and enforce a type of contract (e.g. by Axalto) and some other millions of servents (e.g. by G&D) might adopt different contracts. What can we say about the population as a whole? How will security incidents spread? What kind of private data will be lost?*

If we are able to meet this challenge, then macro-security will be born.

References

1. Channel 4. 4od (2008), http://www.channel4.com/4od/index.html
2. Aktug, I., Naliuka, K.: Conspec - a formal language for policy specification. In: Proc. of the 1st Workshop on Run Time Enforcement for Mobile and Distributed Systems, REM 2007 (2007)
3. Atkinson, B., Della-Libera, G., Hada, S., Hondo, M., Hallam-Baker, P., Klein, J., LaMacchia, B., Leach, P., Manferdelli, J., Maruyama, H., Nadalin, A., Nagaratnam, N., Prafullchandra, H., Shewchuk, J., Simon, D.: Web Services Security. Microsoft, IBM, VeriSign, 1st edn (April 2002) (October 25, 2005), http://www-128.ibm.com/developerworks/webservices/library/ws-secure/
4. Bauer, L., Ligatti, J., Walker, D.: Edit automata: Enforcement mechanisms for run-time security policies. Int. J. of Inform. Sec. 4(1-2), 2–16 (2005)

5. Bielova, N., Dalla Torre, M., Dragoni, N., Siahaan, I.: Matching policies with security claims of mobile applications. In: Proc. of the 3rd Int. Conf. on Availability, Reliability and Security (ARES 2008). IEEE Press, Los Alamitos (2008)
6. Clarke, E.M., Grumberg, O., Peled, D.A.: Model Checking. MIT Press, Cambridge (2000)
7. Courcoubetis, C., Vardi, M.Y., Wolper, P., Yannakakis, M.: Memory-efficient algorithms for the verification of temporal properties. Formal Methods in Sys. Design 1(2-3), 275–288 (1992)
8. Dam, M., Lundblad, A.: A proof carrying code framework for inlined reference monitors in Java bytecode (submitted, 2008)
9. Della-Libera, G., Gudgin, M., Hallam-Bakerand, P., Hondo, M., Granqvist, H., Kaler, C., Maruyama, H., McIntosh, M., Nadalin, A., Nagaratnam, N., Philpott, R., Prafullchandra, H., Shewchuk, J., Walter, D., Zolfonoon, R.: Web Services Security Policy Language. IBM and Microsoft and RSA Security and VeriSign (2005)
10. Desmet, L., Joosen, W., Massacci, F., Philippaerts, P., Piessens, F., Siahaan, I., Vanoverberghe, D.: Security-by-contract on the.net platform. Information Security Technical Report 13(1), 25–32 (2008)
11. Dragoni, N., Massacci, F., Naliuka, K., Siahaan, I.: Security-by-Contract: Toward a Semantics for Digital Signatures on Mobile Code. In: López, J., Samarati, P., Ferrer, J.L. (eds.) EuroPKI 2007. LNCS, vol. 4582, pp. 297–312. Springer, Heidelberg (2007)
12. Erlingsson, U., Schneider, F.B.: SASI enforcement of security policies: A retrospective. In: WNSP: New Security Paradigms Workshop. ACM Press, New York (2000)
13. Erlingsson, U., Schneider, F.B.: IRM enforcement of Java stack inspection. In: IEEE Symposium on Security and Privacy, pp. 246–255 (2000)
14. Ferrari, G.L., Gnesi, S., Montanari, U., Pistore, M.: A model-checking verification environment for mobile processes. ACM Trans. Softw. Eng. Methodol. 12(4), 440–473 (2003)
15. Gong, L., Ellison, G., Dageforde, M.: Inside Java 2 Platform Security: Architecture, Api Design, and Implementation. Addison-Wesley Professional, Reading (2003)
16. Goth, G.: The ins and outs of it outsourcing. IT Professional 1, 11–14 (1999)
17. Hamlen, K.W., Morrisett, G., Schneider, F.B.: Computability classes for enforcement mechanisms. TOPLAS 28(1), 175–205 (2006)
18. Handy, C.: Trust and the virtual organization. Harvard Business Review 73, 40–50 (1995)
19. Hendry, M.: Smart Card Security and Applications, 2nd edn. Artech House (2001)
20. Howard, M., LeBlanc, D.: Writing Secure Code, 2nd edn. Microsoft Press, Redmond (2002)
21. Kaminski, M., Francez, N.: Finite-memory automata. Theor. al Comp. Sci. 134(2), 329–363 (1994)
22. Karabulut, Y., Kerschbaum, F., Massacci, F., Robinson, P., Yautsiukhin, A.: Security and trust in it business outsourcing: a manifesto. In: Etalle, S., Samarati, P. (eds.) Proceedings of STM 2006. ENTCS. Elsevier, Amsterdam (2006)
23. Karjoth, G., Pfitzmann, B., Schunter, M., Waidner, M.: Service-oriented Assurance - Comprehensive Security by Explicit Assurances. In: Proc. of QoP 2005 (2005)
24. LaMacchia, B., Lange, S.:NET Framework security. Addison Wesley, Reading (2002)
25. Massacci, F., Siahaan, I.: Matching midlet's security claims with a platform security policy using automata modulo theory. In: Proc. of The 12th Nordic Workshop on Secure IT Systems, NordSec 2007 (2007)
26. Massacci, F., Siahaan, I.S.R.: Simulating midlet's security claims with automata modulo theory. In: Proc. of the 2008 workshop on Prog. Lang. and analysis for security, pp. 1–9. ACM, New York (2008)
27. Montanari, U., Pistore, M.: History-dependent automata. Technical Report TR-98-11, Dip. Informatica, University of Pisa, 5 (1998)
28. Necula, G.C.: Proof-carrying code. In: Proc. of the 24th ACM SIGPLAN-SIGACT Symp. on Princ. of Prog. Lang, pp. 106–119. ACM Press, New York (1997)

29. CNET Networks. Channel 4's 4od: Tv on demand, at a price. Crave Webzine (January 2007)
30. Neven, F., Schwentick, T., Vianu, V.: Finite state machines for strings over infinite alphabets. TOCL 5(3), 403–435 (2004)
31. Schneider, F.B.: Enforceable security policies. TISSEC 3(1), 30–50 (2000)
32. Sekar, R., Venkatakrishnan, V.N., Basu, S., Bhatkar, S., DuVarney, D.C.: Model-carrying code: a practical approach for safe execution of untrusted applications. In: Proc. of the 19th ACM Symp. on Operating Sys. Princ., pp. 15–28. ACM Press, New York (2003)
33. Smans, J., Jacobs, B., Piessens, F.: Static verification of code access security policy compliance of.net applications. Journal of Object Technology 5(3), 35–58 (2006)
34. Talhi, C., Tawbi, N., Debbabi, M.: Execution monitoring enforcement under memory-limitation constraints. Inform. and Comp. 206(2-4), 158–184 (2007)
35. Vanoverberghe, D., Philippaerts, P., Desmet, L., Joosen, W., Piessens, F., Naliuka, K., Massacci, F.: A flexible security architecture to support third-party applications on mobile devices. In: Proc. of the 1st ACM Comp. Sec. Arch. Workshop (2007)
36. Vanoverberghe, D., Piessens, F.: A caller-side inline reference monitor for an object-oriented intermediate language. In: Barthe, G., de Boer, F.S. (eds.) FMOODS 2008. LNCS, vol. 5051, pp. 240–258. Springer, Heidelberg (2008)
37. Vanoverberghe, D., Piessens, F.: Security enforcement aware software development. Information and Software Technology (2008), doi:10.1016/j.infsof.2008.01.009
38. Veanes, M., Campbell, C., Schulte, W., Tillmann, N.: Online testing with model programs. In: ESEC/FSE-13: Proceedings of the 10th European software engineering conference held jointly with 13th ACM SIGSOFT international symposium on Foundations of software engineering, pp. 273–282. ACM, New York (2005)
39. Wallach, D.S., Appel, A.W., Felten, E.W.: Safkasi: a security mechanism for language-based systems. ACM Trans. Softw. Eng. Methodol. 9(4), 341–378 (2000)
40. Yee, B.S.: A sanctuary for mobile agents. In: Vitek, J., Jensen, C.D. (eds.) Secure Internet Programming. LNCS, vol. 1603, pp. 261–273. Springer, Heidelberg (1999)

e-Services in a Networked World: From Semantics to Pragmatics

Jaap Gordijn, Sybren de Kinderen, Vincent Pijpers, and Hans Akkermans

VU University Amsterdam
De Boelelaan 1081
1081 HV, Amsterdam, The Netherlands
{gordijn,sdkinde,pijpersv,elly}@few.vu.nl

Abstract. Today's economy is a service economy, and an increasing number of services is electronic, i.e. can be ordered and provisioned online. Examples include Internet access, email and Voice over IP. Typically, e-services are offered as bundles consisting of more elementary services, offered by different suppliers, forming a network. This allows for best-of-breed solutions, in which the customer selects the best services from different suppliers to satisfy his need, and in which the supplier can focus on his core-competences. The research question is then how to compose such a multi-supplier service bundle. In this paper, we argue that first understanding of the context of the service is important. We propose a framework of ontologies, called $e^3 family$, which can be used to reason about the contextual socio-economical aspects of e-services. This framework can be used to elicit customer's need, to compose service bundles satisfying such a need, and to reason about profitability of the found service provisioning network. We illustrate $e^3 family$ by presenting two of its core-ontologies: $e^3 value$ and $e^3 service$.

1   Introduction

Today's economy, is a service economy, and an increasing number of services is electronic, i.e. can be ordered and provisioned online. As an example consider an Internet Service Provider (ISP). An ISP satisfies the customer need of 'communication at a remote distance' via a variety of alternative services. Core services include raw bandwidth, IP connectivity, and Domain Name resolution. Additional services may be offered, such as an email box, a chat box, Voice over IP (VoIP), or Instant Messaging (IM).

Although many customers deal with just one ISP for all their Internet-related services, this is not strictly necessary. The mentioned ISP services can *all* be provided in their own right, and so by different suppliers. For example, the customer may obtain raw bandwidth from supplier S_1, IP connectivity and Domain Name resolution from supplier S_2, and an email box from yet another supplier. Actually, *partnership*, being cooperating suppliers who jointly offer something of value to the customer which they never could have done alone, is frequently seen in eCommerce settings [27]. Partnering enables suppliers to satisfy complex

J. Domingue, D. Fensel, and P. Traverso (Eds.): FIS 2008, LNCS 5468, pp. 44–57, 2009.

customer needs, and allows customers to obtains a bundle of services which more closely satisfy customer's need, as compared to a single supplier bundle.

The online nature of e-services requires online ordering by the customer, and online provisioning of those services. Therefore, ordering and provisioning processes should be facilitated by computational support as good as possible. Note that traditional services, such a hair cut, or cleaning of a hotel room, do not have this online characteristic. Envisioned computational support is first about need/want/demand reasoning. Such reasoning aims at understanding the customer, ultimately in terms of desired positive and negative consequences by that same customer. Second, reasoning should be able to *configure* a bundle of services that satisfices these consequences. The bundle consists of elementary services, each of which can be provided by different suppliers. And third, reasoning has also a supplier perspective. For instance, a single supplier may decide for commercial or technical reasons, to offer a bundle of services only in combination, and not as separate units. A large Dutch telecommunication provider offers VoIP only in combination with raw bandwidth, whereas other providers do just the opposite.

In this paper, we argue that ontologies for e-services should focus on the perceived economic value and desired consequences of those services for the customer, the potential profit for the service supplier, and the ability to match desired consequences with available services in the market in the first place. In other words: the *pragmatics* of the service, in terms of customer goals enabled, and positive and negative consequences for the customer is important, in addition to goal satisfaction of the suppliers (usually profitability).

In the past few years, we have developed a series of ontologies, called $e^3family$ to reason about service pragmatics. These ontologies are used during business development of e-service offerings, but are also used to compose multi-supplier service offerings online. In section 2 we will overview the $e^3family$ ontology suite. Then, in section 3, we focus on the two ontologies of e^3value most relevant for e-services, namely e^3value and $e^3service$. The e^3value ontology is intended to model networks of enterprises, jointly offering services. Its main purpose is to support business development processes, so before business starts running. The $e^3service$ ontology allows online elicitation of consumer needs and desired positive and negative consequences. Furthermore, $e^3service$ can be used to match these customer oriented catalogs with available services, and finally allows to reason about possible service bundles from a supplier perspective. This paper ends with a discussion section.

2   The $e^3family$ Ontologies for Modeling and Reasoning about Context

In the recent past, many approaches for understanding semantics of web-services such as WSMO [25], WSDL [6], BPSS [9], BPEL4WS [2], WSCI [3], and WS-Coordination [7] have seen the light. Obviously, these approaches are important to arrive at composition, orchestration, and monitoring of web-services in

Fig. 1. The e^3*family* ontologies

complex settings. We argue however for e-services, being commercial services which can be ordered and provisioned online, understanding of pragmatics of services is also needed. To that end, we have developed e^3*family* (see figure 1).

Understanding of the pragmatics of e-services is about understanding the context of these e-services. This means that we are primarily interested *how* e-services contribute to reaching goals by parties, being customers or suppliers. In the field of Requirements Engineering, a significant amount of work has been done on goal modeling (see e.g. *I**/Tropos [28,8] and KOAS [19]) in general. Our ontologies allow reasoning about goals also, but more specifically related to e-services.

e^3value. The e^3*value* ontology [12] is one of the key ontologies in e^3*family* and represents a network of enterprises producing and consuming objects of economic value. The instantiation of the ontology can be represented as a graphical model, allowing for easy communication during workshops with executives.

Figure 2 shows an educational e^3*value* model. The model states that the buyer (an actor) has a consumer need (bullet eye), and in order to satisfy this need, the buyer has to obtain an object of economic value (here: a good) for a seller (also an actor). However, the buyer has to pay for the good. In e^3*value* , the payment is considered as a reciprocal value object for the good; furthermore it

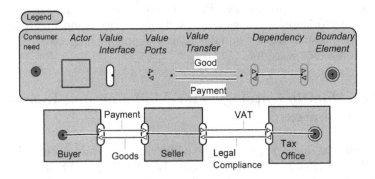

Fig. 2. An educational e^3*value* model

is assumed that if the good is provided the payment always will be done, and vice versa. In other words: e^3value assumes an ideal world, in which all parties provide a reciprocal object (e.g. money) if they obtain another object (e.g. a good). Reciprocity is represented by the value interface, the rounded rectangle superimposed on the actors. Value interfaces include value ports, which provide or request value objects from their environment. Value ports are connected via value transfers. The seller, providing the good, has to pay Value Added Taxes (VAT) to the tax authority, to obtain legal compliance. This is modeled by connecting the two value interfaces of the supplier by means of a dependency path.

In the realm of services, we consider e-services as a kind of value objects. The ontology can be used to reason about profitability for the enterprises involved, or to reason about the economic utility of final customers. It is our claim that for a successful e-service network, *all* enterprises in the network should be economically sustainable. The e^3value ontology comes with software tool support for graphical modeling and model analysis such as profitability assessment and sensitivity analysis (see http://www.e3value.com/ and section 3).

e^3control. The e^3value ontology supposes an ideal world, meaning that economic reciprocity is always maintained. This assumption is convenient for the development of business models for e-services, as the main concern is first and foremost commercial viability of all the actors in the network. The notion of economic reciprocity relates to the idea of 'one good turn deserves another'; if an actor provides an object of value to its environment, it request an object of value in return, which at least has the same economic value to the actor as the provided object.

As soon as the e^3value model is agreed upon by the stakeholders, it is time to relax the constraint of economic reciprocity. We then assume that the world is not ideal anymore, meaning that some actors may obtain objects from their environment, and do not provide the reciprocal object in return. Such behavior is considered as fraudulent behavior. The $e^3control$ ontology allows to model such ideal behavior, by relaxing the reciprocity constraint.

In figure 3 a sub ideal situation is modeled for the ideal e^3value model in figure 2. The dashed value transfer indicates that the seller does not pay taxes, which considered as sub ideal. We have experienced in case studies [17] that analysis of ideal e^3value models for sub ideality is often a first step towards the design of business processes between the actors in the network, as many solutions to avoid sub ideal behavior have a foundation in sound business processes.

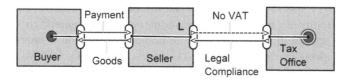

Fig. 3. An educational $e^3control$ model

However, in the same case studies, we have found also solutions that are on the level of the e^3value model itself; as penalties and rewards can be used to reduce sub ideal behavior. To reason about solutions for sub ideal behavior, the $e^3control$ ontology proposes a series of patterns, which are grounded in inter-organizational auditing and control [17].

e³strategy. An e^3value model can also be used to reason about the strategic positioning of each actor in a service network. The $e^3strategy$ ontology extends the e^3value ontology by modeling strategic motivations of actors that stem from environmental forces. The $e^3strategy$ ontology models various forces between actors, based on the theory of Porter. Porter distinguishes five kinds of forces [16,23,24]: *bargaining power of suppliers, bargaining power of buyers, competitive rivalry among competitors, threat of new entrants* and *threat of substitutions*. Questionnaires are used to determine the strength of these forces, as exercised by actors on a focus actor. Understanding of these forces can drive re-design of the corresponding e^3value model, e.g. in terms of alternative partners, different services to be sold, of different customer groups.

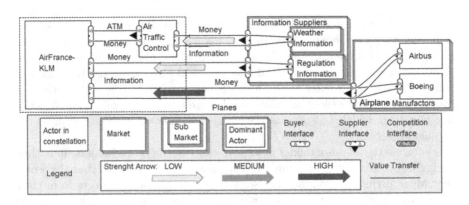

Fig. 4. A partly $e^3strategy$ model

Figure 4 shows a fragment of strategy analysis for the Dutch aviation industry. Here, the forces exercised by suppliers on AirFrance-KLM are shown (by the arrows) and analyzed (see also [21]).

e³domain. The ontologies which are part of the $e^3family$ series are generic in the sense that the ontologies do not include knowledge about a specific industry. We have experienced that, to enable the use of the ontologies for practitioners, at least industry specific guidelines on the use of the ontologies are needed, and also model fragments of their specific industry are convenient to increase re-use. For one specific domain, namely the domain of renewable energy, we have developed a specialization of e^3value [11], called BUSMOD. BUSMOD contains guidelines, specifically for the field on renewable energy, on developing e^3value value models, and comes with an extensive library of model fragments that can be re-used.

e^3service. Whereas the e^3 *value* ontology is used to represent and reason about networks of enterprises exchanging objects of value with each other in general, e^3 *service* focuses on services, and specifically e-services. In e^3 *service*, we understand services as in marketing; economic activities, deeds and performances of a mostly intangible nature [20,14], but with a focus on those services that can be ordered and provisioned (nearly) online. The e^3 *service* ontology consists of a few sub ontologies, of which the customer [18] and supplier [1] ontologies are the most important ones. The idea behind e^3 *service* is that customers and suppliers express their service needs and service offerings in different ways, and in a different granularity. The customer states a need, with associated desired positive consequences, and also acceptable negative consequences (e.g. a price to be paid for service provisioning), for the instance a need to communicate with family living abroad. Suppliers usually list their services in catalogs, and each service in the catalog can be ordered as a separate commercial unit. Examples include Internet access, VoIP, and an email box. The e^3 *service* ontology allows for expressing these two different perspectives on services, and also assists in bridging the customer and supplier perspective. For instance, the need to communicate with family abroad may be satisfied by the service bundle Internet access plus VoIP, or by the bundle Internet access plus email box. Usually, there is a mismatch between the set of consequences as desired by the customer, and the services available in the market that can realize the requested consequences. For a specific service, the set of consequences can be too broad or to narrow. The e^3 *service* ontology can first elicit the desired consequences by employing various marketing techniques (e.g. laddering [4]), and thereafter can configure a minimum multi-supplier service bundle, satisfying the requested set of consequences.

e^3alignment. All the fore mentioned ontologies take different perspectives on the same artifact: the network of e-service customers and suppliers. Although these perspectives separate concerns of different stakeholder concerns, they need to be aligned while exploring and operating networks of e-services. Moreover, as each e-service relies on ICT, there should also be alignment with the technical solutions chosen to provision the e-service at hand.

To this end, we are developing e^3 *alignment* , a framework to reason about the alignment of strategy, business value, cross-organization processes, and ICT [22]. In brief, the e^3 *alignment* approach explores an e-service network by considering each perspective iteratively, and refining each perspective if problems or stakeholder concerns are found in other perspectives.

Discussion. The ontologies in e^3 *family* all have different concerns. The e^3 *value* ontology is used to reason about long term sustainability for all actors in the e-service network. Opportunistic behavior of actors is addressed by e^3 *control.* The e^3 *strategy* ontology evaluates the strategic positioning of actors in a network of service providers and consumers. Customer needs, desired consequences by the customer, bridging these to available commercial e-services in the market, and configuring multi-supplier service bundles is the focus of e^3 *service.* All the ontologies focus on the context, or pragmatics of the service; how does service provisioning contribute to the goal (need satisfying, increase of economic utility) of a customer, and how does service provisioning contribute to the goal (profitability) of the suppliers. Finally, the $e^3 alignment$ ontology assists in keeping consistent all $e^3 family$ models for a case at hand, as these models refer to same artifact being a network of service suppliers and customers, consuming and providing services. Also, $e^3 alignment$ is the bridge to ICT oriented perspectives, showing how services are provisioned in practice, by using software and hardware components.

3   Reasoning about e-service Networks: The $e^3 value$ and $e^3 service$ Ontologies

To show the $e^3 value$ and $e^3 service$ reasoning about e-service networks, we use a case study. The customer wants to communicate over a distance. There are various ways to accomplish this, including via email or Voice over IP (VoIP). An important, usually positively valued customer-consequence for email is that the text can be sent and received. For VoIP, the consequence is to hear and speak voice. The customer considers payment as a negative consequence. From a supplier perspective, there are many parties offering services that may satisfy the fore mentioned need (partly), including KPN (Internet access, email), Google (email) and CozyHost (customized domain). The latter is a service that allows the customer to use a customized domain name (e.g. his own name) for email addresses.

3.1   The Service Catalogs

Reasoning about configuration of e-service networks supposes first service catalogs of suppliers. Our catalogs focus on the economic value aspect of services, in terms of valuable consequences for the customer, and on opportunities to bundle services. Bundling is important because then a more complex customer need could also be satisfied by a supplier, which would otherwise not be possible and thus missed as a commercial opportunity. So, our catalogs differ significantly from catalogs as they are used in the field on web-services.

We assume that suppliers all use the same terminology and structure for expressing their catalogs. Based on these catalog, we generate all possible service bundles. Bundle generation can be done on before hand, or on-the-fly on a per need basis. A fragment of such a pre-generated multi supplier service bundle can be found in figure 5.

Figure 5 uses both constructs from the $e^3 value$ and $e^3 service$ ontologies. Services are seen as value activities that produce resources, such a a valuable service outcome, and require other resources (e.g. money). The resources are offered or requested via ports (graphically shown as arrows) to the environment. The notion of service interfaces (graphically shown as rounded rectangles) shows that if the incoming resources are transfered, the outgoing resources are transfered also, and vice vera. The $e^3 value$ ontology can represent partnerships; enterprises which jointly offering something of value to their environment. We use this feature to represent multi-supplier service bundles. For example, figure 5 shows that

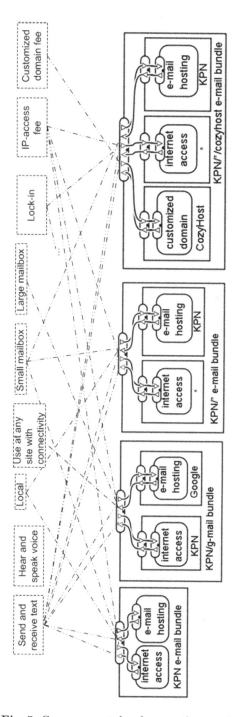

Fig. 5. Consumer catalog for e-mail example

KPN and Google offer together a service bundle, consisting of internet access and email. The e^3 *service* ontology adds the notion of consequences to resources offered or requested. For instance, email hosting of Google has the consequences 'send and receive text' and 'use at site with connectivity'. Furthermore, the e^3 *service* ontology is capable of representing various kinds of constraints between elementary services. These constraints can be used to generate various multi-supplier services on before hand, or on-the-fly. As figure 5 shows the resulting bundles service only, the elementary services and their contraints are not visible (see [13] for more details).

3.2   Reasoning about Customer Needs and Desired Consequences

The reasoning about the customer need is summarized in figure 6. The customer start with a selecting a need from the catalog. Then the customer is presented

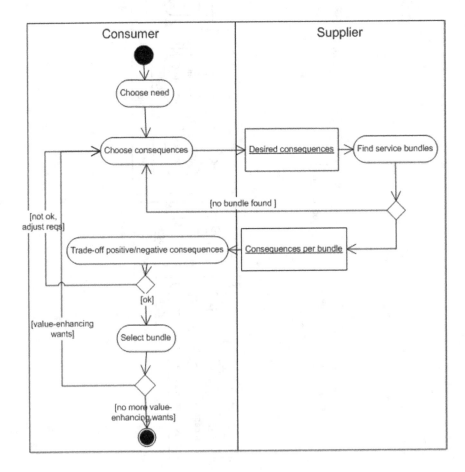

Fig. 6. The generic reasoning structure of e^3 *service*

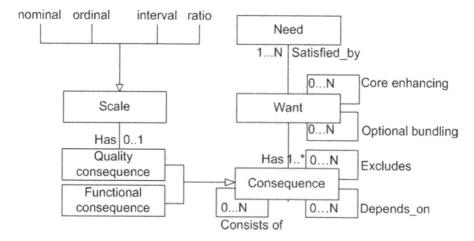

Fig. 7. The customer perspective of the $e^3 service$ ontology

with a series of wants and their consequences. A want is a (partial) solution for the problem indicated by the need. Therefore, the want corresponds to a service, without having a specific supplier in mind. Also, concrete properties (in case of Internet access for instance the bandwidth) are not filled yet. The presented wants should be seen as a bootstrap step to elicit other consequences, perhaps implied by related wants. It is reasonable to expect that the customer has already a notion of solution (want) for his need in mind; as often people are thinking in problem-solutions frames rather than just in problems.

Figure 8 shows a partial instantiation of the $e^3 service$ ontology, specifically the customer perspective of the ontology. The ontology itself is presented in figure 7. The need is to 'communicate over a distance'. There are two alternative wants: 'Email access', and 'VoIP'. Based on the selected wants, a first set of service bundles are generated.

The generated service bundles have consequences, which are presented to the customer. Consequences are expressed on a certain scale, for instance in case of an email size on an ordinal scale.

The customer then scores the presented consequences. This is a subjective process, as each customer has different preferences. Also, the customer decides whether consequences are perceived as positive or negative. The $e^3 service$ ontology only represents consequences themselves, and does say anything about their (positive or negative) value.

It is possible that consequences result in other, more concrete consequences, and so on. The reasoning process elaborates such a series of consequences. This technique is in Marketing called 'laddering' [15].

Based on ranking methods, which are a combination of compensatory decision techniques from [10][5], and the non-compensatory decision techinque MoSCoW from DSDM[26], the customer then selects a set of desired consequences, initially a subset of the consequences of the consequences contained by the bundle. This

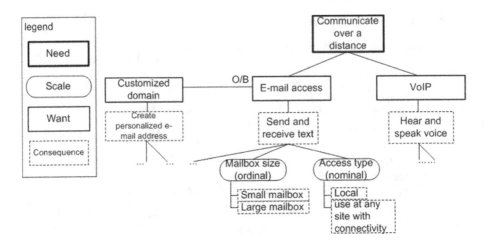

Fig. 8. Example instantiation of the e^3 *service* ontology

set of consequences is then matched with the pre-generated multi-supplier service bundles as explained in section 3.1. Sometimes, the resulting services bundles contain fewer services than the initial proposal, and also different suppliers. In such a case, a better match between the desired consequences and the service bundles containing these is found.

These reasonings steps are repeated to find value-enhancing services and optional services. This refers to what in marketing is called up-selling and cross-selling. For instance, if an email box is selected as service, a value enhancing service could be a spam-filter. The e^3 *service* ontology allows for such reasoning also.

During each iteration, the customer is asked to rank and prioritize the consequences. In other words, the process does not wait until the end before involving consequences. We have learned from our case studies that specifically negative valued consequences should be involved early in the process to discard many potential bundles, which are too expensive.

So, in sum, the reasoning process can be characterizes as as a series of bundle proposals, which are critiqued by the customer by ranking and prioritizing them, and the prioritization is used by the suppliers to come up with modified service bundles.

3.3 An e-Service Network

By ranking the consequences of the alternative service bundles, the customer selects a service that he orders and so should be provisioned. Figure 9 shows an example service network, as an e^3 *value* model cf. the e^3 *value* ontology. The standard reasoning techniques present in e^3 *value* , such as profitability assessment can be used to analyze the network further.

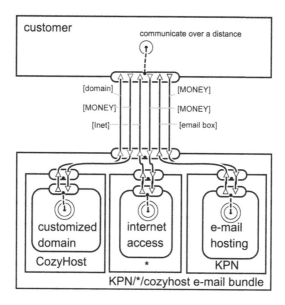

Fig. 9. Example service network

4   Discussion and Conclusion

We have presented in this paper a series of ontologies, all part of $e^3 family$. The $e^3 family$ ontologies have in common that they all focus on the *pragmatics* and and the *context* of innovative IT, which can be offered as bundled e-services.

Concerning the context of e-services, the customers and suppliers are first class citizens. To find appropriate e-services for a specific customer, it is first important to understand the customer need more detailed. The $e^3 service$ ontology does precisely that; Needs are elaborated into desired consequences, which are prioritized. Reasoning steps are borrowed from marketing, and refer to laddering, up-selling, and cross selling. Moreover, the reasoning is an interaction between customer and suppliers, in which the suppliers propose a solution, which is critiqued by the buyer, so that the supplier can offer a modified version of their e-service bundle.

A selected e-service bundle is typically provided by a few suppliers, operating as partners. For the partnership at hand, an $e^3 value$ model can be build. This model shows the actors involved, the service outcomes they consumer or produce and the reciprocal objects (usually money). One of the analysis tools of the $e^3 value$ is then to do a profitability assessment for all the actors involved. The partnership can only survive on the long term if all actors in the partnership can achieve economic sustainability. Such a profitability assessment is another example of understanding the context of e-services, rather than the e-services themselves.

The other ontologies part of $e^3 family$ have similar goals: $e^3 strategy$ reasons about appropriate strategic positioning of an actor in a network, $e^3 control$

analyzes fraudulent behavior of actors, and finally e^3*alignment* keeps the various perspectives on the same e-service artifact consistent.

Acknowledgements. This research has been partly funded by EU-FENIX and by NWO/STW/Jacquard as the projects VITAL, COOP, and VALUE-IT.

References

1. Akkermans, H., Baida, Z., Gordijn, J.: Value webs: Ontology-based bundling of real-world services. IEEE Intelligent Systems 19(44), 23–32 (2004)
2. Andrews, T., Curbera, F., Dholakia, H., Goland, Y., Klein, J., Leymann, F., Liu, K., Roller, D., Smith, D., Thatte, S., Trickovic, I., Weerawanara, S.: Business Process Execution Language for Web Services Version 1.1. Technical report, BEA Systems, IBM, Microsoft, SAP, Siebel (May 5, 2003)
3. Arkin, A., Askary, S., Fordin, S., Jekeli, W., Kawaguchi, K., Orchard, D., Pogliani, S., Riener, K., Struble, S., Takasci-Nagy, P., Trickovic, I., Zimek, S.: Web Service Choreography Interface (WSCI) 1.0. Technical report, BEA Systems, Intalio, SAP, SUN Microsystems (August 8, 2002)
4. Arndt, J.: How broad should the marketing concept be? Journal of Marketing 42(1), 101–103 (1978)
5. Barron, F.H., Barrett, B.E.: Decision quality using ranked attribute weights. Management Science 42(11), 1515–1523 (1996)
6. Booth, D., Liu, C.K.: Web services description language (wsdl) version 2.0 (2007), http://www.w3.org/TR/2007/PR-wsdl20-primer-20070523/
7. Cabrera, L.F., Copeland, G., Cox, W., Feingold, M., Freund, T., Johnson, J., Kaler, C., Klein, J., Langworthy, D., Nadalin, A., Orchard, D., Robinson, I., Shewchuk, J., Storey, T.: Web Services Coordinatioon (WS-Coordination). Technical report, BEA Systems, IBM, Microsoft (September 2003), ftp://www6.software.ibm.com/software/developer/library/ws-coordination.pdf
8. Castro, J., Kolp, M., Mylopoulos, J.: Towards requirements-driven information systems engineering: the tropos project. Information Systems 27, 365–389 (2002)
9. ebXML Business Process Specification Schema Version 1.01 (May 11, 2001), http://www.ebxml.org/specs/ebBPSS.pdf
10. Fishbein, M.: Belief, attitude, intention and behavior: an introduction to theory and research. Addison-Wesley, Reading (1978) (third print)
11. Gordijn, J., Akkermans, H.: Business models for distributed energy resources in a liberalized market environment. The Electric Power Systems Research Journal 77(9), 1178–1188 (2007); Preprint available. doi:10.1016/j.epsr.2006.08.008
12. Gordijn, J., Akkermans, J.M.: Value-based requirements engineering: Exploring innovative e-commerce ideas. Requirements engineering 8(2), 114–134 (2003)
13. Gordijn, J., de Kinderen, S., Wieringa, R.: Value-driven service matching. In: RE 2008 (accepted, 2008)
14. Grönroos, C.: Service Management and Marketing. Lexington Books (1990)
15. Gutman, J., Reynolds, T.J.: Laddering theory-analysis and interpretation. Journal of Advertising Research 28(1), 11 (1988)
16. Johnson, G., Scholes, K.: Exploring Corporate Strategy. Pearson Education Limited, Edinburgh (2002)

17. Kartseva, V.: Designing Controls for Network Organization: A Value-Based Approach. Ph.D thesis, Vrije Universiteit Amsterdam (2008)
18. de Kinderen, S., Gordijn, J.: Reasoning about substitute choices and preference ordering in e-services. In: Bellahsène, Z., Léonard, M. (eds.) CAiSE 2008. LNCS, vol. 5074, pp. 390–404. Springer, Heidelberg (2008)
19. van Lamsweerde, A.: From system goals to software architecture. In: Bernardo, M., Inverardi, P. (eds.) SFM 2003. LNCS, vol. 2804, pp. 25–43. Springer, Heidelberg (2003)
20. Normann, R.: Service Management - strategy and leadership in service business, 3rd edn. Wiley, Chichester (2000)
21. Pijpers, V., Gordijn, J.: E3forces: Understanding strategies of networked e3value constellations by analyzing environmental forces. In: Krogstie, J., Opdahl, A.L., Sindre, G. (eds.) CAiSE 2007 and WES 2007. LNCS, vol. 4495, pp. 188–202. Springer, Heidelberg (2007)
22. Pijpers, V., Gordijn, J., Akkermans, H.: Aligning information system design and business strategy - a starting internet company (accepted, 2008)
23. Porter, M.E.: Competetive Strategy. Techniques for analyzing industries and competitors. The Free Press, New York (1980)
24. Porter, M.E.: Competitive advantage. Creating and sustaining superior performance. The Free Press, New York (1985)
25. Roman, D., Keller, U., Lausen, H., de Bruijn, J., Lara, R., Stollberg, M., Polleresa, A., Feier, C., Bussler, C., Fensel, D.: eb service modeling ontology. Applied Ontology 1(1), 77–106 (2005)
26. Stapleton, J.: Dynamic Systems Development Method. Addison Wesley, Longman, Reading (1997)
27. Tapscott, D., Ticoll, D., Lowy, A.: Digital Capital - Harnessing the Power of Business Webs. Nicholas Brealy Publishing, London (2000)
28. Yu, E.: Towards modelling and reasoning support for early-phase requirements engineering. In: Proceedings of the 3rd IEEE Int. Symp. on Requirements Engineering (RE 1997), pp. 226–235. IEEE Computer Science Press, Los Alamitos (1997)

Hierarchical Modelling and an Approximate Analysis of Parallel Queues Models to the NGN SCEs

Natalia Kryvinska[1], Christine Strauss[1], Lukas Auer[1], and Peter Zinterhof[2]

[1] Department of eBusiness, Faculty of Business, Economics and Statistics,
University of Vienna,
Bruenner Strasse 72, A-1210 Vienna, Austria
`natalia.kryvinska@univie.ac.at, christine.strauss@univie.ac.at,`
`a0700895@unet.univie.ac.at`
[2] Department of Computer Sciences, University of Salzburg,
Jakob-Haringer-Str. 2, 5020 Salzburg, Austria
`peter.zinterhof@sbg.ac.at`

Abstract. The new-emerging inventive technologies that bring together the richness of IT applications with the superiority and intelligence of next-generation networks bring also about a dramatic jump in services value for all types of enterprises and carriers. It is seen by fundamental changes in the way applications and services are designed, developed, delivered, and used. With this new age comes a set of demanding technical challenges along with significant opportunities for technology innovation. Thus, we address here these challenges by evaluating NGNs service platform in terms of functionality, programmability, flexibility, openness, and inter-operability. Besides, in NGNs even a simple service has a complex structure. It consists from a lot of building blocks, which create hierarchical models with a lot of parallel subsystems. Thus, the NGN SCE has to be based on multiprocessing technology and parallel programming environments. And, our particular interest is in understanding and modeling the performance of parallel queuing models.

Keywords: Hierarchical modeling, Next Generation Network (NGN), Parallel queues, Queuing theory, Service Creation Environment (SCE).

1 Introduction

The ICT technologies industry moves ahead towards the drastic transformations in the communications business. It can be noticed by the fundamental changes in the way applications and services are designed, developed, delivered, and used. New-emerging inventive technologies that bring together the richness of the Internet applications along with the superiority and intelligence of next-generation communications networks bring also about a dramatic jump in services value for enterprises and carriers of all types, as well as costumers. With this new era comes also a set of demanding technical challenges along with significant opportunities for technology innovation [1, 4].

Next Generation Network (NGN), in this context, can be seen by network operators and service providers as a new revenue stream from their potential to increase

J. Domingue, D. Fensel, and P. Traverso (Eds.): FIS 2008, LNCS 5468, pp. 58–71, 2009.

service offerings. Therefore, it is very important to understand how proposed solutions in NGN can enable flexible and easy service creation both to service providers and third party application developers [2, 3].

NGN application development has many common features with Internet application development. And, It is accessible to a broad community, because of:

- *easiness* - the need for knowledge that is specific to telecommunications is less than before;
- *productivity* - relies on the fact that a specific SCE is not provided commonly, some systems provide several levels of APIs. This brings the flexibility of choosing the most appropriate level of abstraction for a given application;
- *creativity* - can increase because there is a move to the use high-level application environments that can be deployed across different vendors [2, 5].

2 Evaluation Criteria for Service Creation Technologies

The evaluation criteria used for classification and comparison of different service creation technologies are, as follows:

- *network capabilities* - based on the abstraction of underlying network infrastructure that can be used to exploit network functionalities; they can represent both functional (e.g. call control) and non-functional (e.g., authentication, logging) aspects.
- *reference architecture* - defines which place a technology covers in the categorization (Fig. 1), depending on its characteristics: application server layer includes technologies used to execute services, programmed with tools, represented by the application creation environment layer; call server layer includes technologies handling routing and delivery of voice calls; media server layer represents technologies involved in multimedia communications, and messaging server stands for entities handling messaging and asynchronous communications. Media gateway layer represents networks related technologies.

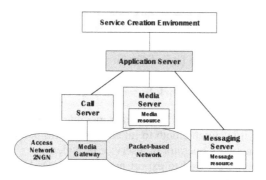

Fig. 1. Reference architecture

- *interfaces and description languages* - The kind of interface (KOI) describes the communications method by which the technology is exposing network capability to external systems.
- *suitability for third party development* – (e.g., programmability) - describes the qualification of the technology in support of application development by third party developers, and the suitability to third party service providers [2 ÷ 6].

3 Technologies for Service Creation in NGN

3.1 Open Service Access (OSA)/Parlay

The OSA/Parlay identifies and specifies a programming network interface in order to easily create applications using the network services (Fig. 2) provided by the communication networks. The set of service capability features (SCFs) could be incrementally extended, because one of the aims of OSA/Parlay is to provide an extendible and scalable interface that allows for inclusion of new functionality in the network in future releases with a minimum impact on the applications using the OSA/Parlay interface.

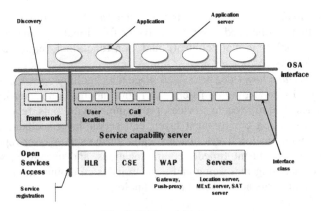

Fig. 2. OSA architecture

A Parlay/OSA APIs provide a medium level of abstraction of the network capabilities. They provide an abstraction from different specific protocols [2, 7, 8].

3.2 Interoperable Services Network Based on Web Services

The web services architecture realizes an interoperable network of services focused on service reuse and it is suitable both to interact with third party applications and to export services by a network operator or a service provider.

The web services can be used to export network services by exposing its WSDL (web services definition language) interfaces; these services communicate using SOAP (simple object access protocol), a protocol used to transport data between web services; service discovery and service registration are implemented accessing to the

UDDI (universal discovery, description and integration) registry; XML is used as data format for SOAP messages that rely on existing internet protocols like HTTP. Web services implementations need that the language-dependent API must be translated in WSDL and the application server where web-services are deployed must translate incoming SOAP messages to the underlying interfaces (e.g., Java, CORBA).

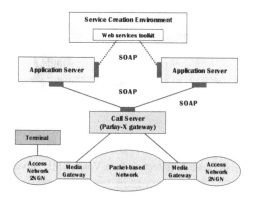

Fig. 3. Web services in reference architecture

Considering the reference architecture, services running on different application servers could communicate using SOAP messages; another scenario can be made by a call server exposing WSDL interfaces (Fig. 3) that offers network connectivity to a 3rd party service running in an application server external to the call server domain; intra-domain connectivity among different components can be obtained migrating to web services, when different technologies must communicate [2, 9 ÷ 11].

3.3 Voice Extensible Markup Language (VoiceXML)

VoiceXML is a technology that allows a user to interact with a web server through voice-recognition technology, which exploits media server capabilities. VoiceXML can also be described as a phone markup language that can be used for voice applications that provide phone access to content and information, so it supports the network capability previously defined as generic user interaction (GUI).

The VoiceXML interpreter can be seen as an enhanced feature of a media server, but its internal architecture is made of different parts (Fig. 4):

- voice browser - software that renders the VoiceXML as a sequence of two dialogs between the system and the user.
- web server - where the application pages reside. The application pages can be VoiceXML files, ASP, JSP, or PHP to dynamically create VoiceXML pages.

The user dials in to a particular phone number or SIP URI corresponding to the voice browser. The voice browser sends an HTTP request for the VoiceXML document to a server determined from the dialed number.

VoiceXML makes it easy to rapidly create new applications and shields developers from low level programming issues. VoiceXML also executes logic: main components of a VoiceXML-based speech service include tags, forms and rules that define the content and a speech browser for interpreting and presenting audio content [2, 13, 14].

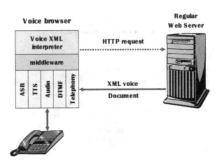

Fig. 4. Basic Architecture for a Voice XML Service

4 Key Aspects for Deploying NGN Services Platform

We highlight here some key aspects that have to be considered when deploying NGN service platforms:

- *SIP tools* - are the means to the communications needs of an NGN deployment. There are however, still several major issues that SIP must support before they may be considered mature enough for scalable, multi-service, managed networks. Functions in support of service selection, QoS, billing and security are such areas of required attention.
- *intelligence balance* - location of intelligence is no longer restricted to the core-operating network. If compared to PSTN networks, NGNs are enriched by much more powerful terminals enabling the provision of new and innovative services. This means that massively used simple services with simple billing policies demand much less resources from the service providers than PSTN services.
- *APIs availability* – a variety of APIs are emerging in NGN providing different levels of functional abstraction. It can be confusing to community when having to choose which API to use for a particular service. But, at the same time it means that the same service may be implemented in many different ways allowing service providers better chance to differentiate themselves from each other.
- *open source software* - open source applications play an important role in NGN systems. However operators of NGN services have to recognize this as a valid deployment model especially given the effective extensibility and tailor made adaptations that this approach offers.

Regarding to the key aspects mentioned above, the development of NGN services is accessible in many ways. And, it is close to the web and IT developer community approach [2, 14].

5 NGN Service Creation Environment (SCE) Modeling

In NGNs even simple service has complex structure. It consists from a lot of building blocks, which create hierarchical models with a lot of parallel subsystems. Thus, the NGN SCE is based on the multiprocessing technology, parallel programming languages, and parallel programming environments [15, 17 ÷ 20].

Furthermore, as mentioned in previous sections, NGN converges different media types onto the single platform (e.g., data, voice, video, interactive multimedia communications). So, the same protocols and service creation technologies are engaged, independently of media type.

5.1 Achieving Performance Efficiencies in NGN Applications Using Parallel Processing

Telecommunications operators rely on personalized services, such as broadband Internet access, mCommerce applications, and ring-back tones and many others, also called "lifestyle services" to grow revenue by addressing niche markets.

However, these new types of services require managing and maintaining increasing amounts of customer data. With some operators having million customers, customizing these services for specific characteristics such as age or special interests requires an intense data processing workload. Regulatory reporting is also adding new data processing on top of existing workloads. In some cases, there are tight windows within which these reports must be completed, and late delivery of reports to agencies can carry big fines.

To support these new business opportunities and increased regulatory requirements is possible by continuing to increase the transaction volumes processed by IT systems. Existing Operations Support Systems (OSS) and Business Support Systems (BSS) may already be at or near capacity, so it can be difficult to expand the transaction workload without addressing the space, power, and cooling capacity of existing data center facilities. With limited budgets and no easy way to expand data center capacity, service providers are faced with the increasingly difficult challenge of squeezing more performance and greater utilization out of their existing IT systems and applications.

Addressing these challenges requires a new approach to developing and deploying business applications - an approach that can more efficiently deliver high volume throughput and better utilize computing resources. A methodology based onto the parallel processing can enable businesses to achieve the benefits without a major redevelopment effort.

Traditionally, parallel processing has been used for massively parallel applications such as genetic research or other scientific applications. Compute grids have also been used effectively for running many small batch jobs that can execute independently of one another.

To show how parallel processing can be useful in practice (e.g., for business purposes), we consider the following example. A cellular carrier that offers pre-paid minutes must be able to track a customer's usage and calculate the minutes remaining in the customer's account in real-time. If the customer initiates a second call immediately after completing the first call, the system must have an accurate account of the minutes remaining in the user's account before initiating the call.

These calculations could be accomplished on a centralized back-end computing system as long as response time is predictable and there is a mechanism to verify that there are no pending end-of-call transactions for a given user before initiating a new call for that user. This is an ideal application for the parallel processing because transaction volume is highly variable, response time is critical, and enforcement of key business rules is essential.

The business/service process for this example consists of the following steps:

- *authenticate* - validate the user account and capture the minutes remaining on account;
- *initiate call* - record start time of the call and compute the maximum number minutes the call can proceed without going beyond the available balance;
- *monitor* - continuously compare the call time against the maximum minutes;
- *end call* - record the call completion time and deduct the total minutes from the user's account.

First, the traditional design of a monolithic, tightly coupled, centralized software component is shown in Figure 5.

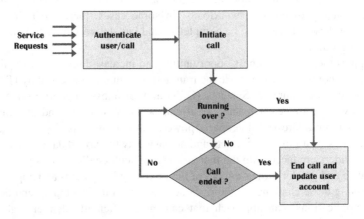

Fig. 5. Monolithic software application (all transactions are processed sequentially)

However, it is obvious that such a design results in every user transaction having to wait for any previous transactions to complete. If volume scales dramatically, as in peak periods, and the input flow outstrips the capacity of this single software component to handle the load, a lot of customers will be waiting for calls to be initiated. All too often, waiting customers result in lost customers - a situation that telecom service providers desperately want to avoid.

Using parallel processing, the processing task can be divided into logical units of parallel work. The first step is to decompose the steps required for processing and to decide what portions of the process can be executed in parallel.

In this simple example, the most important idea is that there are no pending transactions to update the user's account before a new call is initiated. There are a number of ways to enforce this service logic, but one simple way is to keep the initiate call and the end call portions of the transaction in the same parallel channel and then enforce FIFO processing within that channels pool. This ensures that each "end call" for a specific customer account is processed before a new "initiate call" is processed.

The process of authenticating users can be broken out into a separate channel because there is no concern about the order in which authentication requests are performed. Thus authentication can be executed in parallel with other parts of the service logic.

Figure 6 shows how this service logic could be represented to enable parallel processing of the steps identified above.

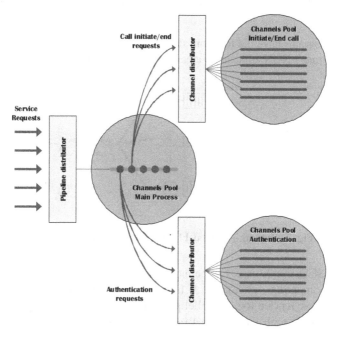

Fig. 6. Service logic to enable parallel processing (example: authentication performed in parallel with other parts of the service logic)

From this picture we can see that there are multiple levels of parallel processing. First, the two separate channel pools enable parallel processing of different segments of the incoming transactions. Authentication requests are processed in parallel with the steps of each transaction that represent the initiate call through end call steps.

Secondly, since each channel pool maintains FIFO order, it is possible to execute the initiate to end call steps for multiple customers at the same time, provided that no two transactions for the same account are performed out of sequence (or simultaneously). This presents a FIFO requirement, a key bottleneck in parallel business applications. A single channel for the initiate to end call sequence is used to distribute this process while enabling parallel processing. The FIFO requirement is supported through the channels distributor which is designed to ensure order of processing for transactions that flow through a given channels pool.

By enabling parallel processing on multiple levels, it is possible to process a far greater number of transactions per unit of time, allowing significantly greater scalability than a traditional monolithic design. Because channel pools can also be assigned to specific hardware resources, enormous scalability can be achieved by replicating channels and assigning additional hardware resources to the replicated software components. This approach can be used to achieve up to an order of magnitude improvement in application throughput [25, 26].

5.2 An analytical Framework for the NGN Services Creation and Modeling Environment

The parallel programs have the fork-join structure and this type of parallel program paradigm arises in many NGN application areas, as mentioned above (Fig. 7) [15, 17 ÷ 20].

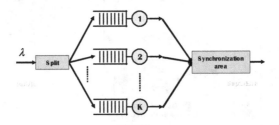

Fig. 7. The fork-join model for service logic parallel program

The NGN SCE, in this case, can be modeled as follows. We assume that SCE multiprocessing computing system has K homogeneous servers, each with an infinite capacity queue. A service logic parallel program arrives to the multiprocessing computing environment with mean arrival rate λ. Upon the parallel program's arrival, it splits into K independent tasks t_i, $1 \leq i \leq K$ and task ti is assigned to the ith server. Each task's service time is k-stage Erlang distributed with a mean service time of $1/\mu$. Each server uses the first-in-first-out (FIFO) scheduling discipline to service its tasks. When a task is finished and if there are any tasks belonging to the same parallel program still in service, the finished task will wait in the synchronization area. The parallel program is considered complete and it departs from the computing system only when all its tasks have been completed.

This type of work is closely related to fork-join queuing systems. The exact analysis is possible when the system is significantly simplified, for example, if it is assumed the job arrival process is Poisson with tasks having exponential service time distribution and the number of servers, K, is equal to two. For more than two servers, approximation and heuristic techniques are used to solve the problem [16, 17, 20].

Thus, we take into consideration a system which consists of K identical parallel queuing systems as shown in Fig. 7. Service requests arrive in a time-invariant, state-independent Poisson fashion with rate λ. Upon arrival, a service request forks into K tasks. Task k, $k = 1, 2, \ldots, K$, is assigned to the kth queuing system which consists of a single server and an infinite capacity queue. The service times of tasks are independent and exponentially distributed with mean $1/\mu$. The server utilization is denoted by $\rho = \lambda/\mu$. A job (e.g., service request) leaves the system as soon as all its tasks complete their service. In other words, tasks of the same job joined before departing the system [21, 22].

The state of the system explained above can be presented by the number of tasks in each of the K queuing systems. This results in a K-dimensional Markov process whose analysis seems to be hard, if not impossible, for the general case.

So, we take into consideration the system with $K=2$ queues to obtain the mean time in system of service request processing or response time. The response time of a task consists of two components:

- time spent in an *M/M/1* queuing system, and
- time spent in the system after service completion and before leaving the system. The latter is called synchronization delay; it is non-zero for the task that finishes its service first and zero for its sibling [21 ÷ 23].

The mean job response time equals the mean task response time because each job consists of exactly two tasks. Thus, the mean job response time in two-queue system is the sum of the mean response time in an *M/M/1* queuing system:

$$T_1 = 1/(\mu - \lambda), \tag{1}$$

and the mean synchronization delay S, that is,

$$T_2 = T_1 + S. \tag{2}$$

Using Little's formulae, we can present synchronization delay as follows:

$$S = \frac{N}{2\lambda}, \tag{3}$$

where N is the average number of tasks which have completed and are waiting for their siblings to complete. Let k be any integer and define q_k to be the probability that the number of tasks in the first queuing system exceeds the number of tasks in the second queuing system by k. By symmetry, we have $q_k = q_{-k}$, $k \geq 1$ and thus

$$N = 2\sum_{k=1}^{\infty} k q_k, \tag{4}$$

which implies

$$S = \frac{1}{\lambda}\sum_{k=1}^{\infty} k q_k. \tag{5}$$

The balance equation for the system can show that $q_k = q_{+k} + p_{k,0}$, $k = 0, 1, ...,$ where $p_{k,0}$ is the probability that there are k tasks in the first queue and 0 tasks in the second queue. This implies that

$$q_k = \sum_{i=k}^{\infty} p_{i,0} \quad k = 0,1,... \tag{6}$$

Substituting (6) into (5) and simplifying yields to [21 ÷ 23]:

$$S = \frac{1}{\lambda} \sum_{i=1}^{\infty} \frac{i(i+1)}{2} p_{i,0}. \tag{7}$$

The generating function for $p_{i,0}$ is given by [23]:

$$P(z,0) = \frac{(1-\rho)^{\frac{3}{2}}}{\sqrt{1-pz}}. \tag{8}$$

Using this to determine the first two moments of $p_{i,0}$ and substituting into (7) and (2) yields

$$T_2 = \frac{12-\rho}{8} T_1. \tag{9}$$

In Fig. 8, we present results of calculations of eq.1 and 9.

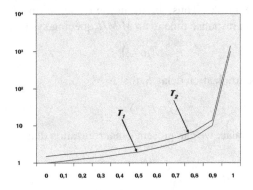

Fig. 8. The first two moments of time in system or response time in two-queue system

The approach to solve the $K > 2$ queue problem is an approximate one. The essence of the approximation method stems from an interesting observation of bounds on T_K. An upper bound is obtained by assuming independent queuing systems and, since the response times in M/M/1 queues are exponentially distributed with mean T_1, is given by

$$T_K \leq H_K T_1. \tag{10}$$

where H_K is the harmonic series [22, 24]. Then the following upper bound holds:

$$T_K \leq H_K \frac{1}{\mu - \lambda}. \qquad (11)$$

The theorem for the expected response time of the queuing system is as follows:

$$T_K = \int_0^\infty G(t)dt \leq \int_0^\infty \left(1 - F^K(t)\right)dt. \qquad (12)$$

The theorem follows from the fact that for the system

$$F(t) = 1 - e^{-(\mu - \lambda)t} \qquad (13)$$

and then [21, 22]:

$$H_K = \int_0^\infty \left(1 - \left(1 - e^{-t}\right)^k\right)dt. \qquad (14)$$

A lower bound, on the other hand, is obtained by neglecting queuing effects. In this case, the response time is the maximum of K exponentially distributed service times each with mean $1/\mu$. Thus, we have

$$T_K \geq H_K \frac{1}{\mu}. \qquad (15)$$

From (10) and (15) we can see that both bounds grow at the same rate H_K. In other words, for large K the bounds are of order $O(\ln K)$. From this observation, we conclude that T_K itself is growing at the same rate. Consequently, knowing the value of T_2:

$$T_K \cong S_K(\rho)T_2, \qquad K \geq 2, \qquad (16)$$

where $S_K(\rho)$ is a scaling factor which grows at rate $O(\ln K)$. We seek an approximation of the following form is

$$S_K(\rho) = \alpha(\rho) + \beta(\rho)H_K, \qquad K \geq 2. \qquad (17)$$

By substituting $S_2(\rho) = 1$, which is true by definition, in the above equation we have that $\beta(\rho) = (1 - \alpha(\rho))/H_2$, and thus,

$$S_K(\rho) = \alpha(\rho) + \frac{1 - \alpha(\rho)}{H_2} H_K, \qquad K \geq 2. \qquad (18)$$

where $\alpha(\rho)$ is to be determined.

And, substituting this into (18) and (16) leads to the following approximate expression for T_K.

$$T_K \cong \left(\frac{H_K}{H_2} + \frac{4}{11}\left(1 - \frac{H_K}{H_2}\right)\rho \right)T_2, \qquad K \geq 2. \qquad (19)$$

The scaling factor in this expression exhibits a logarithmic behavior in K and a linear behavior in ρ, which we can see from Fig. 9 [21 ÷ 24].

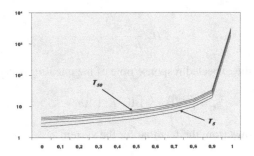

Fig. 9. The mean response or time in system T_K for K identical parallel queuing systems

8   Conclusions and Future Work

In NGNs even simple service has complex structure. It consists from a lot of building blocks, which create hierarchical models with a lot of parallel subsystems. And, particular interest is in understanding and modeling the performance of these subsystems. The fork-join architectures are one of the fundamental modeling structures for parallel processing. According to the correlation of arrival processes to all servers and the infinite queuing capacities at each server, no exact solution exists. In this paper, we have introduced an approximate analysis for a homogeneous fork/join queuing system consisting of K exponential servers.

There are several extensions of this work that are of interest. For example, extending the basic model to the case where the servers are of different speeds, and model a system consisting of non-homogeneous processors.

References

1. Carbone, P., Romagnino, S.: Extreme value from next-generation applications and services. Nortel Technical Journal (5) (2007)
2. Falcarin, P., Licciardi, C.: Analysis of NGN service creation technologies. IEC Annual Review of Communications 56 (June 2003)
3. Eurescom Project P1109: Next Generation Networks: The services offering standpoint, http://www.eurescom.de/secure/projects/ P1100-series/P1109/P1109.htm
4. Quocirca Insight Report: Managing 21st Century Networks - A world of convergence, Quocirca (January 2007)
5. Christian, R., Hanrahan, H.E.: Converging towards Service Centric Networks: Requirements for a Service Delivery Platform Framework. In: Southern African Telecommunications Networks and Applications Conference (SATNAC) 2005 Proceedings, September, vol. 1, pp. 295–300 (2005)
6. Consel, C., Latry, F., Mercadal, J.: Staging Telephony Service Creation: A Language Approach. In: Proceedings of the 1st International Conference on Principles, Systems and Applications of IP Telecommunications (IPTComm), New York, July 19-20 (2007)

7. Bata, Y., Hanrahan, H.E.: Quality of Service in the OSA/Parlay Environment. In: Southern African Telecommunications Networks and Applications Conference (SATNAC) 2005 Proceedings, September, vol. 2, pp. 53–54 (2005)
8. The 3rd Generation Partnership Project (3GPP), Open Services Architecture (OSA)
9. Web Services Description Language (WSDL), http://www.w3.org
10. Simple Object Access Protocol (SOAP) specification,
    http://www.w3.org/TR/SOAP
11. Universal Discovery, Description and Integration (UDDI) specification,
    http://www.uddi.org/
12. Andreetto, A., Licciardi, C.A., Falcarin, P.: Service opportunities for Next Generation Networks. In: Proceeding of the Eurescom Summit conference - 3G Technologies and Applications, Heidelberg, Germany (November 2001)
13. VoiceXML specification, http://www.voicexml.org
14. Bakker, J.L., Jain, R.: Next Generation Service Creation Using XML Scripting Languages. In: ICC 2002 Proceedings (2002)
15. Tanner, M.: Practical Queueing Analysis. IBM McGraw-Hill Series (1995)
16. Schwartz, M.: Telecommunication Networks: Protocols, Modeling and Analysis. Addison-Wesley, Reading (1987)
17. Lui, C.S., Muntz, R.R., Towsley, D.: Computing Performance Bounds of Fork-Join Parallel Programs Under a Multiprocessing Environment. IEEE Transactions on Parallel and Distributed Systems 9(3) (March 1998)
18. Beguelin, A., Dongarra, J.J., Geist, A., Manchek, R., Sunderam, V.: PVM and HeNCE: Tools for Heterogeneous Network Computing. In: Advances in Parallel Computing: Environments and Tools for Parallel Scientific Computing, pp. 139–153 (1993)
19. Hoare, C.A.R.: Communicating Sequential Processes. Prentice-Hall Intel, London (1985)
20. Stonebraker, M.R.: The Case for Shared-Nothing. In: Proc. 1986 Data Engineering Conf. IEEE, Los Alamitos (1986)
21. Thomasian, A., Tantawi, A.N.: Approximate Solutions for M/G/1 Fork/Join Synchronization. In: Proc. 1994 Winter Simulation Conf., Orlando, Fla., December, pp. 361–368 (1994)
22. Nelson, R., Tantawi, A.N.: Approximate Analysis of Fork/Join Synchronization in Parallel Queues. IEEE Transaction on Computers 37(6), 739–743 (1988)
23. Flatto, L., Hahn, S.: Two parallel queues created by arrivals with two demands. SIAM Journal on Applied Mathematics 44, 1041–1053 (1984)
24. Kleinrock, L.: Queueing Systems. Theory, vol. I. Wiley Int'l., Chichester (1975)
25. Isaacson, C., Lasica, S.: Using Intelligent Parallel Processing in a Service Oriented Architecture (SOA) - Achieving Performance Efficiencies in Telco Business Applications, White Paper, Rogue Wave Software (2007)
26. Pipeline (software), from Wikipedia,
    http://en.wikipedia.org/wiki/Pipeline_software

A First Step Towards Stream Reasoning

Emanuele Della Valle, Stefano Ceri, Davide Francesco Barbieri, Daniele Braga,
and Alessandro Campi

Dip. di Elettronica e Informazione, Politecnico di Milano, Milano, Italy
{name.surname}@polimi.it

Abstract. While reasoners are year after year scaling up in the classical,
time invariant domain of ontological knowledge, reasoning upon rapidly
changing information has been neglected or forgotten. On the contrary,
processing of data streams has been largely investigated and specialized
Stream Database Management Systems exist. In this paper, by coupling
reasoners with powerful, reactive, throughput-efficient stream management systems, we introduce the concept of Stream Reasoning. We expect
future realization of such concept to have high impact on the future Internet because it enables reasoning in real time, at a throughput and
with a reactivity not obtained in previous works.

Keywords: Data Streams, Reasoning, Real-time, Throughput-efficiency,
Urban Computing, Pervasive Computing.

1   Introduction and Motivation

Semantics is more and more evoked as a powerful tool to facilitate interoperability, flexibility and adaptability. The growing scalability of reasoning techniques
[1] is key to the relevant role that semantics will play in the future Internet.
While reasoners scale up in the classical, static domain of ontological knowledge,
reasoning upon rapidly changing information has been neglected or forgotten.

Data streams are unbounded sequences of time-varying data elements; they
occur in a variety of modern applications, such as network monitoring, traffic
engineering, sensor networks, RFID tags applications, telecom call records, financial applications, Web logs, click-streams, etc. Processing of data streams
has been largely investigated in the last decade [2], specialized Data Stream
Management Systems (DSMSs) have been developed, and features of DSMSs
are becoming supported by major database products, such as Oracle and DB2.

The combination of reasoning techniques with data streams gives rise to
Stream Reasoning, an unexplored, yet high impact, research area. To understand the potential impact of Stream Reasoning, we can consider the emblematic
case of Urban Computing [3,4,5,6] (i.e., the application of pervasive computing
to urban environments). The very nature of Urban Computing can be explained
by means of data streams, representing real objects that are monitored at given
locations: cars, trains, crowds, ambulances, parking spaces, and so on. Reasoning
about such streams can be very effective in reducing costs: for instance, looking

J. Domingue, D. Fensel, and P. Traverso (Eds.): FIS 2008, LNCS 5468, pp. 72–81, 2009.

for parking lots in large cities may cost up to 40% of the daily fuel consumption. Problems dramatically increase when big events, involving lots of people, take place; a typical Urban Computing problem is to help citizens willing to participate to such events in finding a parking lot and reaching the event locations in time, while globally limiting the occurrences of traffic congestions.

Some years ago, due to the lack of data, solving Urban Computing problems looked like a Sci-Fi idea. Nowadays, a large amount of the required information can be made available on the Internet at almost no cost: computerized systems contain maps with the commercial activities and meeting places (e.g., Google Earth), events scheduled in the city and their locations, positions and speed information of public transportation vehicles and of mobile phone users [5], parking availabilities in specific parking areas, and so on. However, current technologies are not up to the challenge of solving Urban Computing problems: this requires combining a huge amount of static knowledge about the city (i.e., urbanistic, social and cultural knowledge) with an even larger set of data streams (originating in real time from heterogeneous and noisy data sources) and reasoning above the resulting time-varying knowledge.

A new generation of reasoners is clearly needed in order to simultaneously instruct the car GPS of numerous citizens with the fastest route to the most convenient parking lot during exceptional events. Time constraints for such a reasoner are very demanding (i.e., few ms per query) because citizens are continuously making driving decisions and the traffic keeps evolving; therefore, continuous inference is required. In this work, we define Stream Reasoning as a new paradigm, based upon the state of the art in DSMS and reasoning, in order to enable such applications. By coupling reasoners with powerful, reactive, throughput-efficient stream management systems, we expect to enable reasoning in real time, at a throughput and with a reactivity not obtained in previous works.

In the rest of the paper, we identify the problem we want to untangle (Section 2). We introduce a Conceptual Architecture for Stream Reasoning (Section 3) that instantiates the pluggable algorithmic framework proposed in the LarKC project [7,8]. We present two stream reasoning frameworks based on such architecture, one representing an evolutionary approach that combines existing solutions (Section 4), the other representing a revolutionary approach that proposes a new reasoning paradigm (Section 5). We conclude the paper discussing the challenges we are facing while planning our future work (Section 6).

2   Problem Definition

Our attempt to combine data stream and reasoning technologies starts from terminology. Database (DB) and Knowledge Engineering (KE) communities often use different terms to indicate the same concepts. DB community distinguishes among schema and data, whereas KE community distinguishes among factual, terminological, and nomological knowledge. The notion of data is close to the notion of factual knowledge, and similarly the notion of schema is close to the notion of terminological knowledge. Nomological knowledge is information about rules defining actions and action-types and governing means-ends relationships in a given culture or society (e.g., when it rains, traffic gets slower); this notion is somehow captured by constraint languages for DBs, but it is mainly peculiar of KE. For the purpose of this paper, we name *"knowledge"* both terminological and nomological knowledge (thus we include in term knowledge the DB notion of schema) and we use *"data"* as a synonymous of factual knowledge.

Knowledge and data can change over time. For instance, in Urban Computing, names of streets, landmarks, kinds of events, etc. change very slowly, whereas the number of cars that go through a traffic detector in five minutes changes very fast. In order to classify knowledge and data according to the frequency of their changes we first need to introduce the notion of *"observation period"*, defined as the period when we the system is subject to querying. In the context of this paper, we consider knowledge as **invariable during the observation period**; only data can change. Of course, knowledge is subject to change, but then the mutating part of the system is not object of observation. This is not surprising: in the DB context, change of schemas occur by means of create or alter table command; while, for instance, the alter table command is executed all query processing relative to that table is suspended.

Examples of invariable knowledge, in the case of Urban Computing, include obvious terminological knowledge (such as an address is made up by a street name, a civic number, a city name, and a ZIP code), which defines the *conceptual schema* of the application, and less obvious nomological knowledge that describes how the world is expected to be (e.g., given traffic lights are switched off or certain streets are closed during the night) or to evolve (e.g., traffic jams appears more often when it rains or when important sport events take place).

Data can be further classified according with the frequency they are expected to change.

1. **Invariable** data: data that do not change in the observation period, e.g. the names and lengths of the roads.
2. **Periodically changing** data, for which a temporal law describing their evolution is present in the invariable knowledge. We can distinguish:
   (a) *Probabilistic* data, e.g. the fact that a traffic jam is present in the west side of Milan due to bad weather or due to a soccer match is taking place in San Siro stadium;
   (b) *Pure periodic* data, e.g. the fact that every night at 10pm Milan west-side overpass road closes.
3. **Event driven changing** data that got updated as a consequence of some external event not described in the knowledge, which are further characterized by the mean time between changes:
   (a) *Fast*, as an example consider the intensity of traffic (as monitored by sensors) for each street in a city;
   (b) *Medium*, as an example consider roads closed for accidents or congestion due to traffic;
   (c) *Slow*, as an example consider roads closed for scheduled works.

Traditional databases are suitable for capturing relatively small quantity of knowledge in their schema and huge dataset of both invariable data and event driven changing data whose mean time between changes is slow or medium. Periodically changing data can be modeled by means of triggers that perform updates; for example a trigger may update the state of a traffic light when it gets switch off for night-time.

Current reasoners are suitable for capturing large and complex knowledge, but at the cost of small datasets. Complex form of periodically changing data can be modeled by means of rules. However, reasoners cannot capture event-driven changing data whose mean time between changes is fast.

If we consider dynamic query generation, we observe that reasoners are best equipped to execute in reaction to the user's invocation, while many modern applications such as urban computing (but also network monitoring, financial analysis, sensor networks, etc.) require long-running, or continuous, queries or reasoning tasks.

Stream Database Management Systems (DSMS) represent a paradigm change in the database world because they move from persistent relations to transient streams, with the innovative assumption that streams can be *consumed* on the flight (rather then stored forever) and from user-invoked queries to *continuous queries*, i.e., queries which are persistently monitoring streams and are able to produce their answers even in the absence of invocation. DSMSs can support parallel query answering over data originating in real time and can cope with burst of data by adapting their behavior and gracefully degradating answer accuracy by introducing higher approximations.

Is combining data stream and reasoning possible? Can the innovation so far confined within the DB community be leveraged in realizing a new generation of reasoners able to cope with continuous reasoning tasks?

3   A Conceptual Architecture for Stream Reasoning

We are developing the Stream Reasoning vision with the LarKC European Research Project[1]. LarKC proposes [7,8] a pluggable algorithmic framework which will be implemented on a distributed computational platform. The pluggable algorithmic framework ideally includes five steps to be iterated until a good enough answer [9] is found:

1. *retrieve* relevant resource/content/context;
2. *abstract* by extracting information, calculating statistics and transforming to logic,
3. *select* relevant problems/methods/data,
4. *reason* upon the aggregated knowledge, and
5. *decide* if a new iteration is needed.

In Figure 1 we present our vision in plugging data stream technologies in the LarKC framework. The top part of the figure represents the problem space

---

[1] http://www.larkc.eu

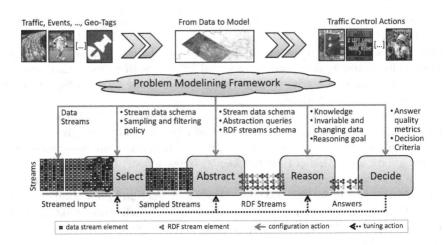

Fig. 1. Conceptual System Architecture

grounded in the Urban Computing field: data from the urban environment (e.g., traffic info, events, geo-tags, etc.) are translated in models and by reasoning on those models traffic control actions can be taken (e.g., controlling traffic lights, showing messages on traffic information panels, asking police intervention, etc.). The bottom part of the figure represents the four pluggable steps of the LarKC approach that we consider for Stream Reasoning[2] interconnected by the data that flow from left to right.

Data arrives to the Stream Reasoner as streamed input. A first step **selects** the relevant data in the input stream by exploiting *load-shedding* techniques [10]. Such techniques were developed to deal with bursty streams that may have unpredictable peaks during which the load may exceed available system resources. The key idea behind load-shedding is to introduce sampling policies that probabilistically drop stream elements as they are input to the selection step. Sampling and filtering policies can be either a) specified explicitly at stream-registration time, or b) inferred by gathering statistics over time, or c) by explicitly including punctuation in streams [11].

An example of sampling and filtering policy could be: if in a city a data stream originates from each traffic control camera, images should be sampled at given times rather than be continuously analyzed; in normal traffic condition, each stream could be sampled every 5 minutes, with options for increasing or decreasing the sampling rates (in congestion condition sample every 2 minutes, at night sample every 10 minutes).

The sampled streams resulting from the selection step are fed into a second step that **abstracts** from fine grain data streams into aggregated events. Such abstraction step can be done either by exploiting data compression techniques or

---

[2] We are explicitly omitting the retrieval step, because data stream retrieval should not be different from any other resource retrieval, therefore we will relay on pluggable components conceived by others.

by aggregation queries. Data compression techniques includes the usage of histograms [12] or wave-lets [13], when the abstraction is meant to be an aggregation (e.g., counting the number of cars running through traffic detectors), and using Bloom filters [14] for duplicate elimination, set difference, or set intersection.

By **abstraction query** we mean, a continuous query that, given a large set of (possibly) unrelated low-level data in the input streams, produces an aggregated event. For instance, the abstraction step may rise a traffic congestion alert for a given street if the number of cars counted by the traffic control camera exceed 100 cars and it has been continuously increasing in the last 15 minutes.

The main proposition brought up in this paper is that, either for doing the abstraction step, or immediately after the abstraction, data streams are consolidated as **RDF streams**. RDF streams are new data formats set at the confluence of conventional data streams and of conventional atoms usually injected into reasoners. At this stage of our research, we envision two alternative formats for RDF streams:

- A **RDF molecules stream** is an unbounded bag of pairs $< \rho, \tau >$, where ρ is a RDF molecule [15] and τ is the timestamp that denotes the logical arrival time of RDF molecule ρ on the stream;
- A **RDF statements stream** is a special case of RDF molecules stream in which ρ is an RDF statement instead of an RDF molecule.

Descending from the two formats, we conceive two different stream reasoning frameworks. RDF molecule streams introduce stream reasoning as a progressive process, allowing for reuse of existing DSMS and reasoners. RDF statements stream introduce stream reasoning as a revolutionary process, requiring upon reasoners the same paradigm shift as the introduction of data streams upon databases. Section 4 and 5 describe respectively the two frameworks.

As last step, before producing the solution of the application problem of our concern (e.g., a congestion situation is monitored and traffic is rerouted according to planning activities), the answering process reaches the **decision** step. In such step quality metrics and decision criteria, defined by the application developer, are used to check if the quality of the answer is good enough and to adapt the behavior of each step (e.g., changing the sampling frequency).

4   RDF Molecules Stream Reasoning Framework

As we have just stated, RDF molecule streams introduce stream reasoning as a progressive process. They allow for reuse of existing DSMS and reasoners by coupling them using a transcoder and a pre-reasoner (see Figure 2).

In particular, the abstraction step can be realized using a DSMS and a transcoder. The DSMS receives the sampled data streams and generates an abstracted data stream by continuously answering the abstraction queries designed by the application developer, which typically perform an aggregation of events. The **transcoder** generates a stream element $< \rho, \tau >$, where ρ is a RDF molecule and the timestap τ typically corresponds to the end of the aggregation interval, and puts it in the outgoing RDF stream.

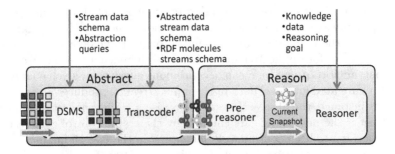

Fig. 2. RDF Molecules Stream Reasoning Framework

We choose RDF molecules [15] as the minimum amount of information, because RDF molecules are the finest component into which an RDF graph can be decomposed without loss of information. Given that a data stream is composed by tuples and each tuple carries a minimum amount of processable information, a direct transcoding of each tuple into an RDF molecule is always possible.

For instance, in our Urban Computing example we may have a system of traffic sensors that feed a data stream by recording every sensed car across a given road. An aggregator associated with each sensor counts the number of vehicles, distinguishing them according to their type; then, the transcoder encodes this information into an RDF molecule stream element. For instance, an RDF molecule for this example is composed of four triples connected by a blank node _:x.

$$\left\langle \begin{array}{lll} \text{http}://\text{uc.ex/tcc}\#123 & \text{uc}:\text{measure} & \_:\text{x}. \\ \_:\text{x} & \text{uc}:\text{numberOfCars} & 120. \\ \_:\text{x} & \text{uc}:\text{numberOfTrucks} & 70. \\ \_:\text{x} & \text{uc}:\text{numberOfOtherVehicles} & 37. \end{array} \right., Jun.17, 09:06:16AM \right\rangle$$

RDF molecule streams are fed into **pre-reasoners** that perform the incremental maintenance of materialized *RDF snapshots*, i.e. RDF views describing the state of the system at a given time, which are given as input to reasoners according to application-specific strategies. Reasoners are not aware of time and produce a set of answers that remain valid until pre-reasoners produce the next snapshot. The efficient incremental materialization of RDF snapshots performed by pre-reasoners is a research challenge under investigation; background studies concern the incremental maintenance of materialized ontologies [16] and indexing of temporal XML documents [17].

5   RDF Statements Stream Reasoning Framework

As we anticipated in Section 3, we are also considering a more revolutionary approach, where streams are directly represented in RDF, and therefore continuous and/or aggregation queries can be directly expressed in RDF languages. Compared to RDF molecule streams, RDF statement streams are fine grain streams of triples. We envision the possibility to define up to eight different types of RDF statements streams depending upon the kind of information that changes at each stream input, ranging from a completely unspecified to a completely specified RDF triple. In the former case, every new element in the stream is an arbitrary RDF triple; in the latter case, every new element in the stream corresponds to the occurrence of an instance of RDF stream which is totally fixed (e.g., another unidentified vehicle seen at a given sensor). The following table summarizes the eight cases:

Name	Subject	Predicate	Object	Denotation
free	-	-	-	free
bound subject	s	-	-	s
bound predicate	-	p	-	p
bound object	-	-	o	o
free subject	-	p	o	po
free predicate	s	-	o	so
free object	s	p	-	sp
bound	s	p	o	spo

For RDF statement streams it is possible to define continuous queries both in terms of a formal abstract semantics and a concrete query language that implements the abstract semantics (namely *C-SPARQL*), following the path already explored in designing CQL [18] for DSMS.

As for CQL, the abstract semantics of such a C-SPARQL language is based on two data types, RDF statements streams (later on shortly named RDFstream) and **instantaneous RDF graphs** (later on shortly named **tgraph**). The two data types are a direct mapping of stream and relation data types in CQL. C-SPARQL queries are executed as trees of fine-grain operators performing selection and abstraction over streams; their optimization and parallelization can be approached by using techniques which are translated from DSMS systems. In Figure 3 we depict how we expect our C-SPARQL engine to share query plans among different registered queries in order to continuously answer in a throughput-efficient manner.

As for CQL, the abstract semantics of C-SPARQL includes operators of three classes:

- A *tgraph-to-tgraph* operator takes one or more tgraph as input and produces a tgraph as output.
- A *RDFstream-to-tgraph* operator takes a RDF statements stream as input and produces a tgraph as output.
- A *tgraph-to-RDFstream* operator takes a tgraph as input and produces a RDFstream as output.

RDFstream-to-tgraph operators use *sliding windows* [19] over RDF statements streams; their efficient evaluation can use the fact that stream elements enter into windows and then exit from windows sequentially, according to the

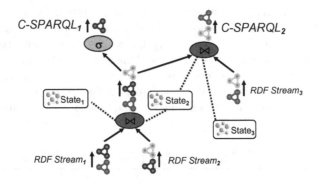

Fig. 3. RDF Statements Stream Reasoning Framework

total order associated with time. RDF data is typically used in the context of ontological languages (e.g., RDF/S and OWL) enabling to describe resources and their properties. The efficient evaluation of multiple queries with several overlapping sliding windows upon both RDF data and language-specific ontological properties is a research challenge currently under investigation; methods presented in [16] can be adapted.

In this framework, scalability will be achieved by distribution and parallelism. Indeed, while each stream should allocated to a given processor, all other operator-based computations can be distributed according to an explicit, well-defined data flow; hence, distributed database methods fully apply.

6   Conclusions and Future Works

In this paper we have presented some preliminary steps toward Stream Reasoning. Our main contribution is an integration architecture, taking advantage of the benefits of both data streams and reasoners, from which two stream reasoning frameworks can be derived.

The one based on RDF molecules is an evolution of the currently available solutions that relies on the possibility to couple DSMSs and state-of-the-art reasoners. This approach requires investigating an appropriate solution for incremental maintenance of time-varying RDF views and engineering throughput-efficient transcoder technology for bridging data streams to RDF Molecules Streams.

The one based on RDF statements is a revolutionary approach to reasoning that requires defining C-SPARQL semantics, studying its computational complexity, defining the concrete C-SPARQL language, and implementing a query processor that heavily exploits the intrinsic characteristic of streams.

Acknowledgements

The work described in this paper is has been partially supported by the European project LarKC (FP7-215535).

References

1. Kiryakov, A.: Measurable targets for scalable reasoning (2007)
2. Garofalakis, M., Gehrke, J., Rastogi, R.: Data Stream Management: Processing High-Speed Data Streams (Data-Centric Systems and Applications). Springer, New York (2007)
3. Kindberg, T., Chalmers, M., Paulos, E.: Guest editors' introduction: Urban computing. IEEE Pervasive Computing 6(3), 18–20 (2007)
4. Arikawa, M., Konomi, S., Ohnishi, K.: Navitime: Supporting pedestrian navigation in the real world. IEEE Pervasive Computing 6(3), 21–29 (2007)
5. Reades, J., Calabrese, F., Sevtsuk, A., Ratti, C.: Cellular census: Explorations in urban data collection. IEEE Pervasive Computing 6(3), 30–38 (2007)
6. Bassoli, A., Brewer, J., Martin, K., Dourish, P., Mainwaring, S.: Underground aesthetics: Rethinking urban computing. IEEE Pervasive Computing 6(3), 39–45 (2007)
7. Fensel, D., van Harmelen, F., Andersson, B., Brennan, P., Cunningham, H., Della Valle, E., Fischer, F., Huang, Z., Kiryakov, A., il Lee, T.K., School, L., Tresp, V., Wesner, S., Witbrock, M., Zhong, N.: Towards larkc: a platform for web-scale reasoning. In: IEEE International Conference on Semantic Computing, ICSC 2008 (August 2008)
8. Fensel, D., van Harmelen, F.: Unifying reasoning and search to web scale. IEEE Internet Computing 11(2), 9695 (2007)
9. Shvaiko, P., Giunchiglia, F., Bundy, A., Besana, P., Sierra, C., Van Harmelen, F., Zaihrayeu, I.: Benchmarking methodology for good enough answers. Technical report, DISI-08-003, Informatica e Telecomunicazioni, University of Trento (2008)
10. Tatbul, N., Çetintemel, U., Zdonik, S., Cherniack, M., Stonebraker, M.: Load shedding in a data stream manager. In: VLDB 2003: Proceedings of the 29th international conference on Very large data bases, VLDB Endowment, pp. 309–320 (2003)
11. Tatbul, N., Cetintemel, U., Zdonik, S., Cherniak, M., Stonebraker, M.: Exploiting punctuation semantics in continuous data streams. IEEE Trans. on Knowledge and Data Eng. 15(3), 555–568 (2003)
12. Thaper, N., Guha, S., Indyk, P., Koudas, N.: Dynamic multidimensional histograms. In: SIGMOD 2002: Proceedings of the 2002 ACM SIGMOD international conference on Management of data, pp. 428–439. ACM, New York (2002)
13. Chakrabarti, K., Garofalakis, M., Rastogi, R., Shim, K.: Approximate query processing using wavelets. The VLDB Journal 10(2-3), 199–223 (2001)
14. Bloom, B.H.: Space/time trade-offs in hash coding with allowable errors. Commun. ACM 13(7), 422–426 (1970)
15. Ding, L., Finin, T., Peng, Y., da Silva, P.P., McGuinness, D.L.: Tracking RDF Graph Provenance using RDF Molecules. Technical report, UMBC (April 2005)
16. Volz, R., Staab, S., Motik, B.: Incrementally maintaining materializations of ontologies stored in logic databases. J. Data Semantics 2, 1–34 (2005)
17. Mendelzon, A.O., Rizzolo, F., Vaisman, A.: Indexing temporal xml documents. In: VLDB 2004: Proceedings of the Thirtieth international conference on Very large data bases, VLDB Endowment, pp. 216–227 (2004)
18. Babu, S., Widom, J.: Continuous queries over data streams. SIGMOD Rec. 30(3), 109–120 (2001)
19. Babcock, B., Babu, S., Datar, M., Motwani, R., Widom, J.: Models and issues in data stream systems. In: PODS 2002: Proceedings of the twenty-first ACM SIGMOD-SIGACT-SIGART symposium on Principles of database systems, pp. 1–16. ACM, New York (2002)

Environmental Content Creation and Visualisation in the 'Future Internet'

Paul Chippendale, Michele Zanin, and Claudio Andreatta

Fondazione Bruno Kessler, TeV group
Via Sommarive, 18, Povo, Trento, 38050, Italy
chippendale@fbk.eu, mizanin@fbk.eu, andreatta@fbk.eu

Abstract. This paper presents a model-based photo registration system for the creation and visualization of environmental content. We utilize freely available Digital Terrain Models of the planet, such as those provided by NASA[1], to generate a three-dimensional synthetic model around a viewer's location. Using an array of image processing algorithms we then align photographs to this model. We will demonstrate the precision of the resulting system through the overlaying of Internet content (such as mountain names and GPS tracks), into geo-referenced photos. Additionally, we will show how a metric can be derived for photos that describes not only which mountains can be seen, but also how visible they are.

Keywords: Geo-referenced, semantic labelling, augmented reality, image processing.

1 Introduction

The desire to overlay virtual content into the 'real-world' is an attractive one, as it is a very intuitive means of purveying information. Although the idea of Augmented Reality (AR) is nothing new and has been researched for many years, accurate and robust automatic image registration remains elusive. For indoor or heavily controlled environments, AR can be seen today on TV [1] in live news shows or sports, where the effects are only visible to TV viewers but not to players or fans at a game.

Registration for outdoor systems cannot exploit the established methods developed for indoor use, e.g. magnetic tracking, fiducial markers. Outdoor AR systems traditionally rely on GPS for position measurements combined with magnetic compasses and inertial sensors for orientation [2]. Examples of systems using such sensors include Columbia's Touring machine and MARS [3,4], the Battlefield Augmented Reality System [5], work by Thomas et al. [6], the Tinmith System by Piekarski [7] and to some extent Sentieri Vivi [8]. Although magnetic compasses, inertial sensors and GPS can be used to obtain a rough estimate of position and orientation, the precision of this registration method (using affordable devices) is insufficient to satisfy many AR overlay applications.

---

[1] http://www2.jpl.nasa.gov/srtm/

J. Domingue, D. Fensel, and P. Traverso (Eds.): FIS 2008, LNCS 5468, pp. 82–93, 2009.
© Springer-Verlag Berlin Heidelberg 2009

The most common interface for AR in the short term will likely be a handheld device, probably something evolved from a mobile phone. In recent years the diffusion of powerful portable technology has increased at a phenomenal rate, furnishing everyday consumers with megapixel cameras and powerful mobile computing devices with gigabytes of storage capacity; GPS is now also commonplace. The Nokia N96 and the Apple iPhone3G are two prime examples of such multifarious devices. Undoubtedly a whole host of other sensors, such as magnetic and inertial, will also one day become commonplace;  until that day however, computer vision methods will have to suffice to estimate device orientation through the correlation of visual features with those in the real world whose positions are known.

The near ubiquitous ownership of digital cameras, their inclusion in virtually every mobile phone on the market combined with the speed at which an image can be taken and shared with the World (via 3G or WIFI and a multitude of photo websites) together promise a new paradigm in environmental observation. Every day millions of geo-referenced images are taken and shared via Internet websites such as Flickr[2] and Panoramio[3], often within minutes of capture; offering an extensive, high-resolution and ground-level coverage of the planet.

The shear volume of data available on the Internet in the near future will make it increasingly difficult to retrieve the information you want and moreover a great deal of valuable content might remain hidden inside non-searchable media. For many years research has been conducted into the semantic labelling of content in photos with increasing success. However due to the complexity of the World, ambiguities will always plague results. Research conducted in the Zonetag project [9] nicely demonstrates how a photo can have content tags auto-generated through proximity to other photos alone, based on social annotation.

In Microsoft's Photosynth [10], highly recognizable manmade features are detected, such as the architecture of Notre Dame de Paris, to align and assemble huge collections of photos. Using this tool, the relative orientation of a photo with respect to a calibration object can be calculated due to its unique and unchanging nature and hence photo parameters and some content surmised. The University of Washington took this idea one step further [11] and created the tool 'PhotoTour' that lets you virtually travel from one photo into another seamlessly. Viewfinder [12] is another research project that aids users to spatially situate their photographs through the creation of a perfectly aligned overlay in a 3D world model such as Google Earth. Although their system is essentially manually, a lot of the hard work of alignment is taken out of the registration process and they say that a 10-year-old should be able to find the pose of a photo in less than a minute.

Our approach to the problem of image registration and content understanding (specifically those photos which contain evident geographical features, e.g. mountains, lakes, etc.) takes a slightly different approach to the aforementioned techniques.

---

[2] http://www.flickr.com
[3] http://www.panoramio.com

We attempt to identify mountains, lakes, villages, etc and assign them their actual names through the automatic identification and alignment of geographic image features (located inside geo-referenced photos) with those in a synthetic model. In this way, we can also attempt to infer foreground content through the occlusion of terrain which we estimate should be visible. Our system relies on the accurate correlation of natural features, extracted from photographs using image processing techniques, with similar corresponding points derived from the synthetic terrain model. Extracting feature points from outdoor environments is however challenging, as disturbances such as clouds on mountain tops, foreground objects, large variations in lighting and generally bad viewing conditions, such as haze, all inhibit accurate recognition. As a result, great care needs to be taken to overcome such inherent limitations and we attempt to overcome this by combining different yet complementary methods.

Behringer [13] uses a similar approach to ours, based on an edge detector to align the horizon silhouette extracted from Digital Terrain Model (DTM) data with video images to estimate the orientation of a mobile AR system. They demonstrated that a well-structured terrain could provide information to help other sensors to accurately estimate registration, but their solution had problems with lighting and visibility conditions. Our approach however incorporates an enriched set of feature points and a more accurately rendered terrain model enhanced by additional digital content such as: lake contours, road or footpath profiles, etc.

In Section 2 we will explain how accurate outdoor photo alignment can benefit the community. In Section 3, we will briefly describe our photo registration technology based on the matching of significant visual topographical features with those computed from a 360 degree model generated from a digital elevation map dataset. Finally, a variety of results are presented, followed by some conclusions and ideas for future work.

2 Bringing Content into Reality

In photos registered by our system, each pixel is tagged with a latitude, longitude, altitude and a distance from the camera. This provides us with the ability to insert any form of geo-referenced data intelligently 'into' the environment. As registered photos exhibit depth, one can choose to overlay only visible data. Fig. 1 shows a good example of how GPS tracks can be drawn into photos in such a 3D manner, taking great care to only draw it where it should be visible.

Naturally, we can also place any geo-referenced hyperlink inside photos straight from the Internet from sites such as Geonames[4] or Wikimapia[5], as is demonstrated in Fig. 1 with the overlaying of mountain refuges and farms.

A team from Nokia's Mobile Augmented Reality Applications (MARA) project [14] has recently created a prototype phone that makes objects in the real world hyperlink to information on the Internet. Using the phone's built in camera, a user can highlight objects on the mobile phone's LCD and pull in additional information about them from the Internet.

---

[4] http://www.geonames.org
[5] http://www.wikimapia.org

In the future when we will have Internet connectivity anywhere, at anytime and in any device and given accurate image registration we could retrieve and accurately overlay online content directly into our vision (perhaps via appropriate eyewear), or more simply, live in the display of a camera or phone. Imagine being able to 'see' others walking across the valley as a consequence of them uploading their current location or maybe even seeing real-time images looking back at you.

One could also think about automatically registering old 'historical' photos (often termed re-photography), adjusted and re-projected into the World in real-time from your current location, one

Fig. 1. Autolabelled photo showing: visible (red) and hidden (blue) footpaths, mountain names, heights, distances and hyperlinks (icons)

possible use being to monitor such things as environmental change or urban growth. Infact, the simple act of sharing our geo-referenced and aligned photos will naturally form an extensive record of the environment for the future on a scale previously unprecedented.

In a recent paper [15], we applied our technology to explore the question: 'Could a similar, more beautiful photo have been taken from somewhere else nearby?' and demonstrated how a 3D 'attractiveness' layer can be created for the planet according to socially derived aesthetic metrics extracted from Photo sharing websites. This gauges the appeal held by a subject for inclusion in a photo.

Fig. 2. Photo attractiveness heat-map

For photos downloaded from Flickr/Panoramio and subsequently registered, an attractiveness value was calculated and draped onto the DTM. The accumulation of many photos taken at other times and from other perspectives naturally generates an attractiveness heat-map (as can be seen in Fig. 2). We calculated an attractiveness value, A, using the following formula: $A=5f\alpha+2c\beta+v\gamma$. Where f is the number of times a photo has been made a favourite; α is a normalizing factor based upon the average number of favourites taken from a random selection of 1000 images from the same website; c is the number of comments made about a photo, likewise β is a normalizing factor for comments, v is the number of views an image has had and γ is a normalizing figure for views.

Using this algorithm, a heat-map can be generated for any area. In Fig. 2, an area around The Matterhorn was analysed in this way using one hundred photos taken from Flickr. The map clearly shows that the appeal of the peak is far greater than its surroundings for photographers. This outcome is of course expected with such an iconic mountain. A similar analysis of less well known areas may help emerging tourist authorities maximise on their assets, perhaps helping site picnic areas, panoramic information points, create new and dynamically changing photo adventure trails which change day-by-day according to photo community trends, etc.

3   The Technology

We register photos by correlating their content against a rendered 3D spherical panorama generated about the photo's 'geo-location'. To do this we systematically load, scale and re-project DTM data onto the inside of a sphere using ray-tracing techniques. In preparation for photo alignment the sphere is 'unwrapped' into a 360° by 180° rectangular window (see a 90° portion in Fig. 3a); each synthetic pixel has its own latitude, longitude, altitude and depth.

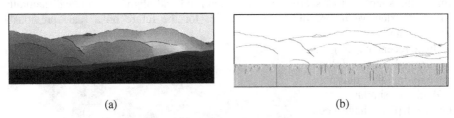

(a)   (b)

Fig. 3. (a) 90° portion of synthetic panorama, (b) Synthetic edges with saliency map below

Placing a photograph into this unwrapped space requires a deformation so that photo pixels are correctly mapped onto synthetic ones depending upon estimated camera parameters, such as pan, tilt, lens distortion, etc. Scaling is estimated from the focal length parameters contained within the EXIF JPEG data of the photo. The problem of accurate photo alignment is the main crux of our research, and is an ongoing challenge. The general approach is structured into four phases: 1) extract salient points from synthetic rendering, 2) extract salient points from the photo, 3) search for correspondences aiming to select significant synthetic/photo point pairs, 4) apply a standard optimization technique to derive the alignment parameters that minimize reprojection error.

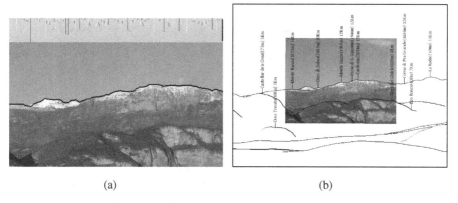

(a)   (b)

Fig. 4. (a) Sky-land profile with saliency map above, (b) Photo auto-aligned with labels

In our current implementation, we extract mountain profiles in both the synthetic panorama and in the photo. While in the first case it is just a matter of detecting abrupt changes of distance between adjacent directions (Fig. 3b), in photos we apply a sequence of machine-vision algorithms: region segmentation, edge extraction, region classification (sky, rock, vegetation, water), and profile extraction, thus profiles are generated at region borders (Fig. 4a). We then analyse both profiles with a multi-scale saliency algorithm that aims to extract important points at different scales. These are shown as horizontal bands in Fig. 3b and 4a; white vertical lines represent maximum points, blacks are minimums, and their length is proportional to importance.

4 Results

Fig. 5 demonstrates how photos registered by our system can easily be inserted into Google Earth. To accomplish this we automatically generate a kml[6] file which exactly describes the photo's placement criteria. Inside the kml we set the fields relating to: position, orientation, field of view, etc.

Google has recently integrated Panoramio's API into Google Maps so that they can place hyperlinks to geo-referenced photos as an overlay (see Fig. 6a). Given that we can assign a latitude and longitude to each pixel in a photo, using the same API generates an explorable 3D interface, as can be seen in Fig. 6b. In much the same way, the size of the icon represents its popularity and all are placed inside this photo exactly 'where' they were taken.

Fig.7 illustrates the 3D nature of the registered photos. In this example the system automatically split the above photo into foreground, midground, background and sky according to the distribution of pixel depths. Fig. 9 shows the depth distribution for this photo as a histogram of pixel depths normalised by the total number of non-sky pixels. The system automatically generated two slicing points for foreground and background at 4.3km and 13.5km.

---

[6] http://www.opengeospatial.org/standards/kml

Fig. 5. Automatic photo overlay in Google Earth

(a)   (b)

Fig. 6. (a) Google Maps Panoramio photo overlay, (b) Our 3D Panoramio photo overlay

In a similar manner we can emphasise which country or province pixels belong to (in Fig.8 country flags can be seen), the distance objects are from the viewer, we could choose to show pixels above 3000m or even change the colour of the sky.

In addition to saying which mountains are visible and where they are in the photo, we can also provide a visibility metric. If we assume that archetypal mountains can be represented as 60° cones, by projecting such objects into a photo in 3D it is possible make a reasonable estimate of mountain visibilities in pixels based on size and occlusion by others.

Fig. 10b illustrates the mountain triangles visible in the photo labelled in Fig.10a. We can then automatically generate a table of meta-data for each photo containing statistics such as visible mountains, each with a size in pixels, a distance from the camera and also from which angle a mountain is being viewed from, e.g. the North face (see Table 1 for the information generated from the photo in Fig.10a).

Fig. 7. Segmented photo according to distance regions

Fig. 8. Labelled image with distances, heights and country flags

The forms of geo-referenced data that can be inserted into registered photos are not limited to the few examples included in this paper. To give a prime example of the potential power of the system, we downloaded a geo-referenced photo from Flickr (http://www.flickr.com/photos/rickpappas/2584664086/) and married it with an alpine ski trail from Giscover (http://www.giscover.com/tours/tour/display/336). The image seen in Fig.11 was automatically produced within a few seconds. In fact, the publication of GPS tracks is becoming very popular and sites such as Giscover[7] and Everytrail[8] offer anyone the possibility to upload and download hikes, cycle rides, horse trails, etc. thus opening up a host of new applications.

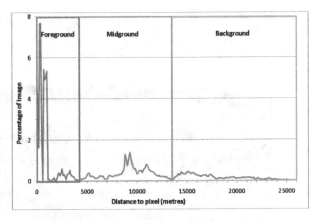

Fig. 9. Histogram of pixel depths from the photo in Fig. 7

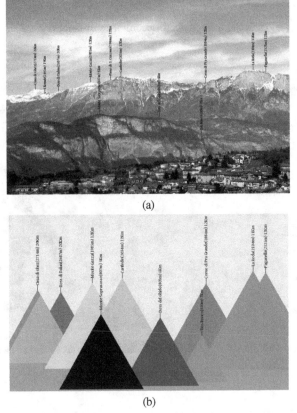

(a)

(b)

Fig. 10. (a) Labelled photo. (b) 60° conic mountains projected into 3D photo.

---

[7] http://www.giscover.com/
[8] http://www.everytrail.com/

Table 1. Meta-data concerning mountain visibility for the photo in Fig.10

Mountain name	Visible area (pixels)	Distance (m)	Angle Mountain viewed from (°)
La Roda	53784	11738	130
Monte Soprasasso	34791	5930	114
Doss del Ghirlo	27134	6410	120
Canfedin	24441	12336	116
Cima Soran	23355	19341	107
Monte Gazza	21555	12859	113
Corno di Pra Grande	20661	12189	125
Dos Ronco	11483	7134	125
Paganella	5965	12272	131
Doss di Dalun	5652	20905	109
Cima di Ghez	3395	20496	107

Fig. 11. Photo with mountain names and GPS track overlaid

Our photo alignment algorithms are constantly evolving, incorporating new data sources and ever more advanced image processing techniques. Current registration time is around 15s, as it is far from optimised.

5   Conclusions

In its current state of development our system is an ideal tool to quickly produce enriched photos with the inclusion of any type of geo-referenced material, e.g. labelled panoramas for tourism, showing how new man-made structures could visually impact on the environment, etc. By placing our system inside a portable device with integrated camera and GPS, our next step is to evaluate performance in the field and to provide a real-time visualisation tool for tourists, geologists, etc...

We have found that problems can arise when the quality and accuracy of the geo-data is poor. For example, if a mountain summit label has been incorrectly placed into the Geonames database, then our system will draw the corresponding point incorrectly. We have implemented a max height function that works on the DEM data in an attempt to re-align peak labels to the closest highest point, with some success. In the future when multiple free-sources of geo-data are available cross-referencing could resolve this issue.

A further source of error that we have encountered is DTM error. To minimise this problem we gather and utilise the best free-sources of data possible, e.g. NASA SRTM, CGIAR-CSI. However, in very rugged mountainous area, the top of sharp peaks are sometimes flattened due to resolution limitations. Small discrepancies in profiles are handled by our system providing that there are other sufficient geographical features present. Similarly, when a mountain profile is modified due to clouds, our system can handle the incongruities providing that the damage is not significant. In future work we plan to use ortho-photo textures to improve the registration process, e.g. the visual appearance of a village on a mountain side could be a good feature to use..

To further exploit our system, we are also investigating its application to environmental monitoring. As we know 'when' digital photos are taken, a spatiotemporal appearance layer for draping onto a DTM can easily be created by synthesising the multitude of geo-referenced photos taken daily. Images taken on the ground provide us with a unique perspective for monitoring erosion on near vertical rock faces or terrain under partial tree cover, for example. Such a layer would automatically evolve helping us to understand snow and glacier coverage or the onset of spring in various geographical locations. For more examples of our research please refer to http://tev.fbk.eu/marmota/.

References

1. Thomas, G.A.: Mixed reality techniques for TV and their application for on-set and pre-visualization in film production, International Workshop on Mixed Reality Technology for Flim-making, University of California at Santa Barbara, USA, October 22 (2006)
2. Azuma, R., Hoff, B., Neely, H., Sarfaty, R.: A motion-stabilized outdoor augmented reality system. In: Proc. IEEE VR, pp. 252–259 (1999)
3. Feiner, S., MacIntyre, B., Hollerer, T., Webster, A.: A touring machine: Prototyping 3D mobile augmented reality systems for exploring the urban environment. In: Proc. ISWC 1997, Cambridge, MA, USA, October 13-14, pp. 74–81 (1997)
4. Hollerer, T., Feiner, S., et al.: Exploring MARS: developing indoor and outdoor user interfaces to a mobile augmented reality system. Computer & Graphics 23, 779–785 (1999)
5. Baillot, Y., Brown, D., Julier, S.: Authoring of physical models using mobile computers. In: Proc. ISWC 2001, pp. 39–46 (2001)

6. Thomas, B., Demczuk, V., Piekarski, W., et al.: A wearable computer system with augmented reality to support terrestrial navigation. In: IEEE Proc. ISWC 1998, Pittsburgh, PA, USA, October 19-20, pp. 168–171 (1998)
7. Piekarski, W., Thomas, B.: Tinmith-metro: New outdoor techniques for creating city models with an augmented reality wearable computer. In: IEEE Proc. ISWC 2001, Zurich, Switzerland, October 8-9, pp. 31–38 (2001)
8. Sentieri Vivi, http://www.sentierivivi.com/
9. Ahern, S., Davis, M., Eckles, D., et al.: ZoneTag: Designing Context-Aware Mobile Media Capture to Increase Participation. In: Proceedings of the Pervasive Image Capture and Sharing, 8th Int. Conf. on Ubiquitous Computing, California (2006)
10. Snavely, N., Seitz, S., Szeliski, R.: Photo tourism: Exploring photo collections in 3D. ACM Transactions on Graphics (SIGGRAPH Proceedings) 25(3), 835–846 (2006)
11. University of Washington, Microsoft: Finding Paths through the World's Photos, http://phototour.cs.washington.edu/
12. University of Southern California: Viewfinder - How to seamlessly Flickerize Google Earth, http://interactive.usc.edu/viewfinder/approach.html
13. Behringer, R.: Registration for outdoor augmented reality applications using computer vision techniques and hybrid sensors. In: Proc. IEEE VR 1999, Houston, Texas, USA, March 13-17 (1999)
14. Kähäri, M., et al.: Mobile Augmented Reality Applications (MARA) project, http://research.nokia.com/research/projects/mara/index.html
15. Chippendale, P., Zanin, M., Andreatta, C.: Spatial and Temporal Attractiveness Analysis through Geo-Referenced Photo Alignment. In: 2008 IEEE International Geoscience & Remote Sensing Symposium, Boston, Massachusetts, U.S.A, July 6-11 (2008)

Having Services "YourWay!":
Towards User-Centric Composition of Mobile Services*

Raman Kazhamiakin[1], Piergiorgio Bertoli[1], Massimo Paolucci[2],
Marco Pistore[1], and Matthias Wagner[2]

[1] FBK-Irst, via Sommarive 18, 38050, Trento, Italy
{bertoli,raman,pistore,traverso}@fbk.eu
[2] DoCoMo Euro-Labs, Landsberger Strasse 312, 80687 Munich, Germany
{paolucci,wagner}@docomolab-euro.com

Abstract. Mobile phones are becoming an essential tool in our life.
They not only act as phones and media players, but more fundamentally
they give us access to variety of services that we use in everyday life, including social networking, personal assistance, entertainment, travelling,
and so on. Unfortunately, while the number of services increases, each
service is narrowly directed to solve a specific user task with no attention
to how the user may utilize these services in combination. At this stage,
the combination of services and the integration of their information flows
must be managed by the user on his own, in a handcrafted way.

To support the user in the composition of services and applications,
we propose to organize the services around a small set of resources -
time, location, social relations, money - which model the essential user
assets handled by mobile services, and which guide the data integration
and service composition.

In the paper, we discuss our current realization of such resource-based,
user-centric service composition approach, detailing the underlying conceptual architecture and discussing the actual execution of the platform
on a set of practical scenarios.

1 Introduction

Mobile phones are becoming an essential tool in our life. They not only act
as phones and media players, but more fundamentally they give us access to
variety of services that we need in everyday life. A simple catalogue of such
services includes ones for travel activities (e.g., navigation and map services,
ticket booking via mobile, SMS notifications of flight delays), social networking,
personal assistance, and entertainment.

While the number of services increases, each service is narrowly directed to
solve a specific need of the user with no attention to how services may work

---

* The research leading to these results has been partially funded by the European
Community's Seventh Framework Programme FP7/2007-2013 under grant agreement 213339 (ALLOW).

J. Domingue, D. Fensel, and P. Traverso (Eds.): FIS 2008, LNCS 5468, pp. 94–106, 2009.

together nor to how the user may utilize these services in combination. For example, even now there exist near-field services that allow us to get information about movies shown in a local theatre, Web services for booking movie tickets, and TelCo services for payment; we can store movie event in the agenda and set up a reminder for it; we can share the information about the movie with the people in our contact list using TelCo services, and finally use map services to route us to the theatre. In spite of the availability of these complementary functionalities, the user has to face the problem of their integration on his own. First, the user has to deal with different services, and consequently, with their specific interfaces, formats, and protocols. Second, the user has to manage by hand the composition of these services and information flow across them. Third, the user has to continuously ensure the consistency of the information used by different services: if the user is not able to go to the movie, he has to take care of propagating the effects of this decision by means of relevant services, i.e., removing the event from the agenda, sending an alert to the friends, cancelling the ticket on-line, and so on.

Ultimately, what is missing is a platform that enables user-centric delivery and composition of mobile services by satisfying the following requirements:

1. facilitate the user activities proactively identifying, interpreting, and addressing the user needs and constraints;
2. support and automatize the information integration so that the user does not have to manually manage and keep track of the data flow between the applications and services involved;
3. provide continuous support for the information consistency through coordinated integration and use of relevant operations and services;
4. foster the user control on the performed activities, requiring that no critical information is transmitted without involving the user, and no actions that are redundant or even harmful for the user are initiated by the platform autonomously;
5. abstract away the heterogeneity of the service implementations making transparent the differences between the protocols and data formats.

Working with the platform, the user activates various services and applications and makes decisions on the information to use and actions to perform in reaction to the results of this work. The role of the platform is to keep track of the data managed by different services and to guarantee its consistency. In this way, the platform has a coherent representation of the undergoing user's tasks and can react to changes in a coherent way by discovering, organizing, and representing the services in a manner understandable by the user, so that the user can make his decisions. In our example, the user decides when to book a ticket and which friends to invite, while the platform has to integrate and pass the relevant data to the payment, agenda, communication, and navigation services. Similarly, the user may decide to remove the event from his agenda, and the platform will take care of cancelling the ticket, notifying the friends, etc.

The key challenge here is how to relate and integrate different applications and services: they are created independently by different parties, represent different application domains, and deal with particular aspects of the user activities. Crucial issue is to identify a set of concepts that are suitable for expressing both the user intentions and the service capabilities, and therefore to form the basis for their integration.

In this paper we present an approach to the user-centric composition of mobile services, where these concepts correspond to the core user assets, or "resources", namely time, location, money and social context. The user activities deal with allocation of such resources, and the key organizational issue for the user is to manage his activities in a way to make a consistent use of his own resources. In practice, most activities have an impact on the user's availability of time and on the requirements on his location; a very relevant set of activities involve monetary exchanges and social networking. Moreover, these resources are already associated with a lot of widely used applications and services, that are operated by the user during his everyday life. Therefore, considering these four resources, we can achieve a major impact on the way the user organizes his activities, providing strong support for the data integration and service composition, while focusing on an agile and manageable set of concepts which can be described and handled in practical ways.

We also present a platform that supports the user in his activities. Based on the notion of resources, the platform enables the information integration and service composition, coherently propagates the use of these resources by the applications, and continuously monitors their evolution in the user context. Finally, we present and discuss the preliminary implementation of our approach on a mobile platform, and show how it may be applied to a set of scenarios.

The paper is structured as follows. In Sect. 2 we present a set of scenarios describing the problems and requirements to the user-centric composition of mobile services. Section 3 presents our resource-driven composition approach, describe the conceptual architecture and prototype implementation of the underlying platform. Section 4 concludes with the discussion on the related works.

2   Motivating Scenarios

We illustrate the problems of providing the user-centric mobile service composition using three scenarios covering different aspects of typical user activities. In particular, the scenarios aim at demonstrating how the information is integrated and maintained across different services, how the user intentions are operationalized through service compositions, and how the dynamically changing context of the user affects and drives the user activities. These scenarios rely on a set of services and applications – agenda, communications, map and navigation, context tracking, payment – that refer to different domains (e.g., travelling, personal activity management, entertainment).

2.1   Data Integration: Booking a Movie Ticket

Passing an interactive poster of the cinema [1], the user decides to go to cinema with his friend. Using the corresponding interaction means (e.g., NFC), the user downloads to his phone an information about the movie show. In order to organize the cinema visit, the user has to perform a set of activities, such as access the booking service (indicated in the above information) to book the tickets, activate the payment procedure, save the movie show in the agenda, share the event with a friend using communication application, add the cinema location to the navigator or map application.

Even if all the above activities are centered around the management of the same object (i.e., movie show), they are not directly related neither to each other nor to this particular object. First, this forces the user to repeatedly input the same data to different applications and services. Second, the actions are performed manually and independently; the associations between the services and objects are not persistent. As a result, if in the future the user decides to cancel the movie show, he has to perform the integration activities again, repeating the data input, and keeping in mind all the relations.

Therefore, the target platform should address the following essential requirements. First, it should provide a means for relating and integrating information entities and services from different domains. Here an important challenge is to achieve a balance between the spectrum of concepts to cover and the simplicity and flexibility of integration provision. Given the diversity and dynamics of the information operated through the mobile device, it is crucial to be able to deal with a compact but rather expressive and pragmatic set of concepts. Second, it should be able to maintain the integration over time so that the related services and objects are managed in a consistent way. Such relations, for instance, would allow one to identify and initiate a new service composition when the user decides to cancel or to change the date of the cinema visit.

2.2   Service Composition: Business Trip

The user receives an invitation to an international event and saves the event in his agenda. If the event takes place in a different city or country, the user has also to organize a trip, since otherwise his future plans become inconsistent with respect to the location of the user. This activity includes several actions (plan an itinerary, search for transportation means, book and pay the travel tickets and a hotel) and involves various services (Web, TelCo, local) that are integrated on purpose of resolving such inconsistency.

In order to support the user in such situations, it is crucial not only to associate and relate different services and information objects, but also to take into account personal information of the user, his requirements and constraints (such as the above inconsistency). That is, the system should be able to identify these requirements, to associate them to the relevant services and applications, and to provide the user with the composed procedures that aim at satisfying the constraints.

A similar situation takes place when the user has to manage conflicting (overlapping) personal activities. For instance, the trip may be in conflict with the movie show, and therefore the latter should be moved or cancelled. Again, the cancellation is driven by the necessity to resolve the inconsistency in personal information of the user, and therefore the platform should be able to detect this and to provide an appropriate solution.

2.3 Monitoring: Trip Cancellation

In many cases the activities are initiated by external events and changes in the user context. For instance, Lufthansa provides a service that sends notification to the subscribed passengers when their flights are being delayed or cancelled. Given the above scenario, when the user is notified about the flight delay, he has to check whether the delay is still safe with respect to the meeting time, and if not, to reorganize or to cancel it. The latter may include removing the trip and the meeting from the agenda, cancelling flight booking, notifying involved people about the problem, etc. Again, the user should take care of the dependencies between the flight and meeting, time constraints, necessity to cancel the booking in order to get money back, making the involved people aware, and so on.

An important functionality that the target platform must provide is the ability to continuously observe the user operational environment and context and to react to the changes and relevant events proactively. In the above scenario, this includes the need to react to the notification about the flight modification; in other situations this might require to track the location of the user through the GPS navigator, etc.

3   Resource-Driven Composition

The presented scenarios give rise to a set of important problems and requirements to the integration and provision of mobile services to users. In order to address these requirements we propose a novel user-centric service composition approach, which is based on the notion of "resources". These resources correspond to the core user assets that he operates and changes during his everyday activities, namely user agenda, location, finances, social network. This compact set of concepts reflects very pragmatic and minimalistic approach to modelling the relevant information: on the one hand it allows for describing a wide range of services, events, and information entities, and on the other hand does not require an exhaustive and very sophisticated models of the real world.

Figure 1(a) represents our resource-driven information and application integration approach, where the resources play fundamental role and perform the following functions.

First, the resources are used to relate different independent application domains: information entities and actions from these domains are interpreted in terms of resources and resource-critical actions (e.g., ticket payment is related to finances, while the show is related to time and location). This provides the basis for the integration of mobile applications and services.

Second, the resources are used to consider and interpret the state of essential user assets in order to align the resource-critical actions with the actual user needs and constraints. In this way, for instance, the approach is able to relate

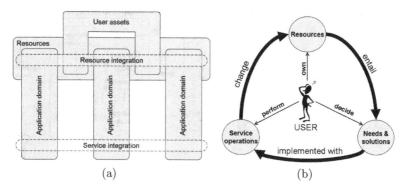

Fig. 1. Resource-driven approach and composition life-cycle

the location of a business meeting with the expected user location, to identify the location problem, and the necessity to integrate various applications in order to organize a corresponding trip.

Finally, the integration performed at the resource level entails the corresponding integration at the level of the actual applications and services. Here the abstract resource-related information and actions are automatically grounded and operationalized using available services, as well as the interactions with the user.

The life-cycle of our resource-driven approach is conceptually represented in Fig. 1(b). The service invocations and the context changes performed by the user are associated with the effects on the owned core resources. These effects are integrated with other resource-critical information, potentially leading to the inconsistencies in the state of resources, and therefore may require new resource-critical activities. The activities are operationalized with the set of available services and applications, and the user decides which of them are relevant and have to be performed.

In the following we present the conceptual architecture and its reference implementation, which supports the presented approach providing the following functionalities:

- represent and associate entities and services from different domains in terms of resources and resource-related actions;
- represent and manage the user resources and their evolution;
- propagate the effect of the actions and operations to the user resources;
- propagate the resource inconsistencies and problems to the user and applications in order to operationalize their resolution;
- continuously monitor the resource-related context of the user in order to synchronize the resource-critical information.

3.1 Platform Architecture

The architecture of the platform (Fig. 2) consists of three main components, namely the *Resource Layer*, the *Control Layer*, and the *Application Layer*. This

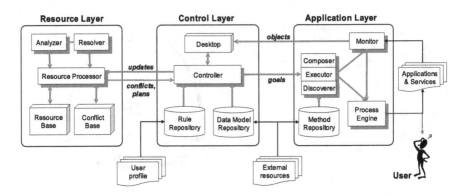

Fig. 2. Platform architecture

decomposition provides a clear separation of concerns in the user-centric operational environment.

Resource Layer. The *Resource Layer* (RL) component keeps track of the use of the core resources and the relations between different resource actions, identifies and analyzes potential inconsistencies, and finds ways of resolving these problems.

When the user resources are modified, the system updates the RL component with the information on the modification: the *Resource Processor* updates the current state of resources (*Resource Base*), analyzes its consistency with respect to a set of resource-specific constraints (*Analyzer*), identifies and stores the resource problems (*Conflict Base*), and looks for the resolution actions on resources (*Resolver*). The information about identified conflicts, as well as the actions needed to resolve them, are returned to the system. This includes the type of the problem (e.g., location inconsistency), its parameters, and a set of abstract, domain-independent resource-related operations needed to make the user assets consistent.

Control Layer. The *Control Layer* (CL) component is used to integrate and harmonize the information from different applications and services according to the model of user resources and their manipulation.

The component continuously processes the information events generated by the applications and by the user context; it integrates various information entities and relates them to the resources and to the resource updates. The information events deliver information about relevant objects as instances of various data structures (e.g., XML document describing the movie ticket) and about their evolution (e.g., change of entity state or modification of relevant information). For this purpose shared data model (*Data Model Repository*) is used. It describes the corresponding data structures from different application domains and their relation to resources.

Information events are published and stored in the *Desktop* and are processed by the *Controller*. Such processing consists of applying a set of associated ECA (event-condition-action) rules stored in *Rule Repository*, which describe the operations and procedures to be executed in reaction to a specific event. This may include invocation of services, execution of service compositions, interaction with the user, etc. The rules may be configured according to the user preferences (*User Profile*); new rules may be installed during the platform evolution.

An important functionality of the CL component includes the interaction with the Resource Layer. It is used to update the RL component with new information regarding user resources and to handle the inconsistencies identified at the level of resources. The inconsistencies and proposed resource actions are related to the concrete objects, and then propagated to the Application Layer, where they are operationalized and executed using available services and applications.

Application Layer. The functionality of the *Application Layer* includes the identification, composition, and execution of the applications and services operated through the mobile phone; interactions with the user and managing his activities and decisions; monitoring and publishing relevant events from applications and user context.

The *Executor* module instantiates and controls the execution of actions specified by the CL component. It validates the availability of known services and find new ones (using *Discoverer* module), creates and adapts service compositions according to the new actions and context changes (*Composer*), and executes these actions and compositions (*Process Engine*). The set of services and applications known to the platform are defined in the *Method Repository*, which defines the service interfaces, protocols/parameters to use, data structure manipulated, etc. This repository, as well as the Data Model Repository, which defines the data structures and ontologies, operated by the platform, are shared among different layers. The repository can be extended with the new information from external sources.

In the AL component a set of *Monitor* plug-ins are installed, in order to track and signal external events, such as the SMS messages received, contextual changes, etc. The events are then forwarded to the CL component for processing.

3.2 System Execution

We illustrate the functionality of the platform using the scenarios presented above. We show how the events are processed, how the objects are related to the resources, and how the resource-driven composition is performed.

Realization of the Movie Ticket Processing. The platform is activated when the movie show information is downloaded and delivered to Desktop (Fig. 3). Using the data model, the Controller identifies the relation of the movie show to a set of resources, namely time (time of the show), location (address of the cinema), money (price of the ticket), and social (public event). These relations trigger the necessity to "allocate" the corresponding resources using available applications and services. The goal is operationalized in AL component by identifying and composing a set of relevant services. This involves booking

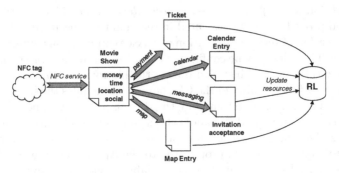

Fig. 3. Movie ticket processing

a ticket, paying it with the appropriate payment service, sending notification to a friend, adding the cinema address to the map, and storing event in the agenda. We remark that these operations are not just atomic service invocations, but complex procedures that include data transformations, interactions with the user, etc. In particular, payment procedure requires (a) asking the user to accept the payment request, (b) creating the payment request object, (c) invoking associated payment service, (d) informing the RL component about the action on the user finances. In a similar way, the update of the calendar and the event invitation/acceptance are followed by the updates of the corresponding resources.

When the procedure is activated (upon the decision of the user or automatically), the composition is executed, and the results of the executions are also propagated to Desktop. In this way, the platform observes the information integration, and relates the different objects and events. These relations are made persistent in order to continuously guarantee the consistency of the managed information entities. For instance, the payment confirmation, the agenda and map entries are associated to the movie ticket: if later on the user decide to cancel the visit to the cinema, the platform will also be able to cancel the payment, notify the friend, and even remove an entry from the map.

Realization of the Business Trip Management. The scenario flow is represented in Fig. 4. When the business meeting is detected, a procedure similar to the one described above is engaged. Besides this, the RL component performs the analysis of the user resources with respect to the meeting information (time and location), and detects the corresponding location inconsistency. The problem is reported to the Control Layer that uses the AL component to operationalize the resolution. Depending on the parameters of the problem, different resolution variants may be defined. In our scenario the resolution includes finding and selecting a flight trip, paying the chosen option, and updating the agenda. As before, the procedure is constructed by the Composer module, and is executed by the Process Engine. In case of positive outcome, the results of the execution will be published in the Desktop, propagated to the Resource Layer, and the user resources will be updated to a consistent state.

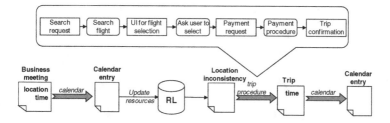

Fig. 4. Managing business trip

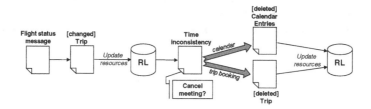

Fig. 5. Flight cancellation

Realization of the Flight Cancellation. The scenario flow is represented in Fig. 5. When the message with the delay information is detected by the monitor, it is published as the flight trip modification event, in particular, its time modification. This modification is propagated to the Resource Layer, and the inconsistency is detected. This inconsistency requires that either the meeting (time) is cancelled or another trip is organized. Both options are operationalized and offered to the user.

We remark that both the proposed solutions include management of other related objects. In case of meeting cancellation, this includes cancelling the trip using the trip booking service, removing the entries corresponding to the meeting and the trip from the user agenda (calendar), etc.

3.3 Platform Implementation

We have implemented a prototype of the conceptual platform for the resources-driven user-centric composition of mobile services. While the prototype is still preliminary, it has already made possible the definition, integration, and delivery of the discussed functionalities on a mobile platform. In the future we plan to extend and enrich the proposed platform with new services and functionalities.

The prototype is designed as a distributed software platform, in which some components are located on a mobile phone, and the others (that require expensive computations and persistence) are accessed remotely. In particular, the RL, CL, and in part AL components are implemented as a Web application, that interacts with a mobile part via a specific protocol. The mobile part contains the platform front-end and the corresponding UI components, which inform the user

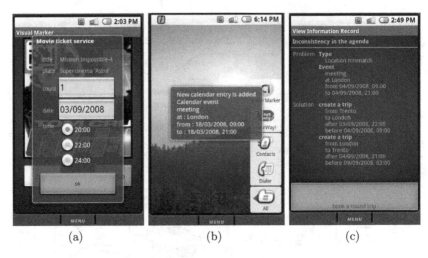

Fig. 6. Platform UI

about various conflicts and important objects, offer different actions to execute, and query additional information required for invocation of services and applications. The mobile part of the platform is implemented on top of the Android platform [2], an open java-based operating environment for mobile phones.

Apart from the applications and facilities provided by the platform (e.g., UI components), the implementation makes an extensive use of remote services and applications. In particular, the Google Calendar application is used in order to manage the user agenda, and the Google Mail application is used to monitor the e-mail messages and notifications from other users. Also, a set of mock-up Web services were implemented for testing/demonstration purposes, such as payment service, movie ticket service, flight search, etc.

Figure 6 shows some screenshots of the platform interface. In particular, Fig. 6(a) represents a dialog window of the movie ticket service. Figure 6(b) shows the notification about the result of the calendar update with the information about the business meeting. Finally, Fig. 6(c) demonstrates the location inconsistency problem identified by the platform, its parameters, necessary actions, and the reference to the trip booking procedure corresponding to these actions.

4 Related Works and Conclusions

We have presented an approach to the problem of user-centric data integration and composition of mobile services. The approach relies on the notion of resources, i.e., a compact set of concepts used to model and represent the important aspects of the everyday activities of the user. This allows for expressive and pragmatic integration of independent application domains, and enables the automated composition of mobile services. The approach also incorporates the management and evolution of the associated user assets, thus providing a way to continuously adapt the service provision and execution to the user activities and needs. We also presented a conceptual architecture for the supporting platform, and discussed its prototype implementation.

So far, research in service composition has focused on the problem of task-centric composition, i.e., on creating a composed process that performs a desired task defined by the composition requirements and interacts with a set of services. The existing approaches target the problem both at the functional level (composition of atomic services, [3,4,5]), and at the process level (take into account stateful behavior of components, [6,7,8]). Our approach is radically different: it starts from the simple requirements, where resources play key role, and from the service descriptions, whose semantics takes resources into account; it considers and integrates all the services related from the resource point of view, even if they perform completely unrelated tasks; it is continuous and is dynamically performed at run-time, when the context and conditions are changing. Our approach also differs from the approaches to the composition of Semantic Web services that take into account user preferences and constraints [9,10]. Our user-centric approach composes services through a set of core resources, which play the crucial role for all the users in general. User preferences may be specified and integrated on top of it.

The way the data is represented and integrated is also rather different from the approaches adopted in Semantic Web services, where the description of services and service data relies on expressive and complex languages and models in order to target automated inference, discovery, and integration of generic services and domains [11,12,13]. In our approach we focus on a compact set of resource-related concepts, targeting a pragmatic and minimalistic description and reasoning on the service and data models. The same holds for the context-related information, where we focus only on the resource-related aspects. This is different from the traditional approaches to the context awareness that define the context in a very unbounded way [14].

References

1. Paolucci, M., Broll, G., Hamard, J., Rukzio, E., Wagner, M., Schmidt, A.: Bringing Semantic Services to Real-World Objects. IJSWIS 4 (2008)
2. Open Handset Alliance: Android mobile phone platform
3. Sheshagiri, M., des Jardins, M., Finin, T.: A Planner for Composing Services Described in DAML-S. In: Proceedings of the Second International Joint Conference on Autonomous Agents & Multiagent Systems, AAMAS (2003)
4. Narayanan, S., McIlraith, S.: Simulation, Verification and Automated Composition of Web Services. In: Proceedings of the 11th international conference on World Wide Web, WWW (2002)
5. Wu, D., Parsia, B., Sirin, E., Hendler, J., Nau, D.: Automating DAML-S Web Services Composition using SHOP2. In: Fensel, D., Sycara, K.P., Mylopoulos, J. (eds.) ISWC 2003. LNCS, vol. 2870, pp. 195–210. Springer, Heidelberg (2003)

6. Pistore, M., Traverso, P., Bertoli, P., Marconi, A.: Automated Synthesis of Composite BPEL4WS Web Services. In: Proceedings of the IEEE International Conference on Web Services, ICWS (2005)
7. Khalaf, R., Mukhi, N., Weerawarana, S.: Service Oriented Composition in BPEL4WS. In: Proceedings of the 12th international conference on World Wide Web, WWW (2003)
8. Berardi, D., Calvanese, D., Giacomo, G.D., Mecella, M.: Composition of Services with Nondeterministic Observable Behaviour. In: Benatallah, B., Casati, F., Traverso, P. (eds.) ICSOC 2005. LNCS, vol. 3826, pp. 520–526. Springer, Heidelberg (2005)
9. Baier, J., Bacchus, F., McIlraith, S.: A Heuristic Search Approach to Planning with Temporally Extended Preferences. In: Proceedings of the 20th International Joint Conference on Artificial Intelligence, IJCAI (2007)
10. McIlraith, S., Son, S.: Adapting Golog for Composition of Semantic Web Services. In: Proceedings of the Eighth International Conference on Principles and Knowledge Representation and Reasoning, KR (2002)
11. OWL Service Coalition. OWL-S: Semantic Markup for Web Services (2003)
12. Roman, D., Lausen, H., Keller, U., Oren, E., Bussler, C., Kifer, M., Fensel, D.: Web Service Modeling Ontology (WSMO): WSMO Working Draft (2004), http://www.wsmo.org/2004/d2/v1.0/
13. Noll, J., Kileng, F., Hinz, R., Roman, D., Pilarski, M., Lillevold, E.: Semantic Service Delivery for Mobile Users. In: Proceedings of the WWRF N17 meeting, WG2 (2006)
14. Dey, A.K., Abowd, G.D.: Towards a Better Understanding of Context and Context-Awareness. In: Proceedings of the Internatonal Symposium on Handheld and Ubiquitous Computing (2006)

Beyond Usability: A New Frontier for User-Centered Design of "Future Internet" Services

Elena Not, Chiara Leonardi, Claudio Mennecozzi,
Fabio Pianesi, and Massimo Zancanaro

Fondazione Bruno Kessler FBK-irst,
Trento, Italy
{not,cleonardi,mennecozzi,pianesi,zancana}fbk.eu

Abstract. This paper proposes a new challenge for the Future Internet initiatives: the need of bridging the digital divide that, even in Europe, still hampers the access to the internet for a large part of the population. As a case study, we discuss the design of communication services for elderly people in northern Italy. The process was conducted by a multi-disciplinary team by involving a large group of stakeholders. The outcome was not just a set of simplified services but a new device offering sophisticated functionalities tailored to the actual needs of the targeted users and respectful of their personal meaningful practices. We argue that such a holistic approach that goes well beyond the objectives of usability and accessibility should become a common practice of approaching the design of new services for Future Internet.

Keywords: User-Centered Design, elders, design of new services.

1 Introduction

There is a wide consensus nowadays that the internet technology has to be redesigned in order to sustain the huge role that the web is currently playing in the world economy. Many Future Internet initiatives around the world are primarily focusing on architectural issues, with some notable exceptions like the ICT Programme funded by the European Commission that has adopted a holistic approach, tightly embedding the network, content, objects, service and security dimensions [1]. In this paper, we argue the necessity to add a new dimension to the issues discussed under the umbrella of Future Internet, namely the need of bridging the digital divide that, even in Europe, still hampers the access to the internet for a large part of the population such as elderly and people with special needs.

Indeed several of the ambitious goals proposed by the Bled Declaration [2] for the Strategic Agendas of the European Technology Platforms may have an impact toward the reduction of the digital divide. For example, the emphasis on open standards and architecture may drastically reduce the costs of access, while the efforts toward adaptable services may eventually benefit the less skilled users. Yet, several recent studies suggest that some types of users often reject technologies because they have different motivation and requirements, and not just because of a lack of skills. Among others, Melenhorst et al. [3] investigated the barriers preventing older adults to use media

J. Domingue, D. Fensel, and P. Traverso (Eds.): FIS 2008, LNCS 5468, pp. 107–116, 2009.

such as e-mail and the internet and their findings suggest that awareness of benefits is a determinant factor for older adults to overcome fears and inhibition toward new technologies. Similarly, Selwiyn [4] observes that older adults' ambivalence with respect to ICT originates from the limited perceived relevance to day-to-day life.

This digital divide may have dramatic effects since it is expected that the Future Internet will help to shape modern society as a whole, especially in the areas of health, education, and government [5]. It is therefore of paramount importance to take into consideration right from the initial phases of the design the values that affect the way people use technology (see also [6] for a manifesto a new roadmap in HCI).

In this paper, we discuss, as a case study, the design of some communication services for elder people in northern Italy. The process was planned to extend beyond the limits, albeit very important, of usability and accessibility to consider the emotional experiences of the targeted users as well as their social practices and cultural schemes. The result was not just the deployment of "simpler" services for less skilled users, but a new device that incorporates advanced features presented with a terminology and a type of interaction which result familiar to the target population. The take-away lesson for this paper is not a set of guidelines to design for elderly people but rather that a User-Centered process should be always put in place when designing for special categories of users.

2 User-Centered Design with Elders

Older adults have a difficult relationship with technology [7], yet the belief that age-related "technophobia" represents the main obstacle to elderly technology usage is progressively disappearing. On the contrary, one of the main reasons for elderly users having been neglected by technology is that hardware and software design, and in particular interfaces, have simply not been designed to suit them [8].

User Centered Design [9] advocates that valuing the users' opinions since the initial phases of the design of a new technology and iteratively throughout the whole development cycle is crucial for both the identification of credible and acceptable technological scenarios and for the assessment of the services and interaction interfaces. However, involving old aged people greatly challenges the applicability and validity of traditional tools used in User Centered Design (e.g., questionnaires, focus groups, interviews, practical workshops, shadowing, cultural probes, mock-ups etc.), due to the peculiar physiologic, psychological, and ethical issues that enter into play [10]. For instance, distress of traveling, unfamiliar environments, or meeting unfamiliar people may be a problem when organizing focus groups or interviews and this psychological discomfort might hamper their willingness to participate and their frank contribution to the discussion [11]. Regarding the in-home observations, which are crucial for an ethnographically based design, it may be difficult get the consent [12]. But, above all, one of the major difficulties in convincing older people to participate to technological R&D is their low confidence in discussing technological issues, and a general underestimation of their own abilities in using new technology.

Involving elders into the process of designing innovative technologies requires the building and nourishing of a long-lasting network of users and stakeholders. This goes well beyond the current practices of sporadically resorting to care givers associations to deal with specific project requirements [13].

In the context of the IST NETCARITY project, we are developing and applying a protocol for the design of advanced web-based communication services targeted to the elderly. The protocol consists in several concrete strategies for motivating the participation of elders in the design team and for establishing a long-term relationship with the elders and the 'experts' while reducing the risk of drop-outs and securing the quality of the information obtained. This protocol distils insights gained in the course of the project by a multidisciplinary team involving interaction designers, social scientists and care givers. It employs the standard UCD tools (in particular, scenario-based focus groups and think-aloud sessions with progressive prototypes) and consists of a sequence of actions aimed at a) securing the endorsement and direct involvement in the project of local authorities and elders associations with the role of mediators and guarantors; b) assuring the constant integration of the design activities with existing daily practices–(in the aggregation centers, by embedding the activities of the design team in regular activities, and at home, by finding suitable time and space slots where testing activities can be carried on); c) seeking a continuous clarification with the elders of how any specific activity (e.g. interviews, focus groups, etc.) contributes to the following steps of the project and to the project as a whole, and how it is linked to previous activities (e.g., through the appropriate selection of the material used– questions, stimuli, props, etc.– and periodic events where findings are presented and discussed with users).

As confirmed by our experience, this is a long and quite complex process, but despite the fatigue required to bootstrap, the initial efforts are well paid back. Of particular importance is the role of the stakeholders that should not be regarded as simple "recruiters" of elders. Care givers, social workers and educators have professional goals – that of improving the psycho-social well-being of elderly people – that naturally integrate with the final goals of technology developers. They have a privileged vision over the social norms, rules, psychological and ethical issues that characterize the aging process. Therefore, they can provide help in tuning the research tools to the old aged audience, avoiding some gross mistakes. For example, they can check that the stimulus material used for focus groups (e.g., terminology, images) does not suggest stigmatization and does not address sensitive topics in an abrupt way. Furthermore, they can provide the continuity and coherence in users' involvement that is crucial for enhancing motivation and long lasting participation.

From the point of view of the technical team, it is important to make elders and stakeholders to perceive how the collected material contributes to the project. It is therefore important to often include references to results emerged from previous activities, strengthening the feeling that elders (and stakeholders as well) are active research partners and that their contribution counts. Periodic events should be organized to present to and discuss with the users the emerging findings. At the beginning of the UCD process, the elders may hesitate to express certain opinions (e.g., about the intrusiveness, uselessness or complexity of the technology) to researchers associated with technology [13], or they may be reluctant to reveal information and opinions that might induce stigmatization (e.g., feelings of loneliness or isolation). However, this behavior reduces as the project progresses, due to the increased involvement and familiarity with the project team.

Fig. 1. An example of a cartoon involving a "persona" in a daily situation

In our experience, we have found that group work, such as focus groups and testing mock-ups in pairs, is particularly welcome by elders because of the socialization "side-effect", even though researchers are faced with the increased difficulty of keeping them focused on the topic of the discussion. Appealing stimulus material, like dramatized stories of technology use, are particularly effective in initiating the discussion on unfamiliar computer-based solutions. Recently, videos and theatre performances turned out to be particularly engaging even if quite expensive [15]. In our project, we conducted a series of successful focus groups based on a cheaper and more flexible approach exploiting personas and narrative scenarios presented through comics. Personas are invented characters with personal features, life stories, goals and tasks [16]. They are introduced to users to favour empathy and identification, encouraging the production of personal interpretations. Several personas were created with the help of care-givers to highlight different typologies of elders, for example Nina exemplifies the active woman with an intense social life, while Piero exemplifies the fragile elder at risk of social exclusion. The personas have been validated in advance with stakeholders to maximize efficacy. Then comic strips are used to show the different personas involved in daily situations (e.g., the phone rings while Piero is cooking, as in 1). Participants are stimulated to discuss about the verisimilitude of personas, and the plausibility of the presented situation, and are encouraged to freely envisage possible solutions (technological and non technological) to the presented problematic situation, expressing their fears, needs and preferences (see fig.1, left). Typically, at this stage of the discussion, many personal stories emerge, and the focus group facilitator has the challenging role of containing the emotional involvement of participants.

Later on, a technological scenario is presented, suggesting a possible role of technology in solving the problem. Participants are then encouraged to express their opinions (with respect to acceptability, perceived usefulness, envisaged changes, and so on) on the introduced services and functionalities. In order to keep older people focused and to facilitate turn-giving, participants are assigned a concrete, manipulative task: they are given green and red tokens to vote on the relevance of the functionalities presented (see fig. 2, right).

Fig. 2. A focus group with elders (left) and voting on a technological scenario

A detailed account of the protocol and its outcomes is reported in Leonardi et al. [17].

3 Design Guidelines for Communication Services for Elders

The analysis process, in the first part of the NETCARITY project, was mainly focused on identifying the requirements for the design of a communication system targeted for elderly people.

An aspect that clearly emerged from the analysis is that the relational universe of elders is heterogeneous and rich. Their social network is segmented into components—relatives, close friends, acquaintances, the group of peers and caregivers—each having its own peculiarities. These relationships are always mediated in a given context (i.e. private vs, public spaces, etc.) and by some artifacts (i.e. telephone, letters, postcards, etc.). Furthermore, they are regulated by social norms and protocols that determine initiation and maintenance of interactions. A technology that aims at facilitating communication should take into account these social norms and integrate rather than replace the existing practices.

Another important aspect is the concept of intimacy. This is an essential component for self-esteem and emotional health. The understanding of the degree of emotional involvement between elderly people and the members of their social network is central for the design of acceptable communication services. For example, it is important to support users in managing access to their private sphere.

As often reported in the literature, we identified anxiety and worries associated with the management of different communicative situations in our user group too. The notion of "Communication Apprehension"— defined as the anxiety associated with either real or anticipated communication with another person [18] —has been used to understand the concerns that can arise, in particular, with technology mediated communication. In our study we investigated which limits and worries elderly people experience in maintaining relationships within their social network.

Finally, any technology designed for elders should take into consideration the age-related changes in perceptual, motor and cognitive abilities. However, the consideration of the decrease of these abilities should be coupled with the appreciation of the compensative processes that older people develop to adapt to these changes: motivation, affection, and experience ("learning by doing") are key aspects that designers should take into account.

3.1 Familiarity as a Design Concept

A familiar technology is a technology that the user is ready to face on the base of a common ground of concepts, meanings and practices that are not conscious but present in a non prominent way [19]. A familiar technological artefact is not perceived just as a jumble of wires and plastic, instead first-time users are able to give it a sense and sometimes even guess its functions. This "familiarity effect" is a powerful tool for the design of new technologies. In the design space we have been exploring in the context of the NETCARITY project, the concept of familiarity is implemented along several dimensions.

The first dimension regards familiarity in personal meaningful practices. We tried to select a context and a domain for our interface which are not only socially and objectively suitable, but also close to elderly people practices, expectations and emotions. We defined and named the tasks in the interfaces accordingly. For example, from the initial analysis it emerged a clear distinction in the practises of communication with the family, with peers and with strangers. We therefore implemented different spaces for these three types of communication.

The other dimension is familiarity in the represented domain. Metaphors are used whereby tasks are represented by real world tasks, and the objects mimic real world objects. For example, the implementation of an email infrastructure are defined in terms of the management of postcards.

Finally, the most crucial aspect of familiarity for this user group is in the implementation of the interaction modality. The well known Direct Manipulation paradigm [20] is applied in a stricter way than the common WIMP—Windows, Icons, Menus and Pointing—interfaces. A touch screen has been used in order to eliminate the mediation of a pointing device such as a mouse. The use of the "click" action has been avoided. Similarly, all the secondary elements, such as menus, toolbars have been eliminated and the use of dialog boxes has been reduced as much as possible. Natural gestures are pervasively used to manipulate objects, for example to delete an object the user has just to scratch on it with a finger or a pen, while in order to create a new object the user has just to draw its contour on the screen (see figure 3). The interface navigation is facilitated by an automatic zooming dynamic: when an element is touched, it is enlarged whereas the dimensions of the other elements are reduced. This guarantees that all the elements visible on the interface are kept available to users, though the attention is focused on the current task.

It is worth noting that the interaction language is not less rich than in the WIMP paradigm (e.g., the range of available actions, like zooming and gestures, is not meagre) nor it is closer to physical reality (e.g., objects in the real world are not created as an effect of a gesture). The very idea of familiarity implies a closeness to users' conceptual world, not necessarily simplified tools..

Fig. 3. Examples of natural gestures for objects creation (left) and deletion (right)

4   The MobiTable

Many design concepts were iteratively generated and evaluated within the stake-holders' group. All the evaluations started from the discussions of scenarios representing the design concepts being used by the personas. As discussed above, in this initial phase cartoons were used to exemplify the scenarios without a real implementation. Then, the most promising ideas were realized as progressive prototypes, from *pen'n'paper* mockups to fully functional prototypes (see fig, 4).

Fig. 4. Users testing an initial *pen-n-paper* mockup (left) and a more advanced prototype (right)

Eventually, the outcome of the process was the realization of a mobile touch-sensitive device, called the MobiTable, implementing four main functionalities: (i) the Social Window which provides access to the social network: through simple gestures on a list of personal contacts, video-communication can be activated and postcards created and sent; (ii) the Public Square which is based on the metaphor of the place where members of local communities physically meet to share knowledge and participate in social activities; (iii) a calendar as a tool to store appointments and commitments coming from the Public Space, it also manages reminders, and finally (iv) a set of Digital Drawers to store media contents exchanged.

Fig. 5. The first prototype of the MobiTable

The physical design of the artifact takes into account the ergonomic constraints emerged during the preliminary mock-up experiments. It is adjustable in height, surface slope and rotation, to get a more comfortable sitting position and a more comfortable vision, focus of attention, and hands usage during the performing of the various tasks (see fig. 5).

A longitudinal evaluation study involving twenty elders in Trento is planned for Fall 2008.

5   Conclusion

This paper reports an experience of value-based design for the development of communication services targeted to elderly people in Northern Italy. The design process was planned in such a way to involve the final users, the elders, since the very beginning. The challenges of User-Centered Design with elderly people are well documented in the literature and we decided to involve a larger group of stakeholders that encompassed social services, families and care-givers. Although quite expensive, this approach was valuable in providing the level of involvement sufficient for reducing the risk of drop-outs and securing the quality of the information obtained. The process was conducted by a multi-disciplinary team and the outcome was not just a simplified interface but a new device offering sophisticated services tailored to the actual needs of the targeted users and respectful of their personal meaningful practices.

Our claim is that a similar process for design of technologies should become a common practise in the development of Future Internet services. If the Future of Internet is going to become even more pervasive than now and to provide access for the crucial areas of health, education, and government, the risk of digital divide cannot be underestimated. The accessibility guidelines and regulation are not enough because, as discussed in this paper, the limited technical capabilities of disadvantaged users are only one aspect of a multi-faceted problem. The only answer is a holistic approach to the design that considers the value system, the emotional experiences, the social practices and the cultural schemes of the users as the basis for the development of effective technologies.

References

[1] Schwarz da Silva, J.: EU approach towards the Future Internet. Eurescom mess@ge (January 2008)

[2] The Bled Declaration (March 2008) (last retrieved, June 2008), http://www.fi-bled.eu/Bled_declaration.pdf

[3] Melenhorst, A.-S., Rogers, W.A., Caylor, E.C.: The use of communication technologies by older adults: exploring the benefits from the user's perspective. In: Proceedings Human Factors and Ergonomics Society (2001)

[4] Selwyn, N.: The information aged: A qualitative study of older adults' use of information and communications technology. Journal of Aging Studies 18, 369–384 (2004)

[5] Mähönen, P., Trossen, D., Papadimitriou, D., Polyzos, G., Kennedy, D.: EIFFEL: Evolved Internet Future for European Leadership. A white paper from the EIFFEL Think-Tank (December 2006)

[6] Harper, R., Sellen, A., Rodden, T., Rogers, Y.: Being Human: Human-Computer Interaction in the Year 2020. Microsoft Research White Paper (April 2008)

[7] Deets, H.B.: Aging and Technology: The Convergence of Two Revolutions. CyberPsychology & Behavior 2(6), 501–503 (1999)

[8] Bucar, A., Kwon, S.: Computer Hardware and Software Interfaces: Why the Elderly Are Under-Represented as Computer Users. CyberPsychology & Behavior 2(6), 535–543 (1999)

[9] User-Centrered Design process for interactive systems, ISO 13407 Model (1999)

[10] Eisma, R., Dickinson, A., Goodman, J., Syme, A., Tiwari, L., Newell, A.F.: Early user involvement in the development of information technology related products for older people. International Journal Universal Access in the Information Society 3(2), 131–140 (2004)

[11] Harris, J.: Usability Stockholm Syndrome (accessed, April 2008), http://blogs.msdn.com/jensenh/archive/2006/03/20/555460.aspx

[12] Dickinson, A., Goodman, J., Syme, A., Eisma, R., Tiwari, L., Mival, O., Newell, A.: Domesticating Technology: In-home requirements gathering with frail older people. In: Proc. of 10th International Conference on Human - Computer Interaction HCI, pp. 827–831 (2003)

[13] Dickinson, A., Arnott, J., Prior, S.: Methods for human-computer interaction research with older people. Behaviour & Information Technology 26(4) (2007)

[14] Rice, M., Newell, A., Morgan, M.: Forum Theatre as a requirements gathering methodology in the design of a home telecommunication system for older adults. Behaviour & Information Technology 26(4) (2007)

[15] Carmichael, A., Newell, A.F., Morgan, M.: The efficacy of narrative video for raising awareness in ICT designers about older users requirements. Interacting with Computers 19(5-6), 587–596 (2007)

[16] Cooper, A., Reimann, R.: About Face 2.0: The Essential of Interaction Design. John Wiley & Sons, Chichester (2003)

[17] Leonardi, C., Mennecozzi, C., Not, E., Pianesi, F., Zancanaro, M.: Getting Older People Involved in the Process of Ambient Assisted Living Research and Development. In: Proceedings of Gerontechnology 2008, Pisa (June 2008)

[18] Reinsch, N.L., Lewis, P.V.: Communication Apprehension as a Determinant of Channel Preferences. The Journal of Business Communication 21(3), 53–61 (1984)

[19] Turner, P., Van De Walle, G.: Familiarity As A Basis of Universal Design. Journal of Gerontechnology 5(3), 150–159 (2006)

[20] Norman, D., Hollan, J., Hutchins, E.: Direct manipulation interfaces. Human Computer Interaction 1, 311–338 (1995)

Unlock Your Data: The Case of MyTag

Thomas Franz, Klaas Dellschaft, and Steffen Staab

University of Koblenz, 56070 Koblenz, Germany
{franz,klaasd,staab}@uni-koblenz.de
http://isweb.uni-koblenz.de

Abstract. The business model of Web2.0 applications like FaceBook, Flickr, YouTube and their likes is based on an asymmetry: Users generate content, Web2.0 application providers own, *(i)*, the access to user content, *(ii)*, the user profiles and, *(iii)*, user interaction data. We argue in this paper that such asymmetry disadvantages the users and prevents innovative applications. We demonstrate an application, MyTag, that is based on a layer for cross-application user profiling and personalization and that exploits web service access to user data. Presenting this application, we conclude that such applications offer additional value to users and usage of such applications on content generated by the users should not be at the disposal of the application provider, but should be a part of users' rights.

Keywords: User-generated content, Web2.0, Mash-ups, User rights.

1 Asymmetry of Efforts and Rights

The success of the internet and in particular of the Web as the most prominent application of the internet is based deeply on the variety of Web applications, stakeholders and users. In fact, this variety has been such a driving force that it is now taken for granted rather than a surprise.

We, however, argue in this paper that such a variety may be fragile and we need innovation of technology and applications as well as development of laws and regulations in order to maintain this variety.

The Winner Takes It All. For example, it has become visible in the Web search market that there is not much room for a variety of search engines. The market is dominated by one player eventually owning a near-monopoly. It has been argued reasonably that such a monopoly may create severe economic and societal problems [6].

User-generated Content, Personalization and Interaction. Until recently, the area of Web2.0 applications exhibited a very different picture. Applications such as Flickr, Delicious or YouTube have been developed by start-up companies creating a new variety of stakeholders and a new set of Web applications attracting site visits at enormous rates. However, (partial) acquisitions of several of the most successful of these companies have led to a situation where not only the index to Web content, but also the user-generated content itself as well as the interaction

J. Domingue, D. Fensel, and P. Traverso (Eds.): FIS 2008, LNCS 5468, pp. 117–129, 2009.

of users with this content is now owned by a few oligopolists. With recent, new types of applications such as Google docs, this development will be further accelerated.

Unlocking Your Data. The oligo-/monopoly in the field of applications is based on the monopoly of data ownership by the oligo-/monopolist — instead of data ownership by the users who generated the data. For example, it will be virtually impossible for an everyday user to unlock his own data from Gmail (Google's mail programme) in order to continue the usage of his own data in a different email client.

To substantiate the discussion, we present in this paper an example application we have developed, i.e. MyTag (http://mytag.uni-koblenz.de). MyTag demonstrates, *(i)*, the need of data ownership by users, *(ii)*, a new application allowing versatile usage of user-generated content and, *(iii)*, further requirements for a variety-rich internet of the future.

In the remainder of this paper, we first introduce our running scenario, based on which we will determine requirements for cross-application usage of content and personalization (i.e. profiles and user interaction). Section 4 describes the MyTag application from the user point of view, Section 5 the architecture of MyTag and Section 6 the personalization capabilities. We describe some lessons learned, before we conclude with a discussion of open technical, application and legal issues to be handled for the future of Web applications.

2   Scenario

The scenario is centered around two global travellers named Tim and Tony.[1] When Tim and Tony approach a town, they use their mobile phone and personal digital assistant (PDA), respectively, in order to access the internet and search and retrieve impressions about the town that may be found in images, videos and Web pages.

Tim also carries a digital camera and often puts images online to share his impressions with friends at home. He has an account for a web application for image sharing for that purpose. Tim likes the application as it is easy to use, enables him to organize his images by simple tags, and offers him to browse for similar images shared by others.

Tony has a digital camera too that she also uses to record short movies. Being interested in professional fotography, she has an account for a web application commonly used by fotographers where members can also discuss about images, e.g. camera settings required to take a photo. Besides that, the application enables sharing and organizing of photos similar to the application used by Tim. For her videos, Tony has an additional account for a web application supporting videos.

After travelling Tony and Tim compile a photo album consisting of the most spectacular places they visited together. As they always tag their photos with

---

[1] The scenario partly overlaps with the scenario developed by the W3C incubator group [1].

the name of the place where it was taken they can use the search functionality of the web applications they use to display such photos.

3   Issues and Requirements Collection

Investigating the scenario, a number of issues with current Web applications, Web2.0 applications in particular, may be noticed:

Lack of task focus: The *task* of the travellers is the retrieval of impressions about a town. As data are locked into several distinct applications, they need to unlock the data manually, because there is no cross-application and cross-media search facility available that could support such a task. A similar case is true for updates. When Tony adds a photo and a video taken at the same place, she needs to create the same geo tag at both the photo and video application. When Tony wants to add a tag *Tim* to photos and videos that show Tim, she needs to execute the same kind of update on both platforms. And also for sharing, Tim and Tony cannot work seamlessly with both photo applications in order to compile an album of their trip. Consequently, users try to avoid switching between applications as much as possible.

Lack of cross use of user-interaction data: Most of the applications they use do not personalize their search to reflect their preferences. Though some more sophisticated applications allow personalization at the level of the individual application (e.g., http://www.bibsonomy.org), the applications do not allow for moving the user-interaction and -personalization data across different applications. Consequently, users have to spend a multiple of user-interaction efforts for unoptimized interaction with different applications.

Lack of cross-application profiles: The applications they use do not allow them to define profiles that are applicable across applications. For sharing content about their travel, they have to explicitly maintain their profile in form of social network data and access rights at different applications. Consequently, users have to spend extra effort for maintaining multiple profiles (if possible at all).

In order to deal with these issues, we have captured the following user requirements. First, we consider traditional ones that exist for single applications:

Personalized Result Ranking: Given personal structures that provide personalized access to content, we derive the requirement for *personalized* ranking to increase task completion efficiency (here, in particular: search). For instance, personalized rankings enable Tony and Tim to find interesting things about a town more quickly as web pages that are more relevant to them will be ranked higher.

Second, we consider user requirements that are derived from the cross-application usage scenario:

Cross-Application Search: To support the task of searching, the travelers need a possibility for cross-application search and results display.

Cross-Application Ranking: Cross-application results display requires intelligent integration of results, e.g. a fusion of collections as discussed in [7].

Cross-Application Profile Management: The sharing of user profiles needs a corresponding cross-application profile management allowing for the sharing of profile data, such as social network data, contact data, login data, etc.

Cross-Application Personalization: Finally, the efficient interaction requires cross application personalization such that the individual application can adapt itself easily according to preferred application-specific and cross-application interactions by the user.

From this requirements collection we may recognize that full benefits from user-generated content in these Web2.0 applications can only be harvested if either one application provider owns a virtual monopoly on these applications and facilitates comprehensive interactions (such as Google does for Google docs) or we may have to come up with new types of applications that fulfill the special needs for cross-application search, ranking, personalization and profiling in a system of distributed applications.

4   MyTag

MyTag [2] is an example of a novel kind of cross-application platform we have built for experimenting and solving limitations of current Web 2.0 applications as discussed in Section 3. MyTag features cross-application search for images, videos, and social bookmarks including capabilities for profiling and personalization. As of now, MyTag integrates Flickr, YouTube, and Delicious to offer transparent access to the information provided by these applications (cf. Fig. 1).

On its start page, MyTag offers its users a single field where search terms can be entered. By default, all platforms currently integrated into MyTag are then searched based on the user input. Search results for each media type are presented as separate result sets in different columns that can be ranked by means such as popularity and creation date (cf. Fig. 1).

For every resource in the result sets, its title, a preview, and the creation date are shown. For bookmarks, the preview is a snapshot of the website that is provided by a mash-up with the service of Snap.com. The snapshot is shown by moving the mouse over the icon next to the title of the bookmark. Furthermore, for each resource its associated tags are shown. Clicking on the preview of a resource opens a new window that offers additional details about the resource and links to its occurrences on the integrated application, e.g. Flickr. Above the results, a tag-cloud is shown that summarizes the most frequent tags in the result set. The font size of each tag is proportional to its occurrence frequency.

In MyTag, clicking on a tag refines the previous search query by adding the tag supporting faceted search for disambiguation of queries. The user can easily explore different directions in adding or removing tags.

Two further modes of operation are available for registered users of MyTag. First, a mode in which only personal media are shown, i.e. only media one

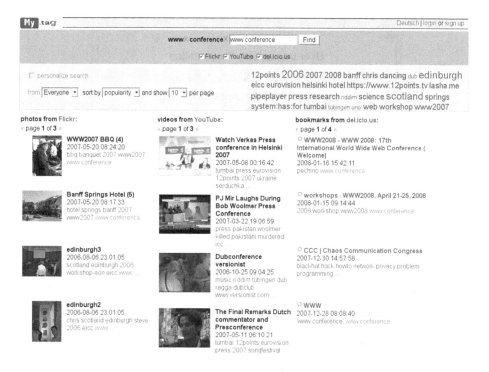

Fig. 1. Screenshot of a MyTag Search Result

contributed to any of the integrated applications. Second, a mode where search
results are ranked based on the personomy of a user. Both search modes are
explained in more detail in Section 6 that deals with personalization features.

5   MyTag Architecture

In the following, we present the conceptual architecture of MyTag and explain
how that architecture supports the integration of existing web applications. Additionally, we point out conceptual improvements we foresee.

5.1   Layers of the Architecture

MyTag was developed utilizing the web-development framework *Ruby on Rails*[2]
to benefit from the maturity, tool support, and lively user community of that
framework. The MyTag architecture realizes the model-view-controller paradigm
(MVC) distinguishing between three conceptual layers as indicated in Fig. 2. The
view layer (shown on the top) is responsible for handling the interaction with the
user such as rendering user interfaces and retrieving user input. The control layer
in the middle implements logical operations and processes data from the model

---

[2] http://www.rubyonrails.org/

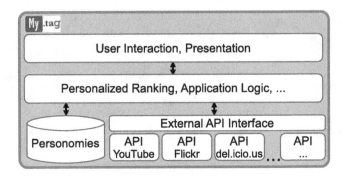

Fig. 2. MyTag Architecture

layer as well as user input from the view layer, e.g. by computing personalized rankings for a search term entered by a user. The model layer provides access to the information processed by the upper layers and consists of two major components: First, the interface to the local database that contains user profiles and personomies. Second, components that integrate applications into MyTag.

5.2   Application Integration

MyTag provides users with unified access to content they contributed to the Internet by the use of different web applications. The integration of such applications is based on the use of web-based application programming interfaces (APIs) that are provided by the tagging platforms integrated into MyTag. Web-based APIs are a common feature of Web 2.0 applications, intended to leverage system integration by enabling programmatic access to the data the applications provide. The utilization of such APIs confronts developers with common issues of integration such as mapping between data structures, data models, and API specifications as well as with further issues, because only a subset of user-generated data is available via the API.

Accordingly, for the development of MyTag, a mechanism was required that maps between the API of an integrated application and the data structures and method calls used by components of the controller layer (cf. Figure 2). MyTag provides a plugin architecture for the integration of applications that provides an abstraction of core aspects of tagging applications as we illustrate in Figure 3. The class `TaggingSystem` provides a common representation for integrated applications while subclasses extend it to provide application-specific details like access credentials. MyTag components communicate to integrated applications by means of common representations of application requests and responses. A `ListRequest` represents a search query that is distributed to integrated applications. It returns a `ListResponse` that contains for each of the integrated applications a `ResultList` pointing to single `Result` instances that provide a common representation for results from different applications. The abstraction of preview requests and responses, i.e. the request for details about a single

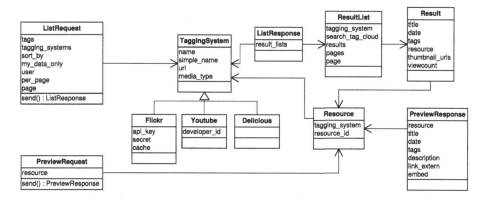

Fig. 3. Unified Model for System Communication

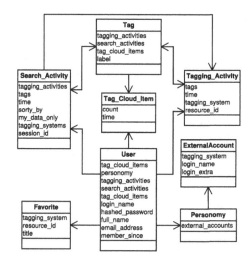

Fig. 4. Unified Model for User and Tagging Data

Resource such as an image on Flickr or a bookmark on del.icio.us, is modeled by the classes **PreviewRequest** and **PreviewResponse**.

Next to an abstraction for cross-application communication, MyTag components build upon a unified data model for users, resources, and taggings (i.e. the association of a tag to a resource by a specific user). Figure 4 shows the classes and properties in UML notation. The class **User** represents a MyTag user identified by its **login_name**. A user is associated to accounts on systems integrated by MyTag via his/her **Personomy**. Favorite resources – e.g. images, bookmarks, videos – are modeled by instances of the class **Favorite**. The class **Tag** models a tag that is identified by its **label**. Tags can be associated to users in three different ways: First, by a **Search_Activity** that models a user's search including the tags entered (**tags**), the applications considered for the search (tagging_systems), and the time at which the search was executed (time). Second by a Tagging_Activity, that stands for a users click on a tag in a result listing of MyTag. Third, tags are associated to users by personal tag clouds that represent the most frequently entered or clicked tags. A tag cloud is represented by instances of a Tag_Cloud_Item that stores how often a tag was used by a given user (modeled by the property count) and when it was last used (modeled by the property time).

6   Personalized Access to User-Generated Content

In Section 4, we introduced two modes of operation that stand for different personalization features of MyTag. In the following, we explain how they are implemented.

6.1   Searching Personal Resources

A user's content is commonly distributed over multiple Web 2.0 applications, e.g. fotos are shared using Flickr, while bookmarks are organized using del.icio.us. To overview the personal content distributed over multiple applications, MyTag supports a cross-application search that considers personal content exclusively. The feature has been implemented reusing functionality already available in many Web 2.0 systems. For example, in Flickr it is possible to restrict a search to one's own photos. If a user wants to take advantage of this feature, he has to enter his account names for the different tagging sites he is member of and which are integrated into MyTag.

6.2   Cross-Application Self-adaptive Personalization

Next to searching personal content as described before, MyTag provides a mode that features *personalized* cross-application search. For instance, Tim and Tony benefit from that mode to retrieve personalized results for preparing their trip to a town. For this personalization approach two different techniques are needed: First, a representation of the user's interests is needed, e.g. in form of a user profile. Second, the user profile has to be taken into account during the ranking of the search results, i.e. the ranking algorithm has to be adapted in order to rank resources higher which are more interesting for the current user.

The approach implemented by MyTag is self-adaptive, i.e. implicit user feedback is used for building a user profile representing his or her interests in form of a personomy. The profile is automatically built based on the tags attached to resources the user picks from the result lists for his search queries. The personomy is modeled as a vector $\mathbf{p}$ of tag frequencies representing the previous search interests of the user. As it is based on implicit feedback no additional user effort is required to specify personal interests, however, implicit feedback may be less robust than explicitly stated interest and requires significant amounts of data to stabilize. The usage of implicit user feedback is a fundamental difference to systems such as Flickr and Delicious, where personalization requires adding resources to the system.

With regard to personalized rankings, MyTag implements a ranking algorithm that combines information from the personomy and the tags assigned to resources of a result set. The tags of a resource are represented as a vector $\mathbf{v}$ of binary values indicating the presence of a tag. The rank r of a resource is computed by the scalar product of the two vectors: $\mathbf{r} = \mathbf{v} \cdot \mathbf{p}$. It is then used for ordering the resources based on their rank value.

While the first type of personalization is widespread, it is not the case for the second type of personalization. It is not available in the "main stream" tagging web sites like Flickr and Delicious but currently only implemented or planned for a few research oriented sites. For example, for the Bibsonomy application a personalized ranking using the FolkRank algorithm (see [5]) is currently considered.

6.3 Cross-Application Ranking

In its current version, MyTag integrates for each of the supported media-types only one tagging platform that is specialized on that type. Search results for different media-types are displayed in separate columns. This setting helps to avoid the fusion of result sets coming from different tagging systems into an overall result set.

To overcome this limitation of MyTag, we are at the moment implementing algorithms for the fusion of result sets. For this purpose, we are extending approaches for collection fusion (see [3] for an example) with capabilities for the personalized ranking of resources (see previous subsection). The new capabilities will directly be used for integrating further applications into MyTag like Bibsonomy, Connotea and Oneview.

Next to the ranking of results across applications, a representation of a user profile in order to implement personalized Internet utilization is limited to management of user identities so far. While the approaches discussed before are based on representations that are specific for the application type, namely tagging systems, other systems will require different representations. Both profile representations and personalization features that are applicable across applications will be needed to support personalized access to information served by a variety of Internet applications. The general user modeling ontology (GUMO) [4] is an example of initial work towards such a reusable profile representation.

7   Lessons Learned

Throughout the development of MyTag, we gathered insight into a variety of challenges that are to be handled in order to provide users with unified access to the information they contributed to the Internet. Challenges range from technological and conceptual constraints to policital, legal, and societal concerns and limitations of existing social platforms.

7.1   Political and Legal Constraints

Terms and conditions of Web 2.0 applications may restrict the implementation of applications that feature cross-application personalization. For instance, StudiVZ[3] forbids its users to access their own content by other means than the native user interface. Hence, applying MyTag on platforms like StudiVZ is legally forbidden while applying MyTag on platforms like Flickr, Delicious and YouTube does not have any legal basis — even if run from a user's PC.

7.2   Access Restrictions

While applications integrated into MyTag provide public APIs for accessing data they store, returned data may be heavily trimmed preventing the development of novel services. For instance, information about the ranking of results may be inaccessible.

In addition to such locking of data, we also experienced the blocking of API requests as another mechanism to restrict access. For instance, the use of some APIs is restricted to a certain number of requests per time unit.

7.3   Standardized APIs for Personalized Access

OpenSocial[4] is an API intended to define a standard interface to social networking platforms to ease the development of web-applications that exploit the data provided by such platforms. At the time of this writing, several platforms support OpenSocial and a JavaScript implementation is available for application development. The development of MyTag, however, could not profit from such a standardization effort: A common representation of user profiles is not foreseen by OpenSocial due to the different user representations on different platforms. Accordingly, we had to implement our own components for matching user profile information from different Web2.0 applications. Furthermore, OpenSocial does not provide interfaces for querying. However, such functionality is required to implement a cross-platform search as provided by MyTag. Moreover, interfaces for personalized search are missing. Accordingly, platforms that offer personalized access can only build upon *non-personalized* results that require further processing in order to adept them to users' preferences. Some applications, e.g. Facebook, provide programming interfaces for building add-ons that can access the data of the underlying application. While such approaches enable to exploit the infrastructure and available data, they lack support for cross-application functionalities and personalization.

7.4   Profile Management Support

Personalized web applications like MyTag require the interplay of different architecture components in order to implement personalization features. User interactions need to be tracked and filtered for generating and updating user profiles. At

---

[3] http://www.studivz.net
[4] http://www.opensocial.org/

the same time they may be accessed and refined by further user interface components as well as components that implement algorithms for personalized ranking and result-set merging. Current development frameworks provide limited support for the tracking, generation, exchange and provision of profile information for use by different architecture components and across Internet applications. While they commonly provide logging interfaces and session management components, they lack support for specific personalization tasks as mentioned before.

7.5   Decentralized Architectures

While MyTag enables transparent access to user-provided content spread over multiple web applications, it still does not change the fact that users have restricted access to the content they contributed. Approaches to distribute content in a decentralized fashion while enabling collaborative access are yet to be examined and constitute an open field of research. During the development of MyTag, we analyzed how to implement MyTag functionality by program code running in the web-browser of MyTag users. In such a decentralized architecture, profiling information could be gathered and stored on the users' clients giving them full-control over profile utilization and distribution. However, security policies implemented by standard web-browsers inhibit the development of cross-platform applications that run inside the user's web-browser. For instance, the *same-origin* policy ensures that program-code can only connect to the web server it was retrieved from. Thus, implementing JavaScript functions that access multiple web sites to implement a cross-platform search is not a viable solution.

8   Requirements for Future Internet Applications

We have presented MyTag, a running application that accomplishes cross-application usage of user-generated content, interactions and profiles in the domain of Web2.0 content sharing applications.

Technological Innovation. We have elucidated user requirements that led us to the development of MyTag capabilities. We have seen that these user requirements lead us to traditional as well as new aspects of needed research and development:

1. Traditional aspects of semantic data integration play a major role.
2. User profiles and user interactions need to be captured and securely managed as part of the user-generated data itself in order that they are applicable across applications. Research in this direction is virtually non-existent (see an exception [4,8]).
3. better support for user's tasks rather than solely the hosting of their data.

Application Innovation. However, we must also concede that the technological innovation achieved by MyTag is far from being sufficient. Though the focus of MyTag is on giving users access to their own content, profile and interaction,

MyTag itself is still a centralized application that locks such data. It is necessary to make such data directly available at the individual peers, e.g. by applications that build heavily on Ajax to establish communication between the web browser and Internet services while enabling corresponding local data hosting. This is currently technologically feasible, but very difficult, and hence aggravates the innovation of such applications. Assuming this next, will we be done and happy ever after?

New Legislation. The clear answer must be no. In spite of the fact that some applications provide Web Service access to one's own user data, the availability of these access mechanisms is far from guaranteed. Any successful application, even if run on the users' local PC, will need reliable and legal access to a user's own data.

To achieve this, technological and application innovation need to be accompanied by new laws and regulations. Currently, users of most Web2.0 applications concede the rights of their data, as well as the rights on their profile and their user interaction data to the application host leaving the possibility for hostile legal action by the application provider.

In order to allow for variety of applications in the future, users need to have a right on accessing their own content, their own profile and their own user interaction data in a machine processable manner — useful across applications and useful for the prospering of the future internet.

Acknowledgements. This work has been partially supported by the European projects "Semiotic Dynamics in Online Social Communities" (TAGora, EU IST FP6-2005-34721; http://www.tagora-project.eu/) and by "X-Media — Large Scale Knowledge Sharing and Reuse across Media" (EU IST FP6-26978; http://www.x-media-project.org). MyTag has been jointly developed by the authors of [2].

References

1. Anadiotis, G., Franz, T., Boll, S.: W3C Multimedia Semantics Incubator Group: Tagging Use Case (2007),
   http://www.w3.org/2005/Incubator/mmsem/wiki/Tagging_Use_Case
2. Braun, M., Dellschaft, K., Franz, T., Hering, D., Jungen, P., Metzler, H., Müller, E., Rostilov, A., Saathoff, C.: Personalized Search and Exploration with MyTag. In: Proceedings of the WWW 2008 Poster Session (2008)
3. Gauch, S., Wang, G., Gomez, M.: ProFusion: Intelligent Fusion from Multiple, Distributed Search Engines. Journal of Universal Computer Science 2(9), 637–649 (1996)
4. Heckmann, D., Schwartz, T., Brandherm, B., Schmitz, M., von Wilamowitz-Moellendorff, M.: Gumo — the general user model ontology. In: Ardissono, L., Brna, P., Mitrović, A. (eds.) UM 2005. LNCS, vol. 3538, pp. 428–432. Springer, Heidelberg (2005)
5. Hotho, A., Jäschke, R., Schmitz, C., Stumme, G.: Information Retrieval in Folksonomies: Search and Ranking. In: Sure, Y., Domingue, J. (eds.) ESWC 2006. LNCS, vol. 4011, pp. 411–426. Springer, Heidelberg (2006)

6. Maurer, H., Balke, T., Kappe, F., Kulathuramaiyer, N., Weber, S., Zaka, B.: Report on dangers and opportunities posed by large search engines, particularly google (September 2007),
   http://www.iicm.tugraz.at/iicm_papers/dangers_google.pdf
7. Voorhees, E.M., Gupta, N.K., Johnson-Laird, B.: Learning collection fusion strategies. In: Proc. of SIGIR, pp. 172–179 (1995)
8. Wenning, R., Schunter, M.: The platform for privacy preferences 1.1. W3C Working Group Note 13 (November 2006)

A Framework for Selecting Trusted Semantic Web Services[*]

Stefania Galizia and Alessio Gugliotta

Knowledge Media Institute
The Open University, Walton Hall, Milton Keynes, MK7 6AA, UK
{S.Galizia,A.Gugliotta}@open.ac.uk

Abstract. Trusted semantic Web services might play a key role in the Future Internet. In this paper, we describe WSTO our comprehensive trust based framework supporting the selection and invocation of semantic Web services. Our framework combines the Web Services Modelling Ontology (WSMO) with a classification framework developed in the IBROW project. Our approach is generic enough to be able to account for a wide variety of trust models including those based on security, policy and end-user recommendations. Expanding on earlier work within this paper, we describe the model in detail.

Keywords: Semantic Web services, Trust, Classification.

1 Introduction

In our vision, the Future Internet will provide an effective and trustworthy environment where people and organizations can easily accomplish their daily tasks, by exploiting thousands of independent computing devices and services. We particularly advocate that the notion of trust will play a fundamental role in the actualization of such a vision. In fact, users accessing Internet will not know a priori most of the available services and computing devices, and thus appropriate mechanisms assuring certain level of trustworthiness in service provision have to be adopted.

Semantic Web services (SWS) technology represents a promising approach for providing users with the most appropriate services. On the basis of formal descriptions with well-defined semantics, SWS aim indeed at automating the selection, composition and mediation of available services to achieve a given goal.

In the literature, a number of approaches enhancing SWS with trusts can be found. Many of them [11, 15] adopt policies involving security statements, such as confidentiality, authorization, and authentication. W3C Web service architecture recommendations [18] also propose security statements to address trust, even though the way to disclose security policies is still not completely clear.

Some policy-based models rely on a Trusted Third Party (TTP) [21]. A TTP works as a repository of service descriptions and policies as well as an external matchmaker, which evaluates service trustworthiness according to given algorithms. Further

---

[*] This work was supported by LHDL (Living Human Digital Library) project (FP6 – 026932).

J. Domingue, D. Fensel, and P. Traverso (Eds.): FIS 2008, LNCS 5468, pp. 130–140, 2009.

models of trust are based on reputation [7, 16]; they make use of ratings coming from other agents or a central engine and based on heuristic evaluations of Quality of Service (QoS). Some of the models quoted above are very complex and elaborate, but no one is flexible enough to deal with any trust understanding. Moreover, the most common approaches for describing semantic Web services, such as WSMO [3] or OWL-S [12], do not provide exhaustive means for trust annotation.

We believe that the main issue of representing trust lies in its context-based nature – the same user may have different trust preferences in different contexts.

In this paper, we propose a general approach for managing trust in SWS, which accommodates all of the possible approaches described above. We have developed an ontology – Web Services Trust-management Ontology (WSTO) - which is able to represent trust specifications within a SWS-based interaction context. In WSTO, we characterize trust-based Web service selection as a classification problem – i.e., given a set of user and Web service trust requirements and guarantees, our goal is to identify the class of Web services that match the trust statements of involved interaction participants, according to an established classification criterion. To accomplish this, we have based WSTO on a general purpose classification library, and adopted WSMO as our reference model for describing semantic Web services. An earlier version of WSTO was described in a previous paper [5]. Whereas in [5] we outlined the idea of characterizing trust as a classification process, in the present work we propose a more complex framework, which is able to accommodate monitoring the history of Web services behavior and a reputation module.

It is worth to highlight that the main contribution of our approach lies in its generality; i.e. our model enables participants to represent their needs and guarantees with a high level of flexibility. For example, a user may trust a WS with a highly rated security certificate whenever she has to provide her credit card details. Conversely, in other environments, the opinion of other users that have already experienced an interaction with a given class of Web services is crucial. In this case, reputation evaluation is a priority in the definition of trust requirements. Moreover, different users may privilege distinct trust parameters in the same context; their priority may depend on their personal preferences. In contrast with other approaches, WSTO allows the interacting participants to model and utilize their own conception of trust – both service requester and provider are able to explicitly model their trust guarantees and requirements. This assumption enables our framework to take context into account and alleviates a number of current issues of selecting a "trusted" Web service in a dynamic environment, such as the Future Internet. In the rest of the paper, we outline the basis of our approach (Section 2), describe the classification library that we use (Section 3), and provide details of our methodology in Sections 4. Section 5 contains a comparison with related work. Finally, Section 6 concludes the paper and outlines our future work.

2 Approach Overview

The Web Service Trust-management Ontology (WSTO) is a novel approach for managing trust in semantic Web services. In our model, user preferences are the main elements on which Web service selection depends. Essentially, the user can decide which variables should be taken into consideration, in order to determine which class of Web services is trusted.

WSTO is founded on two ontologies: WSMO [3] and a classification task ontology developed within the European project IBROW [9]. WSMO defines our basic vision of Semantic Web Services and their ontological specification; the classification ontology provides the overall methodology that we have adopted for managing trust. Essentially, we embed trust-based SWS selection invocation into a classification framework.

Classification can be seen as the problem of finding the solution (class) which best explains a certain set of known facts (observables) about an unknown object, according to some criterion.

For our purposes, we classify Web services according to both the user and Web services trust requirements and guarantees. In WSTO, both user and Web service disclose their trust guarantees by means of observables, displayed as feature-value pairs. Additional guarantees concerning historical and reputation evaluations can be provided by a behaviour-monitoring engine and a reputation module, respectively. Conversely, participant trust requirements express conditions on the values that the feature can take. Given observables and conditions, a classification criterion is necessary to classify Web services and find the appropriate class that addresses both user and Web service requirements and guarantees.

The execution environment we use is IRS-III [2], a platform for developing and executing semantic Web services. IRS-III mediates between a service requester and one or more service providers. To achieve this, IRS-III adopts a semantic Web-based approach and thus it is founded on ontological descriptions. A key feature of IRS-III is that Web service invocation is capability driven. An IRS-III user simply requires a goal she wishes to achieve, and the IRS-III broker locates an appropriate Web service semantic description and then invokes the underlying deployed Web service.

Web service selection in IRS-III - up to now restricted to a capability-based model - has become trust-based thanks to WSTO. Given several Web services, semantically described in IRS-III, all with the same capability, but different trust guarantees, the class of Web services selected will be the one that matches closest with the user trust requirements.

There are reasons for using IRS-III as our execution environment. Firstly, this framework has been designed and built within our institution. Secondly, the Web Services Modelling Ontology (WSMO), our underlying SWS ontological model, has been incorporated and extended as the core IRS-III epistemological framework. Moreover, the classification library we use and extend is represented in OCML [8], the ontological representation language adopted by IRS-III.

3 A Classification Library

The classification framework that we use and extend for our work is a library of generic, reusable components whose purpose is to support the specification of classification problem solvers. The basic structure is the UPML framework [4], on which WSMO is based. The library has been specified in the OCML modelling language [8], and implemented in IRS-III [2].

Within the classification framework, we use the term 'observables' to refer to the known facts we have about the object (or event, or phenomenon) that we want to classify. Each observable is characterized as a pair of the form (f, v), where f is a feature of the unknown object and v is its value. Here, we take a very generic viewpoint on the notion of feature. By feature, we mean anything which can be used to characterize an object, such as a feature which can be directly observed, or derived by inference. As is common when characterizing classification problems - see, e.g., [19], we assume that each feature of an observable can only have one value. This assumption is only for convenience and does not restrict the scope of the model.

The solution space specifies a set of predefined classes (solutions) under which an unknown object may fall. A solution itself can be described as a finite set of feature specifications, which is a pair of the form (f, c), where f is a feature and c specifies a condition on the values that the feature can take. Thus, we can say that an observable (f, v) matches a feature specification (f, c) if v satisfies the condition c.

As we have seen, generally speaking, classification can be characterized as the problem of explaining observables in terms of pre-defined solutions. To assess the explanation power of a solution with respect to a set of observables we need to match the specification of the observables with that of a solution. Given a solution, sol: $((f_{sol1}, c_1).....(f_{solm}, c_m))$, and a set of observables, obs: $((f_{ob1}, v_1).....(f_{obn}, v_n))$, four cases are possible when trying to match them:

- A feature, say f_j, is inconsistent if $(f_j, v_j) \in obs$, $(f_j, c_j) \in sol$ and v_j does not satisfy c_j;
- A feature, say f_j, is explained if $(f_j, v_j) \in obs$, $(f_j, c_j) \in sol$ and v_j satisfies c_j;
- A feature, say f_j, is unexplained if $(f_j, v_j) \in obs$ but f_j is not a feature of sol;
- A feature, say f_j, is missing if $(f_j, c_j) \in sol$ but f_j is not a feature of obs.

Given these four cases, it is possible to envisage different solution criteria. For instance, we may accept any solution, which explains some data and is not inconsistent with any data. This criterion is called positive coverage [14]. Alternatively, we may require a complete coverage - i.e., a solution is acceptable if and only if it explains all data and is not inconsistent with any data. Thus, the specification of a particular classification task needs to include a solution (admissibility) criterion. This in turn relies on a match criterion, i.e., a way of measuring the degree of matching between candidate solutions and a set of observables. By default, our library provides a match criterion based on the aforementioned model. In short words, our analysis characterizes classification tasks in terms of the following concepts: observables, solutions, match criteria, and solution criteria. Please refer to [9] for more technical details concerning the classification library we adopt.

4 Embedding SWS Trust Management in a Classification Problem

Figure 1 summarizes how our classification framework is applied within an SWS context. We have characterized trust analysis as a classification process, within which valid solutions are those Web services that match with user requirements, given classification criteria. Candidate solutions - i.e. user requirements - are defined as pairs (feature, condition). In the example showed in Figure 1, they express conditions on QoS, data-freshness and execution-time, and reliability.

The observables are pairs (feature, value) representing Web service guarantees. The possible available guarantees associated with a WS concern data-freshness, execution-time, confidentiality, and WS reliability.

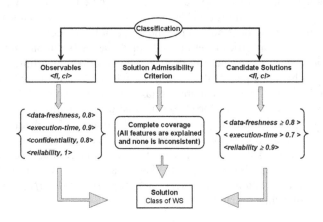

Fig. 1. Classifying Web Services

The chosen solution admissibility criterion, in this example, is *complete coverage*. Our classification goal is to identify the class of Web services that fit with users' trust requirements, given a set of WS trust guarantees. Trust for us is a binary evaluation of trustworthiness: "trust" or "distrust". Whenever conditions for trustworthiness are established, the interaction between participants occurs; otherwise not. Trust as perceived by the user u, can be either strong or weak. It is strong when is adopted complete coverage for classifying Web services. In turn, when the criterion selected is positive coverage, trust is regarded as weak.

Participant profiles. In our ontology (Figure 2), the classes *user*, *ws* and *goal* are key concepts. Both *user* and *ws* are subclasses of *participant*, where *user* denotes the service requester, *ws* is the service provider. In principle, a participant is any actor involved within the interaction. Nevertheless, we distinguish between *user* and *ws* for emphasizing the different perspectives that requester and provider have. Following the basic WSMO notions a *goal* represents the service requester's desire or intention. The *user* usually expresses different trust requirements in achieving different goals. For example, she can be interested in data accuracy when retrieving timetable information, and security issues when disclosing her bank accounts. On the other hand, the *ws* aims to provide a set of trustworthy statements, in order to reassure the requester as well as to appear as attractive as possible.

The participants are associated with trust profiles, represented in the ontology by the class *trust-participant-profile*. A profile is composed of a set of trust requirements and guarantees. *Trust-guarantees* are observables (pairs of feature and corresponding value (f, v)), while *trust-requirements* are candidate solutions (pairs of feature and condition *(f, c))*. We distinguish three logical elements in trust requirements: (i) a set of candidate solutions for expressing conditions on guarantees promised by the relevant parties; (ii) a candidate solution for requesting their reliability; and, (iii) a candidate solution for requesting their reputation evaluation. In a participant profile, the three elements are optional; choice depends strictly on the participant preferences in matter of trust. In turn, the participant trust-guarantees have three components: (i) a set of observables for representing the promised trust guarantees; (ii) an observable corresponding to the evaluation of the participant reliability; and, (iii) an observable for representing the reputation level of the participant.

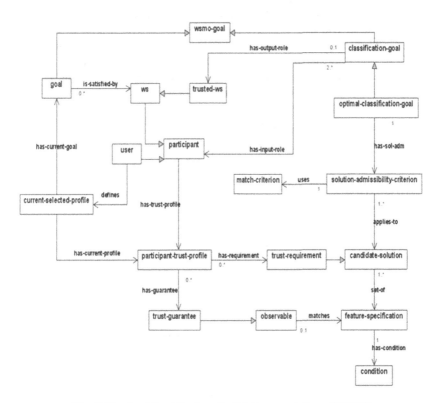

Fig. 2. Trust as Classification: Partial Representation of WSTO

The example displayed in Figure 1 does not include reputation, as optional statement; in turn, the graphical representation in Figure 2 does not show the above-described logical groups of both requirements and guaranties, for improving readability. Whereas the promised trust guarantees are a set of promised values stated by the participant - such as *(execution-time, 0.9)* and *(data-freshness, 0.8)* - reliability and reputation guarantees are computed on-the-fly within IRS-III.

As mentioned earlier, a participant profile is composed of requirements as well as guarantees. For example, a Web service may expose high *data-freshness* and strong *confidentiality* as guarantees. Moreover, the same Web service may define security requirements, such as conditions under which a service requester can access it. However, in the rest of the paper we assume that requirements are only part of the user profile, while a WS profile is composed solely by guarantees. The reason for this choice lies in the fact that we classify objects according to observables we know, and our aim is to find the class of Web services that best explains a set of guarantees - i.e. observables – according to the user requirements. This assumption simplifies the classification process, makes it user centric - since we consider only user trust requirements - and it is not restrictive. Whenever both user and Web service trust profiles are composed of guarantees and requirements, we apply the classification process twice. The second classification process verifies the user guarantees with the class of those WS considered trusted during the first classification process.

Listing 1 shows two user profiles, represented in OCML, within IRS-III - *trust-profile-USER1-A* and *trust-profile-USER1-B*. Both the profiles are associated with the user *USER1* and only her trust requirements are specified. The class *requirement-USER1-A* concerns security needs, in particular, the encryption algorithms used by the WS and the certification authority, which issued the WS security certificate.

```
(def-class trust-profile-USER1-A (trust-profile)
  ((has-trust-guarantee :type guarantee-USER1-A)
   (has-trust-requirement :type requirement-USER1-A)))

(def-class trust-profile-USER1-B (trust-profile)
  ((has-trust-guarantee :type guarantee-USER1-B)
   (has-trust-requirement :type requirement-USER1-B)))

(def-class requirement-USER1-A (trust-requirement) ?req
  ((encryption-algorithm :type algorithm)
   (certification-authority :type ca)
   :iff-def (and (exists ?x (encryption-algorithm ?req ?x)
                    (> ?x 0.9))
                 (exists ?x (certification-authority ?req ?x)
                    (> ?x 0.8)))))

(def-class requirement-USER1-B (trust-requirement)
  ((datafreshness :value high)
   (execution-time :value low)
   (reputation :value high)))
```

Listing 1. User Profiles

The class *requirement-USER1-B* expresses the user needs around general WS performance and WS reputation. Note that whereas the former requirement class expresses conditions through real normalized values, the latter performs qualitative constraints. Representing user requirements in a qualitative way facilitates end-user comprehension. In IRS-III, implemented heuristics act as translators from a quantitative to a qualitative representation. The user can adopt the heuristics, or define new ones, sharing her expertise and knowledge with other users. Optionally, she can express her requirements in a precise, quantitative way, by specifying the exact values expected from Web service guarantees.

Profile Selection. The diagram in Figure 2 shows that, as participants, both WS and user have a trust profile. However, whereas a WS discloses, at design time, only one profile, the user publishes in IRS-III one or more profiles, which may be adapted from previously published profiles. Indeed, a user can associate distinct profiles to different goals by defining multiple definitions of *current-selected-profile*. This choice allows our model to include context.

Classification criteria. The classification match criterion we apply is the one described in Section 3, although other classification criteria can be represented in WSTO. As solution admissibility criteria, we can apply *complete coverage* and *positive coverage*. The former demands that all requirements of the interaction have to be satisfied; the latter accepts that some requirements are fulfilled and no inconsistencies exist. Our classification library implements two different classification methods: *single-solution-classification,* and *optimal-classification*. The former implements a hill climbing algorithm with backtracking to find a suitable solution, the latter executes an exhaustive search for an optimal solution. In turn, the two classification tasks implemented in IRS-III are: *optimal-classification-task* and *single-solution-classification-task*, respectively solved by the two methods described above, according to the UPML framework [4].

We make use of the optimal-classification-task and redefine it as WSMO goal[1], *optimal-classification-goal* (see Figure 2), whose *participant-profiles* and *trusted-ws* represent the pre-conditions and post-conditions of the goal, respectively.

5 Related Work

There is a growing corpus of literature on trust, and different approaches focus on how trust assumptions are made and enforced. A number of current approaches model social aspects of trust [6], while some recent efforts in the last few years concern service-oriented views of trust [1]. However, few approaches provide methodologies for managing trust in a SWS context, and none comprehensively incorporate all possible approaches of trust (policy, reputation TTP), as we do in WSTO.

The work proposed by Vu and his research group [16, 17], who use WSMX [20] as an execution environment, is closely related to the work reported here. Vu et al. [16, 17] propose a methodology for enabling a QoS-based SWS discovery and selection, with the application of a trust and reputation management method. Their approach yields high-quality results, even under behaviour which involves cheating. With respect to their work, the methodology we propose is less accurate in terms of service behaviour prediction. However, their algorithm is wholly founded on reputation mechanisms, and is therefore not suitable for managing policy-based trust assumptions. Currently, policy-based trust mainly considers access control decisions via digital credentials. Our framework, by enabling participants to declare general ontological statements for guarantees and requirements, is also able to accommodate a policy-based trust framework.

Olmedilla et al. [11] propose a methodology for trust negotiation in SWS. They employ PeerTrust [10], a policy and trust negotiation language, for establishing if

---

[1] WSMO goals can be seen as an evolution of UPML tasks.

trust exists between a service requester and provider. The main issue that distinguishes their methodology from ours is that they assume that trust is solely based on policy. They do not propose any mechanism for managing reputation or monitoring past service behaviour, as we do. Similar to our approach, though, they use WSMO as the underlying epistemology. Moreover, they assume delegation to a centralized trust matchmaker, where the participants disclose policies. Similarly, in our approach, we assume that IRS-III plays the role of trust matchmaker. Furthermore, they also address negotiation, which is an important issue in SWS interaction. We do not propose a formal negotiation mechanism here, but, as both requester and provider disclose their guarantees, as credentials within IRS-III, we are able to automatically enable an implicit negotiation process.

There are other approaches for managing trust in SWS that are less closely related to ours, such as KAoS [15]. Within KAoS a set of platform-independent services which enable the definition of policies ensuring the adequate predictability and controllability of both agents and traditional distributed systems is proposed. Even though they present a dynamic framework, and recognize trust management as a challenge for policy management, the framework is not specifically tailored to trust management in an SWS context.

6   Conclusions and Future Work

In this paper, we have presented a framework for managing trust in SWS and have envisaged Web service selection and invocation as a classification problem, where the solution takes the form of a class of Web services matching participating trust profiles. Embodied within the trust profiles are the participant priorities with respect to trust, which can be related to reputation, credentials, or actual monitored behavior. Our conception of trust is described through a binary measure: whenever participant trust profiles match, a trusted interaction can occur, otherwise trusted interaction is deemed to not be feasible.

Trust has different meanings within different contexts: trust can be based on service ability or on reliability. In other contexts, trust can be related to reputation or delegated to TTP evaluations. The main contribution of our approach is to provide a framework that enables a comprehensive range of trust models to be captured.

In order to showcase the benefits of our approach we have deployed two prototypes available at public URLs: http://lhdl.open.ac.uk:8080/trusted-travel/untrusted-query and http://lhdl.open.ac.uk:8080/trusted-travel/trusted-query. The former implements a virtual travel agent based on the standard IRS-III goal invocation method. The latter introduces a trusted goal invocation, according to our trust framework, and taking into account three different user profiles.

Future work will extend our implementation to incorporate a comprehensive management suite for WS reputation and reliability. Additionally, we also plan to import a range of sophisticated reputation algorithms, and to improve the monitoring component.

References

1. Anderson, S., et al.: Web Services Trust Language (WS-Trust), version 1.1 (May 2004), http://msdn.microsoft.com/ws/2004/04/ws-trust/
2. Cabral, L., Domingue, J., Galizia, S., Gugliotta, A., Norton, B., Tanasescu, V., Pedrinaci, C.: IRS-III: A Broker for Semantic Web Services based Applications. In: Cruz, I., Decker, S., Allemang, D., Preist, C., Schwabe, D., Mika, P., Uschold, M., Aroyo, L.M. (eds.) ISWC 2006. LNCS, vol. 4273, pp. 201–214. Springer, Heidelberg (2006)
3. Fensel, D., Lausen, H., Polleres, A., De Bruijn, J., Stollberg, M., Roman, D., Domingue, J.: Enabling Semantic Web Services: Web Service Modeling Ontology. Springer, Heidelberg (2006)
4. Fensel, D., Motta, E., Benjamins, V.R., Decker, S., Gaspari, M., Groenboom, R., Grosso, W., Musen, M., Plaza, E., Schreiber, G., Studer, R., Wielinga, B.: The Unified Problem-solving Method Development Language UPML. IBROW3 Project (IST-1999-19005) Deliverable 1.1 (1999)
5. Galizia, S.: WSTO: A Classification-Based Ontology for Managing Trust in Semantic Web Services. In: Sure, Y., Domingue, J. (eds.) ESWC 2006. LNCS, vol. 4011, pp. 697–711. Springer, Heidelberg (2006)
6. Golbeck, J., Hendler, J.: Inferring trust relationships in web-based social networks. ACM Transactions on Internet Technology (2006)
7. Maximilien, E.M., Singh, M.P.: Toward Autonomic Web Services Trust and Selection. In: Proceedings of 2nd International Conference on Service Oriented Computing (ICSOC 2004), New York (November 2004)
8. Motta, E.: Reusable Components for Knowledge Models: Principles and Case Studies in Parametric Design Problem Solving. IOS Press, Amsterdam (1999)
9. Motta, E., Lu, W.: A Library of Components for Classification Problem Solving. In: Proceedings of PKAW 2000 - The 2000 Pacific Rim Knowledge Acquisition, Workshop, Sydney, Australia, December 11-13 (2000)
10. Nejdl, W., Olmedilla, D., Winslett, M.: PeerTrust: Automated Trust Negotiation for Peers on the Semantic Web. In: Jonker, W., Petković, M. (eds.) SDM 2004. LNCS, vol. 3178, pp. 118–132. Springer, Heidelberg (2004)
11. Olmedilla, D., Lara, R., Polleres, A., Lausen, H.: Trust Negotiation for Semantic Web Services. In: Cardoso, J., Sheth, A.P. (eds.) SWSWPC 2004. LNCS, vol. 3387, pp. 81–95. Springer, Heidelberg (2005)
12. OWL-S working group. OWL-S: Semantic Markup for Web Services. OWL-S 1.2 Pre-Release (2006), http://www.ai.sri.com/daml/services/owl-s/1.2/
13. Sierra, C., Debenham, J.K.: An Information-Based model for Trust. In: proceedings Fourth International Conference on Autonomous Agents and Multi Agent Systems AAMAS 2005, Utrecht, Netherlands, July 25-29, p. 497–504 (2005)
14. Stefik, M.: Introduction to Knowledge Systems. Morgan Kaufmann, San Francisco (1995)
15. Uszok, A., Bradshaw, J.M., Johnson, M., Jeffers, R., Tate, A., Dalton, J., Aitken, J.S.: KAoS Policy Management for Semantic Web Services. IEEE Intelligent Systems 19(4), 32–41 (2004)
16. Vu, L.H., Hauswirth, M., Aberer, K.: QoS-based Service Selection and Ranking with Trust and Reputation Management. In: Meersman, R., Tari, Z. (eds.) OTM 2005. LNCS, vol. 3760, pp. 466–483. Springer, Heidelberg (2005)
17. Vu, L.H., Hauswirth, M., Porto, F., Aberer, K.: A Search Engine for QoS-enabled Discovery of Semantic Web Services. International Journal of Business Process Integration and Management, IJBPIM (2006)

18. W3C. Web Services Architecture. W3C Working Draft 11 (February 2004),
    http://www.w3.org/TR/ws-arch/
19. Wielinga, B.J., Akkermans, J.K., Schreiber, G.: A Competence Theory Approach to Problem Solving Method Construction. International Journal of Human-Computer Studies 49, 315–338 (1998)
20. WSMX working group. Overview and Scope of WSMX (2005),
    http://www.wsmo.org/TR/d13/d13.0/v0.2/
21. Zhengping, W., Weaver, A.C.: Using Web Service Enhancements to Bridge Business Trust Relationships. In: Fourth International Conference on Privacy, Security, and Trust (PST 2006), University of Toronto, Institute of Technology, Markham, Ontario, Canada, October 30-November 1 (2006)

Future Internet Collaboration Workflow

Darko Anicic and Nenad Stojanovic

FZI Forschungszentrum Informatik, Karlsruhe, Germany
`name.surname@fzi.de`

Abstract. The Future Internet predicts more and more networked devices on the Internet. These devices interact, exchange knowledge, and
cooperate in a dynamic environment, changing their states. Each state
change may be signified by an event. In scenarios, where a number of
devices collaborate on a common goal, it is a challenge to capture relevant complex changes, and abstract them in particular collaboration
situations. Further on, it is even more challenging to put those changes
in a relevant context, and to reason about collaboration situations before
adequately reacting on events (changes). We present a novel event-driven
reactivity model for Future Internet collaborations. We implement a flexible collaborative workflow in a declarative way, solving before mentioned
challenges. Particularly, Concurrent Transaction Logic is used for specification, reasoning, and execution of ad-hoc collaborative workflows.

1 Introduction

One of main goals of the Future Internet is to "dynamically support the operations of businesses organisations and the everyday life of citizens in a seamless
and natural fashion" [1]. It would require the transition from a passive system in
which users initiate activities (as Internet is today), to an active environment in
which associated software agents find, organize and display information/services
on behalf of users. The Future Internet predicts more and more devices and sensors
connected to the Internet. All of them will be capable to send and/or to receive
messages or signals. If these signals are seen as events, we need novel Complex
Event Processing (CEP) techniques which will enable detection of "interesting"
situations from those events. In the nutshell of this process is the ability of a Future Internet system (i.e., an agent or a service) to sense, reason, and respond on
billions of signals[1] coming from different sources in different forms.

Further on, the interaction between agents (or services) cannot be fully structured and planned. More realistic are networked services with *an ad-hoc interaction*, where events offer means to realise an unstructured collaboration activities.
In this paper we talk about a *collaboration* on the Internet which is not completely prespecified as in a classical workflow. Instead we need a more dynamic
collaborative workflow. While a workflow is a collection of cooperating, coordinated activities designed to carry out well-defined complex processes, a collaborative workflow is to focus on working together (i.e., more than one participant)

---

[1] Gartner: Large companies experience 0.1M - 10G business events per second.

J. Domingue, D. Fensel, and P. Traverso (Eds.): FIS 2008, LNCS 5468, pp. 141–151, 2009.

towards common goals. They can be small group of companies, project-oriented research teams, to widely dispersed industries with common interests. Effective use of collaborative workflow is now considered a vital element in the success of enterprises of all kinds. Workflow can be represented by a sequence diagram, a collaboration diagram, a Petri net or an activity diagram. Collaborative workflow is a new type of workflow that allows an organisation or enterprise to be added to the existing workflow model. Therefore collaborative workflow exceeds the boundaries of a single organization, and deals with business processes across organisations. Moreover it acts as a workflow broker between separate workflows of participating organisations. With these properties, collaborative workflow may be used in a virtual organisation (VO) which purpose is to establish cooperation between organisations working on a shared process (goal). More broadly, collaborative workflows will be used for any kind of collaboration on Internet which need to automatically respond on certain events, activities and their changes.

We believe that a novel conceptualization of process management is needed to overcome the limitation of conventional approaches in workflow management systems (WFMS). In a business process context, an exact execution order of activities may be impractical, while the interaction or relationship between the environment and activities is more reliable in determining how to orchestrate tasks; i.e., the question of which task to execute and when to execute it is dependent on the current environment and underlying business logic rather than a static process schema. From this point of view, the rule/knowledge-based approach improves upon the traditional workflow approach by supplying real-time reaction to certain events that occur. Our method tries to go further by incorporating events into a *context* that watches over the environment, and exercises timely decision-based control of the execution of business processes. Our approach is used to manage complex business activities based on *situational awareness* and real-time decisions. In a cognitive system, the relationship of the system to its environment is of vital importance, while, in a business process context, information about the process environment (such as events and the state of activities and resources) is collected as perception-based knowledge; business logic concerning process routing, operational constraints, exception handling and business strategies is used to make decisions about tasks based on situation awareness. By extending process management from process logic to business logic, the approach offers more flexibility, agility and adaptability in complex process management.

Our longer-term goal is to realize an approach for the ad-hoc collaborative workflow management which will support the service collaboration in the Future Internet, sketched in Figure 1. The figure depicts cooperation between a collaborative workflow (in the center) and internal workflows from other participants. On the other side, it assumes a workflow triggered by events which are sent by contributing partners (represented by dashed arrows). Events represent not just atomic changes but also more complex situations. They are processed in certain contexts enabling automated *reasoning* before undertaking any action in the workflow.

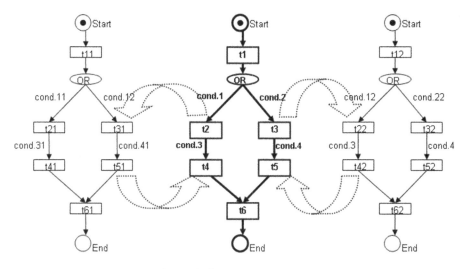

Fig. 1. Collaborative Workflows

The paper is organised as follows: In the second section we briefly overview Concurrent Transaction Logic ($\mathcal{CTR}$), as a logic which provides a unified framework for specifying collaborative workflows, reasoning about their properties, and workflow execution. Further, the logic can be used for modeling complex events, contexts, and situations, as well as for implementation of reactive rules. Third section explains the role of complex event processing (CEP) and reactive rules in collaboration on Internet. Their implementation with $\mathcal{CTR}$ is also provided. Forth section presents our Internet Collaborative Workflow in more details. Fifth section discusses related work, while the final section gives the main conclusion and future work.

2   CTR Overview

Concurrent Transaction Logic ($\mathcal{CTR}$) [2] is a general logic designed specifically for the rule-based paradigm, and intended to provide a declarative account for state-changing actions. A model and proof theory of $\mathcal{CTR}$ has been defined in [2]. It is an extension of Transaction Logic ($\mathcal{TR}$) [3], with its "Horn" fragment defined. In this section we will informally introduced syntax and semantics of $\mathcal{CTR}$. For further considerations related to the semantics of $\mathcal{TR}$ the reader is referred to [3].

Syntax. The atomic formulas of $\mathcal{CTR}$ has the form $p(t_1, ..., t_n)$, where p is a predicate symbol and the t_i's are function terms. More complex formulas are built using connectives and quantifiers.

The same as in classical logic, $\mathcal{CTR}$ has $\wedge, \vee, \neg, \forall$, and $\exists$. Unlike in classical logic, $\mathcal{CTR}$ has two connectives, $\otimes$ (serial conjunction) and $|$ (concurrent conjunction); modal operators, $\diamond$ (executional possibility), $\square$ (executional necessity) and $\odot$ (isolated execution).

Informal Semantics. In short, it is a logic for state-changing actions. The truth of $\mathcal{CTR}$ formulas is determined over *paths*. A path is a finite sequence of states. If a formula, ψ, is true over a path $< s_1, ..., s_n >$ it means that ψ can be executed[2]e s_1. During the execution, ψ will change the current state to $s_2, s_3, ...$ and finally terminate at the state s_n. With this in mind, the intended semantics of $\mathcal{CTR}$ connectives and modal operators can be summarised as follows:

- $\phi \otimes \psi$ means: execute ϕ, then execute ψ;
- $\phi \mid \psi$ means: execute ϕ and ψ concurrently;
- $\phi \wedge \psi$ means: ϕ and ψ must both be executed along the same path;
- $\phi \vee \psi$ means: execute ϕ or ψ nondeterministically;
- $\neg \phi$ means: execute in any way, provided that this will not be a valid execution of ϕ;
- $\odot \phi$ means: execute ϕ in isolation of other possible concurrently running activities;
- $\diamond \phi$ means: check whether it is possible to execute ϕ at the current state;
- $\square \phi$ means: check necessity to execute ϕ at the current state.

The logic has notions of *data* and *transition* oracles. The *data* oracle, $\mathcal{O}^d(\mathbf{D})$, is used to solve queries on a particular state $\mathbf{D}$. Likewise, the *transition* oracle, $\mathcal{O}^t(\mathbf{D}_1, \mathbf{D}_2)$, is used to specify an update (transition). For example, if $a \in \mathcal{O}^t(\mathbf{D}_1, \mathbf{D}_2)$, then a is an elementary update that changes state $\mathbf{D}_1$ into state $\mathbf{D}_2$. The transition oracle can be defined to insert and delete Horn rules from $\mathbf{D}$. For further details about $\mathcal{CTR}$ semantics, its "Horn" fragment, workflows analysing with CTR, the reader is referred to [2] [3] [4], and to [5] for an extended proof theory involving classical conjunction.

For instance, the formula below represents the collaborative workflow from Figure 1 (the middle workflow):

$$start \otimes t_1 \otimes ((cond_1 \otimes t_2 \otimes cond_3 \otimes t_4) \vee (cond_2 \otimes t_3 \otimes cond_4 \otimes t_5)) \otimes t_6 \otimes end$$

where every task t_i may further be defined as a subworkflow.

3   Event Processing and Reactive Rules

Event-driven architecture (EDA) represents a new hype in enterprise information systems, that complements the service-oriented architecture. Event-driven applications trigger actions as a response to the detection of events. The *event* signify a problem or an impending problem, an opportunity, a threshold, or a deviation.

The Future Internet predicts more and more devices and sensors connected to the Internet. All of them will be capable to send and/or to receive messages or signals (containing data). If these signals are seen as events, Complex Event Processing (CEP) techniques provide an approach to handle those events. CEP is focused on detection of complex event patterns from atomic events. Signals

---

[2] $\mathcal{TR}$, and hence $\mathcal{CTR}$, have a notion of *executional entailment*, i.e., a logical account of transaction formulas execution [3].

may be seen as atomic events. To create more meaningful pieces of data (knowledge) from signals it is necessary to put them in a certain *context*. This gives us a possibility to detect more interesting *situation*, to *reason* about them, and finally to *react* on them adequately (e.g., to monitor market prices and react on significant changes).

In our use case scenario (Section 4.1) a number of sensors is used to detect a spill in a chemical factory. They are measuring what chemicals have escaped as well as the severity of the exposure, location etc. Signals emitted by those sensors are combined to form more complex events (using CEP techniques). Complex events are further utilised to trigger a collaborative workflow, and hence provide an automated information system capable to detect, reason, and react on certain changes. Using $\mathcal{CTR}$ we can realise such a system. Particularly in this section, we focus on a capability of $\mathcal{CTR}$ to detect changes (events) and react on them.

Each task, $t(x)$, in a collaborative workflow may be accompanied with two events $t\_start(x)$ and $t\_done(x)$, giving us a possibility to react just before and after $t(x)$. This is accomplished by replacing $t(x)$ with the following formula:

$$t\_start(x) \otimes t(x) \otimes t\_done(x)$$

The same applies for conditions[3], or any other formula, which might change during the collaboration:

$$cond\_start(x) \otimes cond(x) \otimes cond\_done(x)$$

In this way, we enable the collaborative workflow to react on events, i.e., relevant changes. Events are further associated with active rules, which accomplish certain actions as reactions on events. For instance, every time before executing a task, $t(x)$, we want to execute a set of actions $a_1(x), ..., a_n(x)$[4]:

$$t\_start(x) \leftarrow a_1(x) \otimes ... \otimes a_n(x)$$

where each action a_i is defined as an active rule:

$$a_i \leftarrow \text{if } condition \text{ then } action$$

Each event (e.g., $t\_start(x), t\_done(x)$) may be modeled as a complex event [6]. In the context of collaborative workflows, it is not sufficient to respond only to an event, but also to more complex situations. We model these situation via complex events being put within certain contexts. For instance, a task $t(x)$ in a collaborative workflow needs to happen after being approved from a collaboration party A, followed by approval from another party B. These two approvals may be seen as two atomic events (e.g., $eventA$, and $eventB$) which constitute a complex event (e.g., $eventC$). $eventC$ in the context of the task t constitutes a situation s_1 which needs to be handled in a different way from, for instance, situation s_2 which represent the same event in the context of another task (e.g., $t^1(x)$.

---

[3] A condition is assumed to be a Horn rule from **D**.
[4] Different orders of action executions are possible.

If we use the same notation as in [4], i.e., $\nabla\phi \equiv path \otimes e \otimes path$ denoting an event e which must happen on an execution path of the workflow, we can demonstrate $\mathcal{CTR}$ capabilities for complex event modeling. For instance, in the previous example the complex event $eventC$ would be modeled as $\nabla eventA \otimes \nabla eventB$. If we wanted to ensure both events to happen, no matter in which order, we would write $\nabla eventA \wedge \nabla eventB$. Another example, $\nabla \odot (eventA \otimes eventB)$ is a complex event which is detected if $eventB$ occurs right after $eventA$ with no event in-between etc.

4   Event-Triggered Reactive Workflow

A *workflow* is a collection of cooperating, coordinated activities designed to carry out *well-defined* complex processes. A classical workflow is well-defined in a sense that it is described using a particular process specification formalism (e.g., Petri-nets, state charts, process algebras, UML diagrams etc.). However, in order to use a workflow collaboratively in a VO, we need a more flexible workflow.

An *ad-hoc collaborative workflow* is a more flexible workflow which has ability to change its initial specification (e.g., according to collaboration partners' review decisions etc.). The collaboration process, such as an order or an instruction, is assigned to multiple collaboration partners for review and approval (at run time). Partners can be assigned for these tasks in a specified or unspecified order. Partners further, depending on various constraints (e.g., their own knowledge or interest), may change the flow of the current execution. Ad-hoc workflows are more flexible and user-oriented. Therefore they may be applied to more realistic situations in Business Process Management.

An ad-hoc collaborative workflow in a VO may be seen as a formal specification of the best practices w.r.t a particular collaboration processes. Each such a workflow defines collaboration procedure in an appropriate collaboration context. In our framework we follow a logic-based approach for the workflow specification [4]. More precisely, $\mathcal{CTR}$ (Section 2) has been chosen as a formalism for implementation of ad-hoc collaborative workflows. Our decision is driven by a number of arguments. First, $\mathcal{CTR}$ is an appropriate and unified formalism for specifying, analysing and executing workflows [4]. Second, $\mathcal{CTR}$ can represent control flow graphs with corresponding transition conditions. Third, $\mathcal{CTR}$ can be used for detecting events and specification of active rules (e.g., ECA rules). Forth, $\mathcal{CTR}$ has a number of temporal capabilities. Fifth, a logic based formalism, such as $\mathcal{CTR}$, allows for reasoning about workflow properties. Additionally it handles three important problems in workflow management: consistency (determine whether the given workflow is consistent w.r.t a given set of constraints), verification (e.g., check whether every legal execution of the given workflow specification satisfies a particular constrain) and scheduling (e.g., find a possible execution schedule such that the given workflow specification and a given set of constraints are satisfied).

A very important feature of $\mathcal{TR}$, and hence $\mathcal{CTR}$ too, is the ability to allow configuration of transition oracle such that insertion and deletion of Horn rules from $\mathbf{D}$ is also possible. This feature essentially allows manipulation with database rules in the same way as with database facts. We utilise this $\mathcal{TR}$ property to create more dynamic workflows. More precisely we implement a workflow which is capable to send and receive an event and thus to dynamically change conditions in the workflow. By dynamic change of conditions, we effectively may change the run-time workflow execution. Events, received by the workflow, come from the collaboration partners who have the permission to influence the current process execution. On the other side, our collaborative workflow may also send an event. This happens whenever the workflow cannot proceed with the ongoing execution due to some unfulfilled condition. In order to resolve the "obstacle" (e.g., approval from a collaboration partner, a piece of knowledge missing in the current collaboration etc.) the workflow *sends an event* through the collaboration network and receives a response (see Figure 1). Moreover an event may carry (database) *rules* in its body. For instance, if the head of a rule (carried by an event) is $cond_1$ its purpose is to dynamically change the initial definition of that condition. This means that if the event t_1_done (happened just after the task, t_1, has been completed) "hits" the workflow and carries new definitions of $cond_1$ and $cond_2$, then these new rules will be valid definitions for those conditions. New rules replace old ones from the state in which the event happened, and will be valid until another such a change occurs. When the new rule and the database (i.e., the current state of the running workflow) conflict each other, algorithms of reasonable complexity proposed in [7] can be used to solve this problem.

In conclusion, if a collaboration partner decides to change certain conditions, as a part of the approval or review process, he needs to send an event containing one or more new rules. $\mathcal{CTR}$ features capability to delete (e.g., del.$cond_1$ $\otimes$ del.$cond_2$) and insert (e.g., ins.$cond_1$ $\otimes$ ins.$cond_2$) a database rule. Hence once an event (which the workflow is "waiting" for) occurs the old rule will be deleted and the new one will be inserted.

4.1   Case Study

The focus of this use case is to inform and direct first responders and people at risk in case of an incident. Let us assume that there is a major spill in a large chemical factory; sensors at the factory and in the surrounding areas are measuring what chemicals have escaped as well as the severity of the exposure. These measures are organized in a workflow process WF 1 (Figure 2, ad-hoc collaborative workflows[5]) at a location Loc 1 (i.e., location of the chemical factory). Further on, as a part of WF 1, there exist a CEP unit which gets data from the individual sensors and detect a spill situation. If sensors detect a dangerous situation an event will be sent to the center for natural disasters (location Loc 4) where the main workflow will be triggered. The main workflow calculates a plume model, generates possible evacuation plan, and observes the contextual information (in order to detect significant changes in the given situation).

---

[5] Ordinary activities are represented by rectangles, while activities which include sending and/or receiving events are represented by ovals.

In order to calculate the plume model accurately weather information is also needed. This is precisely a role of workflow WF 2 (at location Loc 2), e.g., the wind speed and the wind direction at various surrounding locations is important input for the plume model. The plume model calculates (central workflow, Figure 2) the current exposure depending on events from WF 1 and WF 2 and predicts its development over time.

In parallel to that process, there is a process which generates an evacuation plan (based on the traffic events from WF 3, at location Loc 3). This plan will be used to direct first responders (infoFR, Figure 2), i.e., tell them what happened, where they have to go, what exposure they have to expect and what they are supposed to do. For instance, the plan can be used for evacuating people, directing traffic to speed up the evacuation, transportation of injured people etc. The information is also used to direct people sending them personal messages (sendMsg, Figure 2). Instead of a general evacuation, people will be given precise directives based on their current locations. The intention of this directed notification is to reduce or even to prevent grid lock and to make sure that people do not increase their exposure to dangerous chemicals by evacuating in the wrong direction. Enhanced GPS technology could possible improve directed notifications as each GPS enabled device could be event sources. Additionally the workflow listens to the spill event source during the entire execution. If events signify a change of the current situation or contextual information, the workflow may be restarted.

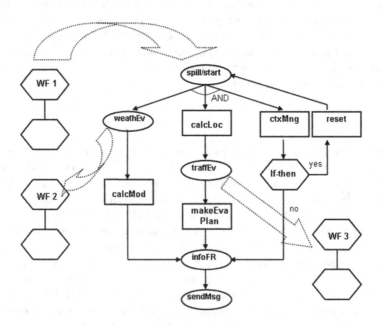

Fig. 2. Ad-Hoc Collaborative Workflows

Let us demonstrate how the main collaborative workflow from Figure 2 can be represented in $\mathcal{CTR}$:

$$spill \leftarrow ((weathEv \otimes calcMod)|(calcLoc \otimes traffEv$$
$$\otimes makeEvaPlan)|(ctxMng \otimes ifThen)) \otimes infoFR \otimes sendMsg \qquad (1)$$

$$weathEv \leftarrow sendWeathEv \otimes getWeathEv \qquad (2)$$

$$ifThen \leftarrow (\diamond ctxChange) \otimes reset \otimes spill \qquad (3)$$

$$ifThen \leftarrow (\Box \neg ctxChange) \qquad (4)$$

Every activity may further be defined as a subworkflow executing other subtasks. For instance, $weathEv$ (rule 2) sends an event to initiate an instance of WF 2, and receives weather information (when WF 2 finishes its execution)[6].

The challenge of this scenario is that there are many components organized in workflows at different location which need to collaborate. They have to work together even though new components are added, some components disappear and existing components change their properties such as availability, location and readiness. The system has to adapt automatically to any change in the number or properties of the components; e.g., if a new sensor is added the plume model should become automatically more precise, as there is an additional event source; if a new police unit is added it will be automatically acknowledged and utilised when searching for the best team to respond to an incident. For this purpose CEP combined with semantics (Section 3) ensures an intelligent event-driven collaboration. Further on, in such a changing environment a number of properties and conditions are changing during the model computation. Therefore we need adaptive and very dynamic workflows where an existing condition may be replaced by another one. For instance, our ad-hoc collaborative workflow is started when an instance of event e_1 occurs. Now imagine a spill happened but conditions are different, e.g., severity of the chemical exposure is not sufficient enough such that the CEP unit in WF 1 triggers e_1. On the other side, the spilled chemical is more dangerous, and in this situation WF 1 triggers an event e_3. To start the plume model workflow, WF 1 now must send an event which also carries a new formula, as a new constraint definition. Therefore the purpose of this event is not just notification: "something has happened", but also a change which needs to take place in the definition of collaborative workflow. This feature is possible to realise, first, due to the fact that declarative programming offers a high, abstract, way to specify workflows. Second, particularly $\mathcal{CTR}$ allows manipulation (e.g., insert, delete and update) of (database) rules in the same way as with database facts.

In general case, changing workflow definitions on the fly may be very useful in dynamic environments such as collaborative workflows. It is not feasible

---

[6] Note that due to simplicity and readability reasons, here, we deal only with propositions. However predicates with function terms may be used without any restrictions. Also note that arrows in Figure 2 do not necessarily represent the direction of events flows. In case of $weathEv$ and $traffEv$, the event communication is bidirectional, while in case of $spill$ event it is one way event flow.

to explicitly specify all collaboration procedures between all partners (as the knowledge base changes during the collaboration). Change of workflow definitions on the fly enables processing of events "not known" to each collaboration party a priori. Instead, our framework can handle events "known" only to one party, which can propagate the "relevant knowledge" further (by sending a $\mathcal{CTR}$ formula to other collaboration parties).

5   Related Work

This section briefly overview current approaches in realizing some aspects related to our work on reactivity-model for Future Internet collaborations. In [8] a Public-To-Private approach is proposed to inter-organizational workflows based on P2P networks. Though it is a comprehensive framework, it clearly misses logic and the reasoning capabilities, as a control mechanism in the inter-organizational workflow realisation. [9] implements the middleware between partners in a VO as web services to provide dynamic and flexible integration between them. There is a semantic model defined for this approach, which has notions of states, state transitions, synchronisation between activities etc. However to the best of our knowledge, the model does not support reactive rules with integrated CEP. [10] is another approach towards realisation of inter-organizational workflow cooperation. The cooperation is based on view concept providing flexibility for participating organizations in terms of the workflow part which is visible to the others. The behavioural aspects of workflow cooperations are based on Petri nets. We believe that our approach based on $\mathcal{CTR}$ provides a simpler and uniform way to describe and reason about collaborative workflows. Finally a cognitive approach in [11] is proposed to manage complex business activities, based on continuous awareness of situations and real-time decisions on activities. The approach also deals with issues of capturing events and changing states of tasks and resources in the business activities execution. The framework, although based on rules and Java Expert System Shell (JESS), cannot handle changes in the definition of workflow on the fly.

6   Conclusion and Future Work

In this paper we proposed a novel reactivity-model for Future Internet collaborations. We explained the role of complex event processing in the future Internet applications, where all devices are networked and capable to send and/or receive events. Semantics play an important aspect in our model, as it enables contextualised event processing. Moreover semantics offers a reasoning service (as a control mechanism) which is performed before undertaking any reaction on events. The reactivity-model is specially suited for collaborative work distributed over Internet (e.g., for Virtual Organisations).

Our work can be extended to handle even more flexible collaborative workflows. Although $\mathcal{CTR}$ offers a powerfull mechanism for specifying dynamic workflows, currently the logic cannot support on the fly update of transaction rules (in the same way as database rules). Transaction rules are crucial components for creation of control flow graphs. Being able to update transaction rules in an ad-hoc manner (i.e., by means of events) would allow us to create truly ad-hoc collaborative workflows. Therefore our future work will be heading toward a $\mathcal{CTR}$ extension in order to accommodate features such as insertion and deletion of transaction rules.

Acknowledgements

This work was supported by European Commission funded projects SYNERGY (FP7-216089), and SAKE (FP6-027128).

References

[1] The future internet: A services and software perspective. Draft reviewed by a working group in Bled (2008)

[2] Bonner, A.J., Kifer, M.: Concurrency and communication in transaction logic. In: Joint International Conference and Symposium on Logic Programming. MIT Press, Cambridge (1996)

[3] Bonner, A.J., Kifer, M.: Transaction logic programming (or, a logic of procedural and declarative knowledge. Technical Report CSRI-270 (1995)

[4] Davulcu, H., Kifer, M., Ramakrishnan, C.R., Ramakrishnan, I.V.: Logic based modeling and analysis of workflows, pp. 25–33 (1998)

[5] Roman, D., Kifer, M.: Reasoning about the behavior of semantic web services with concurrent transaction logic. In: VLDB 2007: Proceedings of the 33rd international conference on Very large data bases. VLDB Endowment (2007)

[6] Anicic, D., Stojanovic, N.: Towards creation of logical framework for event-driven information systems. In: 10th International Conference on Enterprise Information Systems (2008)

[7] Grahne, G., Mendelzon, A.O.: Updates and subjunctive queries. In: Nonstandard queries and nonstandard answers: studies in logic and computation. Oxford University Press, Oxford (1994)

[8] van der Aalst, W.M.P., Weske, M.: The p2p approach to interorganizational workflows. In: Dittrich, K.R., Geppert, A., Norrie, M.C. (eds.) CAiSE 2001. LNCS, vol. 2068, p. 140. Springer, Heidelberg (2001)

[9] Perrin, O., Godart, C.: A model to support collaborative work in virtual enterprises. Data Knowl. Eng. (2004)

[10] Chebbi, I., Dustdar, S., Tata, S.: The view-based approach to dynamic interorganizational workflow cooperation. Data Knowl. Eng. (2006)

[11] Wang, M., Wang, H.: From process logic to business logic: a cognitive approach to business process management. Inf. Manage. (2006)

Towards an Ontological Foundation for Services Science

Roberta Ferrario and Nicola Guarino

ISTC-CNR, Laboratory for Applied Ontology
Via alla Cascata 56C, 38100 Trento
{ferrario,guarino}@loa-cnr.it

Abstract. Most of the efforts conducted on services nowadays are focusing on aspects related to data and control flow, often disregarding the main goal of the future *Internet of services*, namely to allow the smooth interaction of people and computers with services in the actual world. Our main claim is that it is crucial, to achieve such goal, to build a *global* service framework able to account for complex processes involving people and computers, which however have always *people* at their ends. That's why in this paper we mostly emphasize the role of *social* and *business-oriented* services, whose consideration is needed to evaluate the global quality of e-services in relation to their ultimate social benefits, taking the overall impact on the organizational structure into account. Along these lines, the contribution of this proposal is a first concrete step towards a unified, rigorous and principled ontology centred on the notion of *service availability,* which results in useful distinctions between *service, service content, service delivery* and *service process.* Services are modelled by means of a layered set of interrelated events, with their own participants as well as temporal and spatial locations.

Keywords: Ontology, Services Science, Social Service, Service Content, Service Process, Service Description, e-Government.

1 Introduction and State of the Art

Despite the ubiquity of the notion of service and the recent proposals for a unified *Services Science* [1], multiple inconsistencies between definitions of service from different disciplines (and even within the same discipline) still exist ([2], [3]). In particular, despite the general goal of the future *Internet of services* is –arguably– to allow people and computers to smoothly interact with services in the real life, both traditional Web services approaches, as well as the more recent Semantic Web Services (SWS) proposals, seem to focus mainly on the aspects related to *data and control flow*, considering services as *black boxes* whose main characteristic is to interoperate in a well-specified way (see, for instance, [4], [5] [6], [7]). This is certainly very useful, but, according to a recent paper by Petrie and Bussler [8], apparently it seems to work well only within *service parks*, where run-time interoperability is technically feasible because services are very constrained. As the authors put it, "some interoperability among service parks might emerge, but it could take a long time".

J. Domingue, D. Fensel, and P. Traverso (Eds.): FIS 2008, LNCS 5468, pp. 152–169, 2009.

Overall, the current state of the art is well described in a recent note by Katia Sycara [9], who observed that, on one hand, "current Web services proposals don't enable the semantic representation of business relations, contracts, or business rules in a machine-understandable way", while, on the other hand, "current business-process languages [...] are at a low abstraction level and don't provide formal business semantics". In conclusion, "a need exists to model informal business requirements in ways that make it feasible to translate them into precise business-service specifications, including operational interfaces and rules for procedures, timing, integrity, and quality. Such modelling must be driven from the top down, directly from business requirements [...]. The modelling would provide a functionality that's entirely understandable from a business perspective; it would depend on business context, goals, and operational standards, but shouldn't depend on the technology used to implement them. The models would provide business value directly relating to business purposes and could be understood and used without knowledge of underlying IT artefacts".

This is exactly the perspective we are adopting in this paper, which certainly calls for a broad, interdisciplinary effort such as that envisioned by services science [1]. For sure, a proper, general ontological foundation for the notion of service is a fundamental requirement for such endeavour. This is the long term goal of our work.

The present paper aims at establishing a first step in this long-term process, presenting the foundations of a new ontology of services that intends to establish a common, unifying framework for representing services according to different views, based on a vision that considers services as complex systems of commitments and activities, involving real people, organizations, and actual circumstances. In other words, we believe it is crucial, for the future internet of services, to take into account the whole *service system* [2] that interacts with Web services, through complex chains involving people and computers, which however have always *people* at their ends. That's why in this paper we mostly emphasize the role of *social* and *business-oriented* services, although the approach we describe should be ultimately general enough to account for any kind of service. In doing so, we adopt a *global view* of services, which, in a sense, goes against the strict separation between the external and the internal view advocated by SWS standards such as WSMO [10, 11]. The main reason is that the *terminology* needed to properly expose, retrieve and interact with a service, and especially that needed to understand and negotiate Service Level Agreements (SLAs), unavoidably requires a common understanding of the general structure of the service process, and the related activities involving the value exchange process between the producer[1] and the customer. Of course, in some cases services producers may have very good reasons for not exposing their internal workflow details, but the point is that, in general, SLAs *may* refer to some details concerning the *way* the service is implemented and the nature of such details is not specified in advance. So, since the boundaries between the external and the internal service description cannot be defined in advance for all kinds of service, so that a global approach seems to be the only viable alternative for a foundational ontology of services.

---

[1] In literature it is often used the term "provider", where we have chosen to use "producer". The reason for adopting such term instead of the more common "provider" is given by the fact that the latter term is used ambiguously, sometimes to indicate what we have called "producer" and sometimes what we have named "trustee".

A further reason for a global approach lies in the fact that, in many cases, it is important to account for the way a service-based architecture impacts the organizational architecture (indeed, service process re-engineering typically impacts organizational re-engineering). In this case, it is crucial to model in the proper way the links between services, people and organizations. This is especially relevant for application areas such as eGovernment, which is currently our major concern[2], where it is crucial to evaluate the global quality of e-services in relation to their ultimate social benefits, taking the overall impact on the organizational structure into account.

Modelling services according to this global view is not an easy task, however, mainly because the notion of service is a subtle and ambiguous one, so that many researchers simply have given up adopting a clear definition, relying on a variety of intuitive notions mainly coming from practical considerations, which lack unfortunately a coherent framework. In other words, we are still facing the general question: *what is a service?* Is there a single notion behind this term? And if there are multiple aspects, how are they related? How is the internal view of services as *business processes* related to the external view of Web services as exposed (aggregates of) functionalities?

In this paper we shall introduce a novel, general approach to service modelling founded on the basic principles of ontological analysis[3], centred on the notion of *service commitment* as a temporal state resulting from an agent's promise to perform certain actions in the interest of potential beneficiaries in correspondence of certain triggering events. In this view, services are modelled by means of a layered set of interrelated temporal activities, each one with its own participants and spatiotemporal location. This approach shares many similarities, in its main inspirations, with Alter's work on service systems [2], as well as O'Sullivan's work on non-functional requirements for services [12], and Baida, Gordijn and Akkerman's work on the service value chain [13]. While these approaches are however relatively informal, we believe that this proposal is a first concrete step towards a unified, rigorous and principled ontology.

2 The Proposed Approach

2.1 The Basic Idea

If we start from the simple question "what is a service?", it is immediately very evident that there is a huge confusion, not only in the layman's common sense, but also in the way the term is used in the literature. Sometimes the term "service" is used to indicate an *action* (actually performed by somebody), or a generic *type of action* (including in this category data manipulation procedures such as those typically described as Web services) or perhaps the *capability* to perform some action; other times it refers to the *result* of such action, which is typically a *change* affecting an

---

[2] See www.lego-lab.org

[3] Similar efforts are being carried out under the scope of the European project SUPER (   ), which has, among its aims, that of adding an ontological foundation to IT artefacts for business process management, so that these may become more transparent to business people.

object or a person, or just the (subjective) *value*, or utility of such change; moreover, in certain settings (like Public Administrations) the term denotes an *organization* acting (or in charge of acting) in a certain way in the interest of somebody.

In our opinion, all these notions are somehow connected, and contribute to better specify the notion of service, but none of them can be properly identified with what we believe people are commonly referring to when asking for a service. More or less "official" definitions occurring in the ICT literature do not help much.

To start with, the definitions in the W3C glossaries, referred to Web services, present evident ambiguities:

> "[...] a software system designed to support interoperable machine-to-machine interaction over a network".
> *Web Services Glossary*

but also

> "[...] an abstract resource that represents a capability of performing tasks that form a coherent functionality from the point of view of providers entities and requesters entities. To be used, a service must be realized by a concrete provider agent."
> *Web Services Glossary*

It is easy to see that, even in the case of restricted technical domains such as that of Web services, services are sometimes seen as processes, other times they rather resemble agents. WSMO, on the other hand, introduces a radical distinction between Web services and services, stating that the former are "computational entities able (by invocation) to achieve a user's goal", while the latter are "the actual value provided by this invocation" [11]. From a more general perspective, the "Research manifesto for services science" [1] cites Ted Hill's definition [14]:

> "a service is a change in the condition of a person, or a good belonging to some economic entity, brought about as the result of the activity of some other economic entity, with the approval of the first person or economic entity"

On the same line, from the business-oriented perspective, we may mention the comprehensive list of "service concepts" involved in the value chain process discussed in [2], and the service ontology proposed in [13], which however don't attempt a precise definition of service.

Finally, O'Sullivan and colleagues make a suggestion that fits very much our intuition (although the former author avoids to build on it in his recent PhD thesis [12]):

> "a service instance is essentially a promise by one party (the provider) to perform a function on behalf of another party at some time and place, and through some channel".
> [15]

To see how these various definitions are related, let us start with some simple questions, focusing on very general public services such as fire-and-rescue services, snow removal services, children care services, etc. What do we *pay for*, when we fund such services with our taxes? What does it mean that, for instance, in a municipality there are such services, at a certain time? Is anybody extinguishing a fire or removing some snow *at that time*? No, certainly not necessarily. We can legitimately say that *here and now* both a fire-and-rescue service and a snow removal service are *present*, even though there are no lit fires, nor is it snowing. It suffices to say that there is someone (firemen, snow removal operators) who is *prepared* to perform precise actions in case something happens (fire, snow). So our core notion of service is based on the following statement:

A service is present at a time t and location l iff, at time t, an agent is explicitly committed to guarantee the execution of some type of action at location l, on the occurrence of a certain triggering event, in the interest of another agent and upon prior agreement, in a certain way.

So, in a sense, at the core of any service there is a *commitment* situation in which someone (the service *trustee*) guarantees the execution of some kind of *action(s)* (by means of a *service producer*, which may coincide with the trustee or be *delegated* by him) in the interest of somebody who agrees (the *service customer*), at a certain cost and in a certain way. From the ontological point of view, this situation is a static temporal entity, i.e. a *static event* in the sense of the DOLCE ontology [16][4], which involves the participation of a single agent, the *trustee*. This commitment state typically starts at the time of the commitment act, and its duration is determined by the commitment's act itself[5], which typically specifies some constraints concerning the way the commitment will be fulfilled.

As we shall argue in the rest of the paper, service commitment needs to be distinguished from *service content*, which concerns the kind of action(s) the trustee commits to, and *service process*, which is a set of business processes implementing the service commitment (see Figure 1). In turn, we distinguish service commitment from *service availability*, which involves a service process running at a certain time and location: this allows us to account for malfunctioning periods or working pauses, where the commitment still holds but the service is not available. Following [17], [18], [19] and [20], the commitment act can be seen as a *speech act* that most of the times is codified in a *document*, i.e. in an institutional object that can assume many different forms: a contract, an official declaration or deliberation, a service level agreement[6], etc.

In institutional settings, the *trustee*, the agent who commits, is typically a Public Administration. On the other hand, the service *producer* may not necessarily coincide with the trustee, and can be either a PA or another kind of (private) organization, delegated by the trustee; in some exceptional cases even an individual agent. The

---

[4] Although the term "event" has often a dynamic connotation, we use such term in the more general sense of *entity which occurs in time* (also called *perdurant* in the DOLCE ontology). In this understanding, states and processes are considered as special event kinds.

[5] We assume that the commitment act (the *speech act*) is instantaneous, and occurs at a time which does not necessarily coincide with the beginning of the availability state.

[6] In the actual practice, the term "service level agreement" may be typically used to refer to the negotiation that the producer conducts with the user; here we are using the locution in a coarser sense, which includes also the agreements between trustee and producer and trustee and user and, possibly, between trustee and the community to which services are provided.

same holds for the *service customer*, who can in turn be a PA, an organization, or an individual agent, the latter being much more common than in the previous case.

The last element present in the definition is the *triggering event*; two kinds of triggering events can be singled out. The first one, more trivial, is a simple request made directly by the customer (like a parent in need who requires children care); in this case the *service invocation* coincides with the triggering event. The second one is the occurrence of a particular event kind, like the lighting of a fire in a wood, or a difficult situation observed by a social assistant, that triggers the action[7]. Of course, since the occurrence of the triggering event is not known in advance, the action time is in general much shorter than the availability time, so a service may be available at a certain time even if none of its foreseen actions do actually occur.

It is worth stressing an original feature of our definition, namely the inclusion of the triggering event. Traditionally, approaches on services are goal oriented; take for instance this definition from [21]: "A service delivers a process to achieve a certain goal by using resources". Note however that actually the goals may in some cases be just implicit, or even different if you compare the producer's perspective with thecustomer's perspective. In such cases, specifying the service also in terms of the triggering event and the action to be performed in correspondence of such event seems to be less ambiguous. The service's goal doesn't disappear in our approach, it is present in what has been called the service content, but the triggering event allows to justify the passage from service availability to service invocation. Moreover, note that a triggered action may not necessarily succeed. What the trustee guarantees may in some cases be only the action's performance, not its result. This changes also the mechanisms for the evaluation of service quality, which must distinguish between actions/processes and resulting states.

It is interesting to compare our definition with the second W3C definition reported above. We can observe many similarities, the most obvious being the presence of producers and requesters, and the distinction between two levels: an *abstract* level, where functional capabilities find their place, and a *concrete* one, where the functionalities are *realized*. However, our notion of commitment is different from an abstract capability in two ways. First, an agent may be capable of doing something without being committed to do so (for instance, a Web service may be potentially operational but not activated). Second, our definition involves the producer agent (more exactly, the trustee) already in the notion of service, instead of confining it to the service realization only. This means that, in our approach, different agents will always guarantee different services (possibly with the same *content* – see below). This choice seems more intuitive to us: when asking "how many telephone services are there in this country?" the answer can be "Two, but they deliver the same content". Moreover, W3C's definition is terminologically ambiguous, since it adopts the same term for the abstract and the concrete level. For us, services are always concrete: so, for instance, a C procedure, even if endowed with a standard Web interfacing

---

[7] To be more precise, it is the *observation* of such event that triggers the action. It is worth noting that, for this reason, many services include among their supporting activities an explicit monitoring activity, which can be executed by the producer itself or delegated to another agent.

mechanism, is not a service, but rather a *service process description.* When a computer runs this procedure, then it produces a service that complies with such description.

In a sense, our definition binds together the abstract and the concrete levels, which are comprehended in an articulated unitary framework. It is important to underline that this binding is very different from collapsing the two levels: they are kept separated, but they are both taken into explicit account, while in most cases the concrete level, even when mentioned, is then neglected.

2.2   Services and Goods

To better understand the nature of our proposal – that services are temporal entities (events) based on *commitments* – let us briefly discuss the difference between services and goods.   According to the World Trade Organization, services are a sort of intangible goods, so that a service might be defined as anything you can buy, but "you can't drop on your foot" [Shrybman 2001]. Yet, Ted Hill insists on the fact that services are not a special kind of goods, because goods and services belong to quite different ontological categories: goods are both *transactable* and *transferable*, while services are transactable, but not transferable. In Hill's own words, "a surgical operation is not some kind of immaterial drug": when you buy the drug you become an *owner* of it, in the sense that you can decide about its behaviour (i.e., assuming it in your body), while when you pay for the surgical operation you are not actually becoming the owner of it. In support to this argument, we argue that the ontological reason why services are not transferable is exactly because they are events: you cannot *own* an event, since if owning implies being in control of temporal behaviour, then, strictly speaking (at the token level), the temporal behaviour of an event is already determined, and changing it would result in a different event. So events are not transferable simply because they are not "ownable". Since services are events, they are not transferable as well.

So, in conclusion, it seems legitimate to assume that goods are *objects* (endurants, in DOLCE's terms), while services are *events* (perdurants). One may observe however that our economy is full of examples of transactions involving services, where the service seems to pass from hand to hand: certainly somebody may buy AMAZON, for instance: our point is that in this case the transaction involves the AMAZON *company*, not AMAZON's *service*: there is a change of ownership concerning the service producer, but not the service itself, which remains the same.

2.3   The Basic Ontological Structure of Services

Let us continue our analysis with another question: what's happening when a service is *produced*? As we have seen, a service may be concretely available even if it is not actually delivered, or maybe will be never delivered: we keep paying the firemen even if no fires occur. So, in our approach, a service has to be distinguished from its actual *delivery* to a particular customer. Indeed, typically the same service guarantees multiple deliveries. By the way, to avoid confusions, we propose an important terminological distinction: strictly speaking, it is not *the service* which is delivered, but its *content,* i.e., the actions intended to be performed in the interest of the customer. So a service is the concrete commitment (guaranteed by a *trustee*) to produce a certain content, consisting in actions of a certain kind executed in a certain way. Altogether, the various actions that ultimately lead to service production (performed by the service *producer* on behalf of the trustee) constitute the *service process*. We shall say that a service process *implements* a service. The concrete delivery to a particular customer presupposes however a *service acquisition* activity engaged by the latter, which typically negotiates a *service offer* resulting from *service bundling and presentation* activities on the producer's side. Finally, to complete the picture, we have to take into account the activities related to the value exchange chain, which include the service exploitation from the customer's *(customer's exploitation),* the sacrifice needed to access to the service *(customer's sacrifice),* as well as the corresponding activities from the producer's side.

So, as illustrated in Figure 1, a service is conceived as a complex event, with five main proper parts: service commitment, service presentation, service acquisition, service process, and service value exchange. In the following, we shall discuss these notions in more detail, with the aim to establish the basis for an ontology of services able to account both for *service descriptions* from an external point of view (typical of Web services and Service Oriented Architectures) and for *service processes* from an internal, business modelling point of view.

First of all, let us remark that all the blocks described in Figure 1 are *events* (*perdurants,* in DOLCE's terminology). This means that they can be characterized, roughly, by their *temporal location* and by their *participants,* linked to the event by means of what are usually called *thematic relations: agent, patient, theme, instrument...* Specifying a service (or a service kind) amounts to constraining these events by imposing suitable restrictions on their temporal locations and thematic relations. So, for instance, non-functional requirements such as those discussed in [12] are represented as attributes of specific service components, each involving a particular aspect (participant/thematic relation) of a particular service event. The resulting analysis, which we cannot discuss in detail for reasons of space, looks very similar to Alter's *service responsibility tables* [2], where the rows correspond to service components (events), and the columns to specific aspects to be considered (thematic relations). We give therefore a clean ontological foundation to a business-oriented proposal. Moreover, specifying the agents involved in each event allows for a fine-grained account of the *organizational impact* of a certain service. Note that, although the relationships between these various events (for instance, whether or not they involve the same agents) may vary according to the nature of the service specified, there exists a systematic ordering relationship between them, so that a service has a *layered structure*. This ordering relationship is not so much a temporal precedence (indeed most of these events are temporally overlapping), but rather an (existential) *ontological dependence* relationship: in order for an event at a certain layer to occur, some event at the higher level has to occur. Ultimately, all the events belonging to the service process presuppose some acquisition event, which in turn presupposes the service commitment.

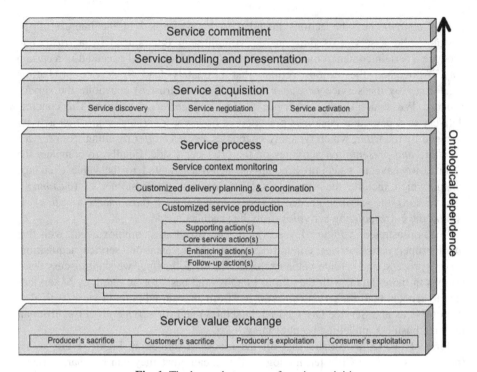

Fig. 1. The layered structure of service activities

At this point it is important to notice the central role played by actions and events in this account for the description of services; this is in contrast with the major trend, which is to describe services in terms of pre-conditions and post-conditions, like in WSMO, where processes are represented as transitions between states [11]. Under a different perspective, the two approaches could also work in conjunction.

There are several reasons why in our opinion it is important to explicitly represent events; first of all, though for the front-office in most cases it is enough to know which is the starting state and which the desired one, for the back-office it is important that the whole process be transparent (to know who does what and when), especially when a failure is at stake. But malfunctioning is not the only reason: without events one does not have sufficient expressiveness to distinguish two different commitments with the same content but different deadlines. Even if one sees these deadlines as non functional properties, it is hard to use them, say, for expressing a SLA without a clear semantics.

Again, in [22] a list of service quality's determinants is given, in which at least a couple of these determinants are strongly space-time dependent: responsiveness, connected with timeliness of service and access, defined by (among others) three items: "waiting time to receive a service [...]; convenient hours of operation; convenient location of service facility."

By using only pre- and post-conditions other subtle but important differences are lost. Take for example these two scenarios: 1. an unemployed woman who becomes pregnant and 2. a pregnant woman who becomes unemployed. In our account, the two scenarios can be distinguished by the fact that in 1 the pregnancy is the triggering event, while in 2 it is the unemployment. This difference may result in the activation of different services (for instance, a financial aid in 1 and a help in searching a new job in 2, or a legal enquiry on the employer if there's a suspicion of unfairness). In a pre- post-conditions framework both scenarios have the same pre-conditions and thus should activate the same services. Notably, the literature in economics has since long recognized that comparing the outcomes of services is not enough in order to evaluate their quality. See for instance [22] (similar distinctions appear in [23], [24], and [25]):

> Quality evaluations are not made solely on the outcome of a service; they also involve evaluations of the *process* of service delivery.

Let us now consider the various events constituting the service process internal structure. In Fig. 1, the containment relationship between the various blocks represents the parthood relationship. The core constituent of a service process is a set of basic activities (each called *customized service production*[8]), centered around the delivery of service content to a *single customer*. In addition to the *core service action(s)* depending on the service nature, a customized service production may include *enhancing actions* intended to increase the service value or differentiate it from those of competitors [14] as well as *supporting actions* needed to enable the core service consumption and *follow-up* actions intended to monitor the core action's results. In addition to customized delivery activities, the service process includes various back-office activities concerning *customized delivery planning and coordination*, plus an activity we have labelled as *service context monitoring* – which seems to be neglected by most current approaches and which involves the various actions necessary to detect the event that triggers service production, which can be an external situation or a customer's request: without an explicit modelling of such activity, there would be no way to account for delays or improper management of triggering events.

As a presupposition to service production, typically some *service acquisition* activities are required from the side of the customer[9]. These include *service discovery*, which is the event where the service trustee (or producer) and the service customer first meet together; *service negotiation,* which involves an agreement between the two parties, and *service invocation,* which refers to the event where the customer agrees to the service (not necessarily implying immediate production).

On the other hand, the service production results in a complex chain of transfers of value, which are represented in Figure 1 as the event Service value exchange. With a simplification, this is decomposed in *Producer's cost, Customer's cost, Producer's revenue* and *Customer's revenue.*

While in the case of the producer, most of the times both for cost and for revenue the value has to be intended in terms of money, in the customer's case things are more complicated. For instance, especially for services in the social domain, the customer's cost can be seen as an action whose results go somehow against some of the

---

[8] In the context of public services, a single event of customized service production is often called an *intervention*.

[9] Even in the case of free, public services, it is difficult to imagine a case where the customer is not required to actually discover the service, or make a minimal sacrifice to exploit it.

recipient's desires, but which the customer is still willing to perform, like *service sacrifice* as specified in [11]. Also the customer's revenue sometimes is not expressible in monetary terms, but only as some wellness state. Moreover, even though there's always an ultimate recipient of a service, we could also have indirect recipients, like the community that pays with its taxes for the service and benefits in terms of enhancement of its social conditions.

In conclusion, we can say that a service is characterized in a *prescriptive* way (*commitment level*), while a service process in a *descriptive way* (*implementation level*). The commitment level is where the "rules of the game" are established: what types of action compose the service, what types of agents are entitled to execute those actions, what types of agents may qualify as recipients, what types of events can become triggering situations. It is also the level where legal responsibility is at stake. In fact, from the point of view of the service offering, it is not important who in particular executes certain actions, but rather that a certain kind of action is executed in a certain way, by an agent who displays certain features and has some competences. The agent who is responsible that the required conditions are met is usually an organization, such as for instance a public administration. Such responsibility is usually distributed and assigned according to some structural constraints, i.e. by devising a structure of roles and sub-organizations. The ontological analysis of organizations is thus a topic tightly connected to the ontological analysis of services.

When we come to the actual service process, the various *kinds* mentioned at the commitment level need to be instantiated in concrete *tokens*. Individual agents are those who realize the core actions of service production, whose recipients are, ultimately, concrete agents (citizens); also the triggering situation is the occurrence of a precise (instance of) event. The service production level is thus the *descriptive* level, the one the data that are recorded and transferred belong to.

Finally, let us mention the issue of spatio-temporal location of services. In very general terms, one could say that in most cases when a somebody makes available a service, this availability spans over a spatio-temporal region which includes the spatio-temporal region in which the core service actions will (possibly) be executed; in rare cases, the two can coincide. For some special services, the analysis can be further complicated by the fact that the service may be delivered in a place and at a time and received in another place at another time. We won't enter into these details at present, but the issue needs to be investigated.

3   A Revised Version of Alter's Responsibility Tables

In a recent article, Steven Alter [2] has presented a conceptual instrument that he calls "service responsibility tables" (SRT); these are aimed at facilitating a better under-standing of services primarily based on the responsibilities assigned to each role; moreover, Alter suggests to add as many columns as necessary in order to address dif-ferent aspects of analysis. For instance, in Table 1 below, we have in the rows the various activities constituting a service, in the first two columns the responsibilities that the main actors have been assigned to in each constituting activities (provider in the first and customer in the second), while in the third column Alter records the problematic situations that may emerge in the execution of some activities composing a service. For what concerns the inclusion of additional columns, in another table Alter collects other possible topics, among which: participant or interpersonal issues, goals and requirements, preconditions, triggers, post-conditions, benefits provided to the customer, duration (cycle time), provider cost, customer cost, etc.

In practice, Alter isolates two orthogonal components of services: the constituting actions and, for each of these actions, the responsibilities of the involved stakeholders; he thus describes *how* such stakeholders participate to the various events. These *modes* of participation individuate the *role* the participants play in the various events constituting the service.

Even though the topics suggested by Alter are heterogeneous and sometimes confusing, we are interested in his idea of representing the events composing a service and the role participants have in these events.

In order to represent all this, we take inspiration from a notion introduced in linguistics to account for the internal structure of events: so-called *thematic relations,* expressing the nature of the relationship between an event and its participants. Adding thematic relations to those linking an event to its own qualities (such as temporal and spatial location) we have a full set of attributes at our disposal, among which the following ones appear to be as especially relevant for our purposes:

- Agent (the active role, the one who acts in the event)
- Theme/Patient (the one who undergoes the event; the patient changes its state, the theme does not)
- Goal (what the event is directed towards – typically a desired state of affairs)
- Recipient/Beneficiary (the one who receives the effects of the event)
- Instrument (something that is used in the performance of the event)
- Location (where the event takes place)
- Time/duration (when the event takes place, or how long it lasts)

As a result, in the table we have the main composing events in the rows (service commitment, service acquisition, service process, service value exchange...) and the thematic relations in the columns.

In order to give an idea of the approach, we take an example and we represent it using the tables. The example is directly taken from [14] and it is about a guy who goes to the mechanic's garage to have his car repaired. The aim of Table 2 is that of representing in an explicit way the fundamental constraints that need to be specified in an actual service description. This can bring many advantages both in the comprehension of the service's features and in the many different evaluations of service quality that can be made under various viewpoints.

The table describes the events in which a generic car repair service is articulated. The values we put in the various cells allow us to express the relevant constraints that distinguish this service from others.

We start with service commitment. During the commitment event, that chronologically comes first and is the one that all the other events depend on, the mechanic commits with a Public Administration (for instance the Chamber of Commerce) with a subscription act and his commitment consists in guaranteeing that he will execute a certain type of job (illustrated in the job description, on which he commits) according to the local rules. This commitment is valid in the whole Province (for instance) and starting from that very moment on.

Table 1. Alter's Service Responsibility Tables

Provider Activity or Responsibility	Customer Activity or Responsibility	Problems or Issues
Loan officer identifies businesses that might need a commercial loan.		Loan officers are not finding enough leads
Loan officer contacts potential loan applicant.	Potential loan applicant agrees to discuss the possibility of receiving a loan.	
Loan officer discusses loan applicant's financing needs and possible terms of the proposed loan.	Potential loan applicant discusses financial needs.	Loan officer is not able to be specific about loan terms, which are determined during the approval step, which occurs later.
Loan officer helps loan applicant compile a loan application.	Loan applicant compiles loan application.	Loan applicant and loan officer sometimes exaggerate the applicant's financial strength and prospects.
Loan officer and senior credit officer meet to verify that the loan application has no glaring flaws.		20% of loan applications have glaring flaws.
Credit analyst prepares a loan write-up summarizing the client's financial history, providing projections of sources of funds for loan payments, etc.		10% rate of significant errors, partly because credit analysts use an error prone combination of several spreadsheets and a word-processing program. Much rework due to experience of credit analysts.
Loan officer presents the loan write-up to a senior credit officer or loan committee.		Meetings not scheduled in a timely manner. Questions about exaggerated statements by some loan officers.
Senior credit officer or loan committee makes approval decision.		Excessive level of non-performing loans. Rationale for approval or refusal not recorded for future analysis.
Loan officer informs loan applicant of the decision.	Loan applicant accepts or declines an approved loan.	25% of refused applicants complain reason is unclear. 30% of applicants complain the process takes too long.
Loan administration clerk produces loan documents for an approved loan that the client accepts.		

Table 2. The Garage example

		Agent	Theme/Patient	Goal	Recipient/Beneficiary	Instrument	Location	Time/duration....
Service Commitment		Mechanic	Job description		PA (Chamber of Commerce)	Subscription act	Province/ Region?	Starting from a fixed date before the opening of the garage and until the duration of the license
Service Acquisition	Discovery	Customer	Mechanic	Car repaired				After opening and before actual repair
	Negotiation	Customer, Mechanic	Service customization	(Agreement)			Garage	
	Activation	Mechanic	Internal execution plan				Garage	
Service Process		Mechanic	Car	Car repaired	Customer	Mechanic's tools	Garage	Period in which the repair actually occurs
Service Value Exchange	Producer's sacrifice	Mechanic	Working hours	Being payed			Garage, bank...	A certain time (usually) after that the car has been repaired
	Customer's sacrifice	Customer	Money, car's unavailability, time needed to pick-up car...	Car repaired				
	Producer's exploitation	Mechanic	Money					
	Customer's exploitation	Customer	Car repaired/car availability					

After the commitment, we have the service acquisition, which in turn is composed by three different events: discovery, negotiation and activation. During discovery the customer looks for a mechanic (that is then the theme of his search) with the goal of having his car repaired. Note that not all the cells in this line are filled, meaning that, for instance, the instrument used for the discovery activity is not specified. Should we describe a service based (exclusively) on a certain mediator for the discovery process, the name of such mediator would be specified in the "Instrument" cell.

After the service is discovered, the negotiation between customer and mechanic starts; the goal is (probably) an agreement and the negotiation is on the customization of the service (in other words, how the service type in the job description is tailored to the customer's needs). At that point the mechanic activates the service, i.e., the related scheduling and organization activities. The last two events usually take place in the garage and the whole service acquisition event is performed after the commitment has been taken and before the occurrence of the actual repair.

The actual service process (as can be noted from Figure 1) is a very complex one, consisting of a lot of interconnected activities; here, for simplicity reasons, we choose to represent only the service's core actions.

In the service process event, the mechanic, with his tools and in his garage, performs some actions on the car aimed at having it repaired; this in the interest of the customer.

Finally, there is an articulated service value exchange event, which is constituted by a bunch of activities corresponding to what counts as a "sacrifice" or an "exploitation" from the producer's and consumer's points of view. This is a complex topic, that deserves a more thorough examination, because both the components of cost and those of revenue can be many and different evaluations can be conducted with different purposes.

Simplifying a lot, here we can say that the mechanic counts as a sacrifice his working hours with the goal of being paid, while the customer counts as a sacrifice the money he pays, the time to go to the garage, the time the car is unavailable and so on with the goal of having the car repaired; the mechanic earns money, while the customer's revenue consists in having his car available again.

There are some remarks that can be made; first of all, from the knowledge representation point of view, one thing that can be easily observed is that some values must be the same across multiple cells; for instance, the mechanic plays a role of agent both in the service commitment and process, while he plays the role of patient in service acquisition. This might be a problem as most languages ordinarily used to talk about services (like those based on description logics) are not expressive enough to account for co-reference between variables.

Another remark – a methodological one – is that these tables can be further refined, for example by decomposing the service process event in its internal layers.

Even though the example is quite elementary, it is already possible to see how much additional information the table can convey.

4 Concluding Remarks and Future Issues

In this paper we have proposed a novel framework aimed at constituting a common ontological foundation for services science. Let us briefly discuss what the main contributions of this approach are, and what future research directions we are considering.

1. *Revisitation of the difference between internal and external service views.* We have seen that the black box model of services based on external behaviour is too limited, and that a higher expressivity is necessary both to describe services in terms of their internal structure and to properly characterize SLAs and non-functional attributes.
2. *Improvement of the classic definition of services coming from economics.* We have seen that Hill's definition based on change is not general enough, since, for instance, it does not allow to consider services which do not necessarily produce a change, such as fire control.
3. *Focus on core actions instead of pre- and post conditions.* We have seen how pre- and post- conditions cannot by themselves capture important aspects of services, related to the way the service process is performed.
4. *Activity-based service representation.* We have seen how to describe a service in terms of a layered structure of related activities (events, in the most general sense of this term). The separation of the various activities described in Fig. 1 allows us to properly account for non-functional properties, which instead of generically belonging to the service as a whole are attributes that characterize specific activities. In this way, it is possible to determine what aspect of a given service implementation is responsible for a certain service property. In particular, spatio-temporal attributes can be easily taken into account.
5. *Comprehensive business-oriented approach.* We have introduced a clear distinction between service commitment, service process, and service content, taking also into account important issues affecting service quality and evaluation, such as bundling and presentation activities, acquisition activities, and actions related to the service value chain.
6. *Common framework to describe service according to different views,* in terms of more or less general constraints among the various service activities, providing an ontological foundation to the technique of *responsibility tables* introduced by Alter.

Given the preliminary nature of the present paper, many are the directions in which the analysis can be extended and enriched.

For sure, in order to be effective, this exploratory work needs to result in a formal model, that will constitute an ontology of services that, as a component of a modular social ontology, should be in the end connected with an ontology of organizations.

Acknowledgements

This work is carried out under the scope of the activities of the LEGO lab (www.lego-lab.it), a joint e-government initiative located in Trento, as well as the TOCAI.IT project, founded by the Italian Ministry of Research (Tecnologie Orientate alla Conoscenza per Aggregazioni di Imprese su InterneT) and the project "CSS – Cartella Socio-Sanitaria" founded by the Autonomous Province of Trento. The initial ideas at the basis of this project have emerged from a fruitful collaboration with "Servizio

Politiche Sociali e Abitative" of the Autonomous Province of Trento concerning the revision of a catalog of social services, to be shared among different Public Administrations. The first author is funded by a PostDoc grant from the Autonomous Province of Trento.

References

1. Chesbrough, H., Spohrer, J.: A Research Manifesto for Services Science. Communications of the ACM 49(7), 35–40 (2006)
2. Alter, S.: Service system fundamentals: Work system, value chain, and life cycle. IBM Systems Journal 47(1), 71–85 (2008)
3. Baida, Z.: Software-aided Service Bundling - Intelligent Methods & Tools for Graphical Service Modeling. Vrije Universiteit, Amsterdam (2006)
4. Janssen, M., Wagenaar, R.: From Legacy to Modularity: a Roadmap Towards Modular Architectures Using Web Services Technology. In: Traunmüller, R. (ed.) EGOV 2003. LNCS, vol. 2739, pp. 95–100. Springer, Heidelberg (2003)
5. Papazoglou, M.P., Georgakopoulos, D.: Service-Oriented Computing. Communications of the ACM 46(10), 25–28 (2003)
6. Traverso, P., Pistore, M.: Automated Composition of Semantic Web Services into Executable Processes. In: McIlraith, S.A., Plexousakis, D., van Harmelen, F. (eds.) ISWC 2004. LNCS, vol. 3298, pp. 380–394. Springer, Heidelberg (2004)
7. Vetere, G., Lenzerini, M.: Models for semantic interoperaility in service-oriented architectures. IBM Systems Journal 44(4), 887–903 (2005)
8. Petrie, C., Bussler, C.: The Myth of Open Web Services: The Rise of the Service Parks. IEEE Internet Computing 12(3), 94–96 (2008)
9. Sycara, K.: Untethering Semantic Web Services. In: Martin, D., Domingue, J. (eds.) Semantic Web Services, Part 2, pp. 11–13. IEEE Intelligent Systems (2007)
10. Fensel, D., Bussler, C.: The Web Service Modeling Framework WSMF. Electronic Commerce Research and Applications 1, 113–137 (2002)
11. Roman, D., et al.: Web Service Modeling Ontology. Applied Ontology 1(1), 77–106 (2005)
12. O'Sullivan, J.: Towards a Precise Understanding of Service Properties (PhD thesis). Faculty of Information Technology, p. 232. Queensland University of Technology (2006)
13. Baida, Z., Gordijn, J., Akkermans, H.: Service Ontology. Free University, Amsterdam (2001)
14. Hill, T.P.: On Goods and Services. Review of Income and Wealth 23(4), 315–338 (1977)
15. Dumas, M., et al.: Towards a semantic framework for service description. In: Data Semantics 9: Semantic Issues in E-Commerce 239. Kluwer, Hong Kong (2003)
16. Masolo, C., et al.: The WonderWeb Library of Fundational Ontologies and the DOLCE ontology. WonderWeb Deliverable D18, Final Report (vr. 1.0. 31-12-2003) (2003)
17. Castelfranchi, C.: Grounding We-Intention in Individual Social Attitudes: On Social Commitment Again. In: Sintonen, M., Miller, K. (eds.) Realism in Action - Essays in the Philosophy of Social Sciences, Dordrecht (2003)
18. Jennings, N.R.: Commitment and conventions: The foundation of coordination in multi-agent systems. The Knowledge Engineering Review 8(3), 223–250 (1993)
19. Verdicchio, M., Colombetti, M.: A logical model of social commitment for agent communication. In: AAMAS 2003. Elsevier, Amsterdam (2003)

20. Singh, M.P.: An ontology for commitments in multiagent systems, toward an unification of normative concepts. Artificial Intelligence and Law 7, 97–113 (1999)
21. Cauvet, C., Guzelian, G.: Business Process Modeling: A Service-Oriented Approach. In: HICSS 2008, 41st Annual Hawaii International Conference on System Sciences. IEEE Computer Society, Los Alamitos (2008)
22. Parasuraman, A., Zeithaml, V.A., Berry, L.L.: A Conceptual Model of Service Quality and Its Implications for Future Rersearch. Journal of Marketing 49(4), 41–50 (1985)
23. Sasser, W.E.J., Olsen, R.P., Wyckoff, D.D.: Management of Service Operations: Text and Cases. Allyn & Bacon, Boston (1978)
24. Gronroos, C.: A Service-Oriented Approach to Marketing of Services. European Journal of Marketing 12(8), 588–601 (1978)
25. Lehtinen, U., Lehtinen, J.R.: Service Quality: A Study of Quality Dimensions. Service Management Institute, Helsinki (1982)

Challenges and Opportunities for More Meaningful and Sustainable Internet Systems*

Pieter De Leenheer and Stijn Christiaens

Semantics Technology and Applications Research Laboratory (STARLab)
Vrije Universiteit Brussel
Pleinlaan 2, B-1050 BRUSSELS 5, Belgium
{pdeleenh,stichris}@vub.ac.be

Abstract. Despite its technological success story, the Internet is facing a rampant growth of isolated ontologies and a massive dump of unstructured legacy data. Therefore, architecting the next generation of the Internet will require a paradigm shift that goes beyond technological excellence. This is the main hypothesis we take and defend in this paper. Main drivers behind the dynamics of this future Web 3.0 are the massive and meaningful reconciliation of disparate data sources and service discovery, and the pervasiveness of these processes in daily life and work of on-line communities. Paving our way to more meaningful and sustainable internet systems, we devise a three-dimensional problem space from which we draw challenges and methodological opportunities. Next, based on this, we propose a DNS of Information. Finally, we substantiate our proposal with related research projects, practices, and initiatives that act as main catalysts or adopters.

1 Introduction

In less than two decades, the World Wide Web successfully evolved from a merely static data resource towards a knowledge sharing platform for a seemingly unlimited number of people worldwide. This "second-generation Web" (Web 2.0 [24]) allows on-line communities to emerge all around and massively share ideas, and create knowledge in a usually self-organising manner. This is manifested by an explosion of new tools, platforms, and technologies being developed and shared at little or no cost, that support social applications like lightweight folksonomies, blogs, and wikis.

The emerging range of Semantic Web technologies, pushed by the networked economy, an pulled by the exponential growth of computing power and bandwidth, promises an increase in scale and maturity of the Web 2.0 phenomenon, achieved through collaboration and integration within and between different and diverse communities. Some visionaries hypothesise about a new wave of Internet revolution, which would ultimately take us to the Internet of Services or Web 3.0., where communities will consist of a mix

---

* We would like to thank Felix Van de Maele, Damien Trog, and Robert Meersman for the valuable discussions about the subject. The research described in this paper was partially sponsored by the EU FP6 IST PROLIX (FP6-IST-027905) and FP7 TAS3 project, and the Brussels-Capital Region (IWOIB PRB 2006).

J. Domingue, D. Fensel, and P. Traverso (Eds.): FIS 2008, LNCS 5468, pp. 170–183, 2009.
© Springer-Verlag Berlin Heidelberg 2009

of human and software agents that will communicate and request services from each other, orchestrated by the goals and needs of the community. Through advanced mobile technology, these services would become ubiquitously available on domestic devices other than personal computers, making the latter disappear and become obsolete for end users.

When extrapolating the current pace of the continuous technological development, it seems that the realisation of this Future Internet is at hand. However, we are facing a universal limit on the total amount of information that can be stored and processed in the future, which is expected to put an ultimate time limit on Moore's Law [16]. Furthermore, although XML (and its successor RDF(S)) is becoming a de facto format for data structuring, the degree of shared semantics is still marginal. Therefore, massively distributed information services and semantic re-conciliation of on-line data silos are key drivers that will determine the Web's ability to carry out the envisioned services on the underlying knowledge without the need for human intervention.

Architecting Web 3.0 will require a paradigm shift that goes beyond technological excellence. Paving the way will start with radical, multi-disciplinary reconsideration of the ecology of its first-class citizens, namely (meta-)data, processes, services, and predominantly their owning communities. For example, Web 2.0 made us realise that unleashing ICT on massive communities results in a rapid emergence of invaluable common sense resources in a self-organising manner. Such a manifestation of wisdom of crowds was never thought to be conceivable with traditional AI. Therefore, the basic idea here is establishing the continuous adaptation of knowledge resources to their respective owner communities, and vice versa, as a fundamental property of knowledge-intensive systems. Just as database schemas and ontologies respectively took the data and much of its semantics out of applications, the proposed approach goes further by externalizing also the semantics of the (user) communities themselves.

Ontologies, being formal, computer-interpretable specifications of shared conceptualisations of the worlds under discussion, are an important lever by providing shared resources of semantics [13,11]. While evolution is currently regarded as a pain that must be technically alleviated, a viable methodology makes the evolution of knowledge, caused by passing along knowledge or by adapting it to particular application contexts, the center of representation [5]. If successful, such a fundamental shift towards a deep understanding of real-time, community-centric usage and evolution of structured knowledge has the potential to make a meaningful, pervasive, and evolutive Web more powerful and sustainable over longer periods of time.

In this article, we devise a three-dimensional problem space from which we draw challenges and methodological opportunities. Next, based on this, we propose a DNS of Information. Finally, we substantiate our proposal with related research projects, practices, and initiatives that act as main catalysts or adopters.

2   Problem Space

The state of the art in semantic reconciliation of knowledge is dominated by either (i) a (waterfall-inspired) engineering paradigm, as in ontology engineering performed and biased by a small elite, or (ii) by mining large bodies of data for significant correlations, as in folksonomy or process mining. Both paradigms, however, are quite limited approaches to the underlying problem of carving out and maintaining structure in data, information, and knowledge. They are unsatisfying, both theoretically and as far as the quality of the results is concerned. The main orthogonal vectors of the underlying problem space are as follows.

2.1 The *Co-evolving* Character between Ontologies and Their Owning Communities

In current practices, there is still a strong reductionist push towards universal convergence in the ontology, which is rooted in centennial principles of Taylor's scientific management. *Scientific management*, rooted in the belief that all systems are ordered, served well in the revolution of total quality management and business process reeingeneering in hierarchical organisations, and continues to be applicable in enterprise architecture modelling and enterprise ontology research. However, the tendency towards "simple" models contradicts with the need for pragmatic variety required when managing the knowledge of networks of communities with a common purpose that characterise ecosystems in globalised value networks. In other words, there is little understanding about how to formalise, align and unify relevant inter-subjective representations of meaning from individual perspectives in an adequate manner. Furthermore, evaluating knowledge is only valid in a specific usage context, which is often unknown at the time of producing consensual structures.

One should not focus on the practice of creating and evolving ontologies in a project-like context, that considers the ontology at some stage in its life-cycle to be an end-product [27]. Earlier, an explicitly contradictory model was established in which knowledge was exclusively seen as an "ephemeral, active process of relating" [29]. According to [27], it is not a contradiction, but a paradox that an ontology is to be viewed simultaneously and paradoxically both a *product* and a *flow*. The shared background of communication partners is continuously negotiated, as are the characteristics or values of the concepts that are agreed upon [4].

2.2 The *Bi-sortal* Nature of the Knowledge-Pervasive Internet

The environment in which knowledge-intensive systems are deployed, is populated by human as well as software agents that share and exchange knowledge. Regarding this *bi-sortal* setting, dynamic and absolute meaning is essential for all practical purposes amongst and between humans and computers respectively.

However, in current practice, knowledge representation approaches usually focus on syntactic and formal aspects of concept modelling, with the sole intention to enable computer-to-computer communication. The complementary real-world semantics (of elicitation) and the pragmatics (of application) of these models are often weak or even completely ignored [9]. Consequently, the cost of misinterpretation of available data is very high, and has vast economic consequences. Furthermore, this leads to unnecessary and expensive demands for changes to the ontologies [1].

2.3 The Pervasive *Impedance Mismatch* between Business and IT

There is a pervasive *impedance mismatch* between knowledge created by the domain experts on one hand, and the application and presentation of this knowledge at the (layman) business user level on the other hand. Given the diversity of knowledge domains that need to be accommodated, a convergence-centric approach to ontology engineering often result in monolithic so-called ontologies are often in fact just their author's (extended) data model for a particular, a priori known, application that author has in mind. Furthermore, these ontologies are biased by the strict technical conceptions and terminology and the imposed formal serialization syntax, which can hamper the adoption and usage by the wider target community for contextualized, and meaningful community sense making and reasoning and may impede creativity and innovation, both of which are vital for the competence of a professional community. For example, the requirements for the ontology are usually deduced top-down from the technical web service requirements that were solo-designed by a single application developer, rather than collaboratively grounding them directly bottom-up in the real community needs.

3   Methodological Principles

Our approach aims at supporting stakeholders in interpreting a common ontology base in their own terminology and context, and feeding back these results to the community. Figure. 1 illustrates this spiral-based change process model. The community dynamics is characterised by Nonaka's [23] four basic modes of *knowledge conversion*: *socialisation, externalisation, combination*, and *internalisation*, that drive the ontology evolution processes (*community grounding, rendering, unification, and commitment*). The latter are characterized by a continuous rendering and unification of common and individual perspectives driven by joint action and continuously changing needs, expectations, and opportunities, while supporting new branching and divergence where unification and consolidation limits the community in pursuing their goals. Next, we outline some methodological principles for our approach.

3.1   Ontological Grounding of Communities

Successful knowledge-intensive communities are usually self-organising; driven by implicit community goals such as mutual concerns and interests. Current approaches tend to reduce communities to a large set of contributing individual "entities" only. However, when considering a community as a human complex system, an agent can be anything that has legitimate identity and we continuously flex our identities both individually and collectively. Individually, we can be a parent, sibling, or child, and we will behave differently according to the context [17].

In order to better evolve relevant knowledge in a community-goal-driven way, these community goals must be externalized appropriately. They may then be linked to relevant strategies underlying the collaborative ontology engineering process and its support. This requires modeling communities better (i.e. establish their formal semantics) in terms of their intrinsic aspects such as goals, actors, roles, strategies, workflows, norms, and behaviour, and to so integrate the concept of community as equally relevant as technology in creating and sustaining knowledge structures of the evolving system.

On one hand, many professional communities such as enterprises already contain stable nuclei that are accepted at higher and lower levels of acceptable abstraction and

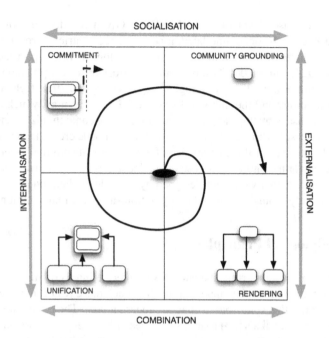

Fig. 1. An ontology evolution spiral model

provide sufficient shared conceptual context to ground an ontological foundation for their community evolution. On the other hand, by spawning common goal statements, the remaining informal sub-populations "swarming" pointless at the community boundaries can be reactivated, without conscripting them, on a voluntary basis. Many organisations are dependent on their informal networks composed from sub-communities within an across enteprises, and the recognition of them are a key competitive advantage in the knowledge-intensive ecosystem. Doing so, the traditional issue of scalability of automation can give floor to the wisdom of crowds to operate [27].

This holistic approach is breaking with current practice, where community information systems are usually reduced to only the non-human parts, with the possible exception of the field of organisational semiotics (e.g., MEASUR by [30] and FRISCO by [9]) and the language-action perspective (e.g., RENESYS by [8]). These bridge the gap between the "reality" of the community and its modelling concepts in particular by adopting socio-technical aspects of communities (e.g., norms and behaviour).

3.2 Community Evolution

An ontological foundation for communities establishes a semiotic grounding for community evolution. Regarding the co-evolutive dimension, the ontology as a flow on one hand asks for a cyclic cultivation and rendering of knowledge resources that is integrated in the operational processes of the community [22]. The ontology as a product on the other hand requires pragmatic perspective unification and persistent version management.

Divergent Perspective Rendering. Regarding the impedance mismatch and the bi-sortal character, the rendering of domain conceptions should not be conducted by external knowledge engineers, but constructively by legitimate domain experts in the community themselves. Only they have the tacit organisational knowledge about the domain and can sufficiently assess the real impact of the conceptualisations and derived communication opportunities on their organisation. A key challenge here is to overcome the *ontology-perspicuity bottleneck* [14] that constrains the use of ontologies, by finding a compromise between top-down imposed highly formal semantics expressed in logic language and bottom-up emerging real-world semantics expressed in layman user language.

Pragmatic Perspective Unification. Disagreements between divergent perspectives on common ontologies require a complex socio-technical process combining ontology alignment and meaning negotiation. Furthermore, sometimes it is not necessary (or even possible) to achieve context-independent ontological knowledge, as most ontologies used in practice assume a certain professional, social, and cultural perspective of some community. The common interest only partially overlaps with the individual interests, and hence the semantic unification of perspectives should only be done insofar necessary for the current pragmatic context. This corresponds to Snowden's application of the just-in-time principle to knowledge management. Finding a careful balance between the common ontology, and the various contextualised perspectives is a key challenge here.

3.3   Human-Computer Confluence

In general, dynamic communities require tools and systems for interaction and exchange. On one hand, computer-supported cooperative work (CSCW) aims at supporting groups in their cooperation and collaboration. On the other hand, the ontology engineering within communities requires a different type of system support. Both types need to be integrated into a holistic knowledge-intensive system, of which humans are part, to be both useful for and useable by such dynamic communities.

Clearly, many of these processes are intrinsically interactive in nature and require a lot of human intervention. This does not mean, however, that we should rule out other approaches that are fully automated. Regarding the bi-sortal character of knowledge-intensive systems, a careful balance and communication is needed between human, semi-automatic (i.e. requiring human interaction) and automatic approaches for semantic reconciliation and service discovery processes.

In order to engage the soft community boundaries (employees) as volunteers in knowledge cultivation, a radical reconsideration of reward and reputation structures, organisational form, and management attitude is required [26]. This would result in a shift in conception of an organisation as an hierarchy towards a complex ecology in which the number of causal factors renders pseudo-rational prescriptive models redundant at best and poisonous at worst. Furthermore, this requires the appropriate tool support that allows humans to denote domain conceptions in a natural and non-disruptive manner, while guaranteeing unambiguous computer interpretation.

4   Implementation of a DNS of Information

In this paper we do not aim at providing a systemic solution, but rather proposing an architecture for the reconciliation and application of semantics for service discovery in the future Internet. We will refer to this framework as the *DNS of information*. We will explain how this DNS can be constructed, taking into account the three problem space dimensions of (Sect. 2) and methodological principles for (Sect. 3) the future of Internet.

Figure 2 shows an overview on the DNSoI concept framework. A traditional Domain Name System (DNS), connects on-line information to Internet domain names, via un-ambiguous mappings of human-friendly host names (e.g., www.semanticweb.org) into machine-interpretable IP addresses. The concept of a DNS of Information (DNSoI) that we introduce here, works in a similar manner: bi-sortal communities have common goals they want to realise, and in terms of semantics, these goals are related to a certain set of concepts that can be used to semantically weave and publish the requested information services.

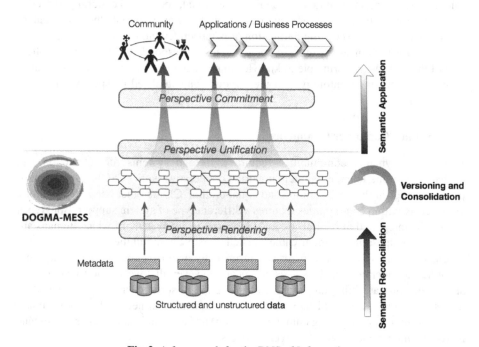

Fig. 2. A framework for the DNS of Information

Evolution lies at the heart of the DNSoI framework: it controls the human-driven semantic reconciliation and machine-driven service discovery processes that are orchestrated by the community needs. The key goal is to find a right balance between multiple plausible "flowing" ontological perspectives to coexist in the ontology base and a minimal effort to unify relevant parts of these divergent perspectives resulting in shared ontological commitments, that are transparantly published as "products" serving acute application purposes for people and processes.

We describe a step-wise procedure to reconcile and apply semantics, that extends DOGMA-MESS, which we introduced [7], formalised [3] and validated [2] earlier. Furthermore, our procedure partly draws on some best practices from some of the following methods:

- DOGMA [18,19] adopts on its turn principles from the following methodologies [28]:
  - TOVE [12]: the use of competency questions as a means to scope the problem and domain of interest and to evaluate the resulting conceptualisation.
  - Enterprise Ontology [33]: the concept of brainstorming, the middle-out approach, and the grouping of terms. The comprehensive documentation of the full-cycle engineering process is also included.
  - the "unified methodology" [32]: the specification of target applications as a way to scope the semantic space.
  - Methontology [10]: inclusion of management activities.
  - OnToKnowledge [31]" the inclusion of a feasibility study before any ontology engineering process starts.
  - CommonKads [25]: having specific documented deliverables for every activity or task throughout the ontology engineering process.

- RENESYS [6]: the inclusion of insights from social science, and particularly legitimate user-driven system specification processes.
- FRISCO [9]: the consideration of semiotic dimensions in organisational information system modelling.
- AKEM [36]: the inclusion of techniques from linguistics for ontology engineering, including highlighting, paraphrasing, and story building.

Accordingly, the involved activities are grouped in two operational cycles that together establish full-cycle semantics engineering: the semantic reconciliation cycle, and the semantic application cycle respectively. This is illustrated in Fig. 3. The two cycles communicate with each other via the consolidation activity.

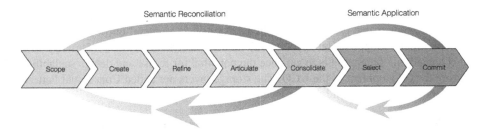

Fig. 3. A step-wise procedure to reconcile, consolidate and apply semantics

4.1 Semantic Reconciliation

The semantic reconciliation cycle starts from scoping the domain by collecting and abstracting facts from, e.g., natural language descriptions, (legacy) logical schemas, or other metadata and consequently decomposing this scope in sub-domains. Next, during the semantic reconciliation (which is constituted of three processes, i.e. creation, refinement, and articulation), the scoped facts are formalized into conceptual patterns. Then, the groups of equivalent patterns are consolidated by removing redundancies. Ultimately, the semantic reconciliation results in a number of reusable language-neutral patterns for constructing business semantics that are grounded in informal meaning descriptions.

4.2 Semantic Application

During the semantic application cycle, the scoped information sources and services are committed to selected consolidated semantic patterns. This is done by first selecting relevant patterns from the pattern base. Next, the interpretation of this selection is semantically constrained. Finally, the various scoped sources and services are mapped on (read: committed to) this selection. The selection and axiomatization of this selection should approximate the intended business semantics. This can be verified by automatically verbalization into natural language, and validation of the unlocked data.

4.3 Semantics Consolidation and Storage

The reconciliation and the application cycles feed back to each other via the business semantics consolidation process. The business semantics consolidation process is the beating heart of the DNSoI Platform as it is responsible for managing the many different versions and views on the business semantics, and rinsing them from possible anomalies or redundancies.

The sequence of the activities emphasises the iterative improvement of the patterns by looping through the cycles. Mess activities are further subdivided in tasks, each producing a number of deliverables. Deliverables range from documentation, such as vision and cost statements, to knowledge, such as structured glossaries and semantically constrained ontological commitments. In this paper will mainly focus on the knowledge deliverables produced.

In order to store the deliverables, the DNSoI framework is constituted of two separate storage layers that establish an explicit separation of (general-purpose) conceptual patterns from its (application-specific) axiomatisation (i.e., semantic constraints). The idea behind this separation is to enhance the potential for re-use and design scalability during the development of the UCO. The storage layers are called Conceptual Pattern Base and the Commitment Layer respectively.

Ontology Base. is a consolidated repository of language-neutral patterns for constructing ontologies, that are grounded in informal meaning descriptions. Examples are plausible fact types such as RDFS triples, or XML metadata tags, possibly articulated with other semantic attributes or media such as constraints, glosses or synsets. These patterns are underspecified which makes them reusable across application contexts. The ontology base is the manifestation of the ontology as a flow. Its evolution is triggered either by *requesters* or *providers*. Providers unlock new knowledge fact types by massively semantically reconciliating their data silos (perspective rendering). Requesters query the DNSoI for particular service concepts that can be linked and combined to satisfy the needs of their community (perspective unification). Doing so, the Pattern Base establishes an extensive and reusable pool of possible vocabularies, providing elementary building blocks for constructing ontological commitments to this Pattern Base (perspective commitment). For guiding the knowledge worker through this very large database, elicitation contexts impose a meaningful grouping of conceptual patterns within the Pattern Base.

Commitment Layer. is a library of ontological commitments to the Ontology Base. An ontological commitment defines a meaningful view or selection of relevant and semantically constrained patterns. Each ontological commitment renders a perspective trivially on the Conceptual Pattern Base or recursively on an arbitrary ontological commitment. Application committers then map their applications to one or more commitments in order to enable the scoped information services. The Perspective Commitment Layer is concerned with the architecture of the conceptual patterns and the interfaces between different ontological commitments.

Following the tradition of decentralized control which has made the current Internet flourish, this layer would be divided over several physical DNS servers, which can be combined in a partner-like structure. Each of these DNS servers contain their part of the ontological base, and the collection of all of them provides a complete, multi-perspective view on aggregated information.

5   Discussion and Related Work

There is a plethora of research projects, practices, joint initiatives, and approaches that serve as catalyst or adopter for our proposed approach. In the following paragraphs we make a non-exhaustive selection.

5.1   Research Projects, Practices, and Joint Initiatives

The COIN project[1] is developing a prototype for collaboration and interoperability services on a generic integrated solution. This corresponds to the community grounding and perspective rendering phases, operationalized in the form of published ontological commitments. Further, the ServiceFinder[2] project aims at developing a platform for service discovery in which web serves are embedded in a Web 2.0 environment. They also recognize the important role of communities and semantics, as they tap into the community proces to support automatic service annotation with ontologies. On a larger scale, the NeOn project[3] aims to create a service-oriented, open infrastructure to support the development life-cycle of semantic applications. The infrastructure described in NeOn corresponds to our DNSoI concept, on top of which applications share evolving semantics with each other through information services.

---

[1] http://www.coin-ip.eu/
[2] http://www.service-finder.eu
[3] http://www.neon-project.org

The SOA4All[4] project will produce a framework and infrastructure that allows a domain independent service delivery platform. The cornerstones of this project are the principles present in the current Web, the human-machine cooperation structured in a Web 2.0 manner, Semantic Web technology and context management to process user requirements. SOA4All envisions the next Web as a global computational resource where services play a key role, and end users cooperate to use them in problem solving. This vision is aligned with our DNSoI concept, that allows cooperative communities to share concepts and publish them as information services.

The OKKAM[5] project, which interprets Ockham's razor as "Entity identifiers should not be multiplied beyond necessity", proposes a three-step roadmap. The first step defines an Entity Name System (ENS). The ENS is a scalable and sustainable infrastructure, that promises to leverage the systematic reuse of global and unique entity identifiers. OKKAM envisions this ENS as a distributed service, providing core services through which to access the system. This goal of the ENS is similar to that of our DNSoI, which serves as an infrastructure through which to access and assemble concepts, and therefore requires a layer that provides collaborative management.

The recently initiated Mature project[6], which focuses on the knowledge maturing process and ways to overcome barriers to it. The projects attempts to produce reusable knowledge maturing services and creating awareness of maturing-relevant individual and community activities.

On a practical level, we can see the importance of the Linked Open Data initiative[7], which aims at using the Web to connect related data that was not previously linked. The initiative attempts to use the web to lower the barriers to linking data currently linked using other methods. In the long term, their methods promise to become a well-established approach, carried out by bi-sortal communities on a global scale. The continuously evolving result of this effort should be made available and governed through a DNSoI architecture. Within Europe, the Semantic Interoperability Centre (Semic.eu)[8] has been launched. This initiative and platform aims to support the data exchange of pan-European eGovernment projects. It presents a repository where communities can share, review and reuse semantic interoperability assets.

5.2   Methodology and Tools

With the DOGMA-MESS methodology and system[9] [7], we provided a Meaning Evolution Support System (MESS) and platform that helps communities of practice consisting of different stakeholders from different organizations to define and evolve shared ontologies that are relevant to their joint collaboration objectives. The systems aims to make the evolution process of a collaborative community as effective and efficient as possible.

---

[4] http://www.soa4all.org/

[5] http://okkam.org

[6] http://mature-ip.eu

[7] http://linkeddata.org

[8] http://www.semic.eu

[9] http://dogma-mess.org/

A similar application is MyOntology[10], that provides wiki-based collaboration and community-driven development of ontological artefacts. The system provides a technical infrastructure for maintaining a tight coupling between an ontology and the individuals creating and using this ontology. As such it tackles issues related to governing the evolving ontology base.

Pinto et al. [35] recognizes ontologies as a moving target, and hence propose the DILIGENT ontology evolution methodology. The user and the usage of the ontologies, and the application goal to have a shared conceptualisation are three important aspects in their approach. In relation to our DNSoI, this supports our view of the Ontology Base as a manifestation of the ontology as a flow, where different perspectives are collected.

Mika [20] describes a model that unifies social networks and semantics, thereby also stressing the need for a social dimension in the more traditional perspective on ontologies. This supports our perspective of DOGMA-MESS, where social dynamics and affordances govern ontological perspectives resulting in emerging "products". Van Damme et al. [34] present FolksOntology as an approach to use social interaction in the building and maintaining of ontologies. The authors use different techniques to achieve this, such as statistical analysis, online lexical resources and mapping and matching approaches. The work they describe also supports our collaborative management layer, which can benefit from these techniques as support mechanisms to the different communities. Haase et al. [ref] present a framework for ontology evolution, that has two main change discovery drivers: usage and data. The data drivers correspond to our provider side of semantic reconciliation, where different data silos are sources for new knowledge fact types. The usage drivers correspond to our requester side of information services, where service concepts are linked and combined according to usage needs.

Summarising, the overview of projects and approaches above hints at the importance of a DNSoI for the information-centric infrastructure or the realization of the information fabric in the future Internet. This is confirmed by independent research by Gartner [21] and Forrester. Concepts such as the information pump [15], which synchronizes the diverse dimensions of the content continuum present in enterprises, and techniques for metadata management, are on the top ten list of strategic technologies for today[11]. As such, they are important milestones in the realization of a DNS of Information.

6   Conclusion

Architecting the next generation of the Internet will require a paradigm shift that goes beyond technological excel. This is was the main hypothesis we took and defended in this paper. To this end we assumed key drivers behind the dynamics of this Web 3.0: (i) massive and meaningful reconciliation of disparate data sources and service discovery; and (ii) the pervasiveness of these processes in daily life and work of individuals and communities. In order to realise the potential of this Future Internet, we reflected on a three-dimensional problem space in which we proposed an approach and architecture: the DNSoI. Finally, we substantiated this proposal with related research projects, practices, and initiatives that may act as main catalysts or adopters.

---

[10] http://www.myontology.org

[11] http://www.gartner.com/it/page.jsp?id=530109

References

1. Carnap, R.: Meaning and Necessity. University of Chicago Press, Chicago (1947)
2. Christiaens, S., De Leenheer, P., de Moor, A., Meersman, R.: Business use case: Ontologising competencies in an interorganisational setting. In: Hepp, M., De Leenheer, P., de Moor, A., Sure, Y. (eds.) Ontology Management for the Semantic Web, Semantic Web Services, and Business Applications, from Semantic Web and Beyond: Computing for Human Experience. Springer, Heidelberg (2008)
3. De Leenheer, P., de Moor, A., Meersman, R.: Context dependency management in ontology engineering: a formal approach. In: Spaccapietra, S., Atzeni, P., Fages, F., Hacid, M.-S., Kifer, M., Mylopoulos, J., Pernici, B., Shvaiko, P., Trujillo, J., Zaihrayeu, I. (eds.) Journal on Data Semantics VIII. LNCS, vol. 4380, pp. 26–56. Springer, Heidelberg (2007)
4. De Leenheer, P., Meersman, R.: Towards community-based evolution of knowledge-intensive systems. In: Meersman, R., Tari, Z. (eds.) OTM 2007, Part I. LNCS, vol. 4803, pp. 989–1006. Springer, Heidelberg (2007)
5. De Leenheer, P., Mens, T.: Ontology evolution: State of the art and future directions. In: Hepp, M., De Leenheer, P., de Moor, A., Sure, Y. (eds.) Ontology Management for the Semantic Web, Semantic Web Services, and Business Applications. Springer, Heidelberg (2008)
6. de Moor, A.: Empowering Communities: A Method for the Legitimate User-Driven Specification of Network Information Systems. Ph.D thesis, Tilburg University, The Netherlands (1999) ISBN 90-5668-055-2
7. de Moor, A., De Leenheer, P., Meersman, R.: DOGMA-MESS: A meaning evolution support system for interorganizational ontology engineering. In: Schärfe, H., Hitzler, P., Øhrstrøm, P. (eds.) ICCS 2006. LNCS (LNAI), vol. 4068, pp. 189–202. Springer, Heidelberg (2006)
8. de Moor, A., Weigand, H.: Formalizing the evolution of virtual communities. Inf. Syst. 32(2), 223–247 (2007)
9. Falkenberg, E.D.: Frisco: A framework of information system concepts. Technical report, IFIP WG 8.1 Task Group (1998)
10. Fernández, M., Gómez-Pérez, A., Juristo, N.: Methontology: from ontological art towards ontological engineering. In: Proceedings of the AAAI 1997 spring symposium series on ontological engineering, Stanford, USA, pp. 33–40 (1997)
11. Gruber, T.R.: A translation approach to portable ontology specifications. Knowledge Acquisition 5(2), 199–220 (1993)
12. Grüninger, M., Fox, M.: Methdology for the design and evaluation of ontologies. In: Skuce, D. (ed.) IJCAI workshop on basic ontological issues in knowledge sharing (1995)
13. Guarino, N.: Formal ontology and information systems. In: Proc. of the 1st Int'l Conf. on Formal Ontologies in Information Systems (FOIS 1998), Trento, Italy, pp. 3–15. IOS Press, Amsterdam (1998)
14. Hepp, M.: Possible ontologies: How reality constrains the development of relevant ontologies. IEEE Internet Computing 11(1), 90–96 (2007)
15. Know, R.E.: An information-centric infrastructure: the XML pump (2008), http://www.gartner.com/DisplayDocument?id=689307&ref=g %20sitelink
16. Krauss, L.M., Starkamn, G.D.: Universal Limits on Computation. Astro (2004)
17. Kurtz, C.F., Snowden, D.: The new dynamics of strategy: Sense-making in a complex and complicated world. IBM Systems 42(3), 462–483 (2003)
18. Meersman, R.: Semantic ontology tools in is designs. In: Proc. of the International Symposium on Methodologies for Intelligent Systems (ISMIS), pp. 30–45 (1999)

19. Meersman, R.: Reusing certain database design principles, methods and techniques for ontology theory, construction and methodology. Technical report, VUB STAR Lab, Brussel (2001)
20. Mika, P.: Ontologies are us: A unified model of social networks and semantics. Journal of Web Semantics 5(1), 5–15 (2007)
21. Newman, D.: Top view: Definition of, issues with and uses for an information-centric infrastructure (2007),
    http://www.gartner.com/DisplayDocument?id=506444&ref
    =g%20sitelink
22. Nonaka, I., Konno, N.: The concept of "ba": Building a foundation for knowledge creation. California Management Review 40(3) (1998)
23. Nonaka, I., Takeuchi, H.: The Knowledge-Creating Company: How Japanese Companies Create the Dynamics of Innovation. Oxford University Press, Oxford (1995)
24. O'Reilly, T.: What is web 2.0: Design patterns and business models for the next generation of software (September 09, 2005),
    http://www.oreillynet.com/pub/a/oreilly/tim/news/2005/09/30/
    what-is-web-20.html
25. Schreiber, G., et al.: Knowledge engineering and management - the common KADS methodology. MIT Press, Cambridge (1999)
26. Snowden, D.: Cynefin: a sense of time and space, the social ecology of knowledge management. In: Depres, C., Chauvel, D. (eds.) Knowledge Horizons: The Present and the Promise of Knowledge Management. Butterworth-Heinemann (2000)
27. Snowden, D.: Complex acts of knowing: Paradox and descriptive self-awareness. Knowledge Management 6(2), 100–111 (2002)
28. Spyns, P., Tang, Y., Meersman, R.: A model theory inspired ontology engineering methodology. Applied Ontology 4 (2008)
29. Stacey, R.: Complex Responsive Processes in Organizations: Learning and Knowledge Creationvon. Routledge, London (2001)
30. Stamper, R.: Language and computing in organised behaviour. In: van de Riet, R., Meersman, R. (eds.) Linguistic Instruments in Knowledge Engineering, pp. 143–163. Elsevier Science Publishers, Amsterdam (1992)
31. Sure, Y.: Methodology, Tools, and case studies for ontology-based knowledge management. Ph.D thesis, AIFB Karlsruhe (2003)
32. Uschold, M., Grüninger, M.: Ontologies: Principles, methods and applications. The Knowledge Engineering Review 11(2), 93–136 (1996)
33. Uschold, M., King, M.: Towards a methodology for building ontologies. In: Skuce, D. (ed.) IJCAI Workshop on basic ontological issues in knowledge sharing (1995)
34. Van Damme, C., Hepp, M., Siorpaes, K.: Folksontology: An integrated approach for turning folksonomies into ontologies. In: Proceedings of the ESWC Workshop Bridging the Gap between Semantic Web and Web 2.0, Innsbruck, Austria. Springer, Heidelberg (2007)
35. Vrandecic, D., Pinto, S., Tempich, C., Sure, Y.: The diligent knowledge processes. Journal of Knowledge Management, 2005 9(5), 85–96 (2005)
36. Zhao, G.: AKEM: an ontology engineering methodology in FF POIROT. Deliverable 6.8, FFPOIROT Project IST-2001-38248 (2005)

Author Index